Chinatown Quest

Chinatown Quest

One Hundred Years of
Donaldina Cameron House
1874-1974

by Carol Green Wilson
Carol Green Wilson

Revised Edition

California Historical Society
with Donaldina Cameron House
SAN FRANCISCO

Other books by
CAROL GREEN WILSON

California Yankee
Gump's Treasure Trade
We Who Wear Kites
Alice Eastwood's Wonderland
Arthur Fiedler—Music for the Millions
Herbert Hoover—A Challenge for Today

TO THE FAR-SIGHTED WOMEN OF 100 YEARS AGO

WHO

ESTABLISHED THIS MISSION

FOR GIRLS OF ANOTHER RACE

AND THEIR SUCCESSORS

WHO HAVE DEVOTED THEIR LIVES

TO DEVELOPING A CHRISTIAN CENTER

IN SAN FRANCISCO'S CHINATOWN

FOREWORD

THIS BOOK recounts the life work of a woman of great courage and perseverance. For forty-three years (1895–1938) Donaldina Cameron gave herself unstintingly to the often dangerous challenges and changing needs of the Chinese Presbyterian Mission Home at 920 Sacramento Street, San Francisco. To honor her leadership, in 1942 the building and the organization were renamed the Donaldina Cameron House. Through the remaining years of her century-long life, Miss Cameron saw the fulfillment of her work, as Cameron House expanded its services to meet the contemporary needs of the Chinese community.

In its one hundredth year of publishing California history, the California Historical Society is pleased to join the Donaldina Cameron House to publish this revised edition of a book that has become difficult to find but remains rewarding to read. With a Prologue to replace the original 1931 preface and an Epilogue to complete the story of Miss Cameron's life and bring up to date the work of Cameron House, Carol Green Wilson has prepared her book for a new generation of readers.

These chapters present an approach to history and biography strikingly different from what would be produced in the 1970's. Times and values have changed. There is here a sense of simple right and wrong, a revelation of a time when direct action brought perceived direct results, when a woman unhesitatingly set out in the night in the face of bubonic plague to cross roof tops and climb down sky lights, motivated by her compelling realization that "she could not disappoint this trusting child." With "a high, merry heart," Donaldina literally broke into brothels (with armed police aid, often without search warrants), raced down dark passageways, discovered trapdoors and hidden rooms, and almost always rescued the helpless Chinese slave-girls who were then taken to 920 Sacramento Street, there to be trained for a new life. Through it all, for more than forty years of attacking institutionalized slavery and corruption, the simple, trusting spirit of this woman survived undaunted, as she herself—a lady—remained unabashed, unsullied by the sights of degradation she must often have seen and remembered—though they are not here described.

There is in it all a strength, a spirit, a sureness of mind that may seem naïve in our times. But it reads true, and Chinese American scholars who have studied and written the history of their people in California recognize this book as an important historical record of circumstances that prevailed for many years. While these scholars decry the paternalism implicit in Miss Cameron's Christian fervor and while they attest that she was never half so endangered as the many Chinese men and women who helped in her fight against Chinatown corruption, they share our judgment that "*Chinatown Quest*" is a book well worth reading and deserving of this new edition.

J. S. Holliday
Executive Director
California Historical Society

TABLE OF CONTENTS

PROLOGUE

In the late 1920's the Women's Association of Calvary Presbyterian Church in San Francisco asked me to help find a speaker for their Mother-Daughter dinner to be held on May Day. I was then Editor of the Stanford Alumni Magazine and they suggested that I might find a speaker from the campus, but I had another idea. At a recent meeting of General Assembly in our city Donaldina Cameron had brought a bevy of tiny Chinese children to the platform of the Civic Auditorium to sing. I understood that she was known as "The Mother of Chinatown." Perhaps she would tell us how she had acquired this title.

She accepted. Never will I forget that evening. When she finished her tale of adventure in Old Chinatown where she had rescued the mothers of some of these children, and many other victims of the "Yellow Slavery" that characterized early days of illegal importation of girls from across the Pacific, I obeyed an irresistible impulse to join the throng who surrounded the speaker.

"Would you perhaps have time someday to let me jot into my notebook some of the details of these stories you have told us tonight?" I ventured, as I introduced myself. "I would like to try an article for the *Atlantic Monthly* next May on your way of solving the race relations problem."

She smiled and said, "Oh, that magazine was very kind to Jean Kenyon MacKenzie" (daughter of a San Francisco clergyman and an early California writer), and turned to acknowledge the next greeter.

I felt abashed and said no more to anyone except my family. But three weeks later we were picknicking with the pastor of our church, Dr. Ezra Allen Van Nuys, his wife and children. He turned to my husband.

"G.O., go on down and play with the kids on the beach. I have something to ask of your wife and I do not want you to object."

"I better stay," my husband said emphatically.

Our friend continued, "Ever since Donaldina Cameron talked the other night I have been determined that her story should be put between the covers of a book. And Carol is the one to do it."

"Well," agreed G.O., "if you had lived with us for the last three weeks you would know she was going to do just that."

And so my first book was conceived. The birth was not easy. Donaldina Cameron did not agree . . . "you don't write about living people," she demurred, "and anyway I didn't do it alone."

In spite of these objections, however, she did recognize my interest in the Mission work. I practically never saw her alone, although I found myself invited to functions, such as weddings at 920 Sacramento Street, where "her girls" were safely housed; and she herself "gave them away" when the right man appeared. I met her associates, Chinese and American. Among them was Sergeant Manion of the Chinatown Squad. He invited me to his office in the old Hall of Justice and opened his files.

Chinatown seen through Donaldina Cameron's eyes became a new place. For a year of priceless searching I followed the routes of her quest through its alleys and shops, rewarded in the end by intimate knowledge of the Oriental neighbors who give such charm to our city.

Before that year was over I found myself a member of the Advisory Committee on Chinese Work, appointed by General Assembly, and found new allies in preparing the story for what I hoped would be its publication as a winner in the *Atlantic Monthly* Non-Fiction Contest with a deadline for entry of May 31.

Mrs. Lynn Townsend White, wife of a member of the faculty of the San Anselmo Presbyterian Seminary, was Chairman of this Board responsible for the work of the Mission. She suggested that I bring the manuscript—and Miss Cameron—to their home for dinner so that her husband could listen to it. To my amazement Miss Cameron agreed; but when I called for her to drive to the Sausalito ferry, she had a missionary from China with her. The quiet visit I had counted on as we crossed the Golden Gate was not to be! Finally after dinner when Dr. White had delivered the unexpected missionary guest to other friends, we sat by the fire and I began to read the manuscript, with constant interruptions by Miss Cameron . . . "Oh no, it did not happen that way" and so on. Suddenly Dr. White stopped me and turned to Miss Cameron.

"Dolly, I want you to go into the garden tomorrow morning with Mrs. Wilson and tell her just what did happen. This is a great human document. It must be published."

"But I can't do that," she protested. "I have to meet a boat from China at eight o'clock with the Immigration man."

We did and returned to the Mission Home in time for a Board meeting at ten. I had begged off from the meeting because I wanted to sit somewhere in quiet and jot down some of the things I had heard and seen that morning. I was writing, inspired by the fact that I was sitting at Miss Cameron's desk in the room where she had counseled so many girls. A knock at the door interrupted.

"Please, Mrs. Wilson," a young Chinese girl said, "they need you for a quorum downstairs."

I gathered my papers and followed her. I was needed for another reason. Mrs. White greeted me.

"I want the Board to hear some of what you have written. Can you read us Chapter Twelve?"

When I finished one of the members said, "I will take care of your children if you will drive Miss Cameron up to my brother's ranch at Hopland for a few days and complete this story."

That was too far away for the conscientious Director of the Home, but another member suggested a cottage in Los Gatos, adding that it was near to her sister, Jessie Cameron Bailey. And so I had my subject alone for three unforgettable days. It was here, looking out across the sea of white blossoms in the Santa Clara Valley, that she said on the last morning, "Carol Wilson, if this book is ever published, I hope it will have a jade green cover, with black letters like the teakwood."

And so it has had—published by Stanford University Press (not the *Atlantic*!) where my friends had been following my research with interest, insisting "we want to publish this book as our first venture into the Trade field." There have been two editions, the first in 1931, the second in 1950 to celebrate Donaldina Cameron's 80th birthday.

When I approached her with this idea, she was easier to convince. In fact, she said, "I remarked to a friend the other day Carol Wilson and I literally fought, bled and almost died over the first writing, but I have come to the conclusion that the book should have a codicil."

Now, nearly twenty-five years later the Centennial of the work established in 1874 as the Occidental Board of Foreign Missions by the Presbyterian Church (the only enterprise with "foreign" connotation ever carried on within the confines of the USA) has called for another "codicil." This time it is a paperback, with the hope that a new generation will thus become familiar with what this fearless woman and her successors have accomplished.

If, of necessity, the tongs, child slavery and the highbinders formed the screen against which modern Chinatown shines in bold relief, the essence of this story is not display of evils but praise for the combined efforts of those Chinese and Americans who have evolved law and order out of the welter of pioneer conditions.

Donaldina Cameron was right. The work that justified the faith of those who saw a great need and met it has been carried on by many, but she participated in more years than any other person and lived to see her unfaltering belief in the redemptive power of the Holy Spirit revealed in three generations of those she loved and served. This new edition, like the first and second, is dedicated to those who pay tribute to her in selfless devotion to the principles which motivated her entire life.

CAROL GREEN WILSON

San Francisco
August, 1973

APOLOGIA

When this book was published over forty years ago neither the author, the subject nor the editor recognized that the correct designation for a native or descendant of Scotland is "Scottish," not "Scotch." Since the original edition was published we have been to Scotland to visit the ancestral home of the Camerons in Inverness, and to New Zealand, where we found Clydevale-on-the-Moleyneux, Donaldina's birthplace. For economic reasons the current edition is a photographic reproduction of the original and thus the error persists—with apologies. I just want my readers to realize that I know better now than in those early days.

C.G.W.

CHAPTER I

TITLES FAIRLY WON

"NOW TO GET HOME, fast. Forget the speed laws."

The young immigration official glanced at the tightly pursed lips of the white-haired woman beside him, but he lost no time in obeying. He stepped his engine up to sixty as they sped into the blackness of the night. In the back seat of the closely curtained sedan a sobbing little Chinese girl was still shrieking, "Fahn Quai! Fahn Quai!" as she shrank away from the outstretched hand of the strange foreigner in the front seat. The calm interpreter beside her spoke in soothing native tongue: "But she is not Fahn Quai. She is Lo Mo. She has come to protect you."

The young official could not turn his head as the road stretched out before him, but he could use his ears. This was the first raid he had taken part in with Miss Donaldina Cameron. Until now he had understood little of her eventful career in Chinatown; but as the whirring motor sped them from Stockton to San Francisco he had opportunity to understand why there was such a ring of authority in the quick-spoken command that had started their dash through valley and foothills to the securely bolted doors of the red brick dwelling on steep Sacramento Street where this gallant Scotch gentlewoman harbored her family of Chinese "daughters."

But the story of how she came by both her Chinese names belongs to times that are now almost hidden in memory.

Years ago, when fair smooth cheeks belied the snowy hair that even then set off her eager young face, she had one autumn day joined the scurrying crowds that daily jostled through the San Francisco Ferry Building gates, carefully guiding two small Orientals. They made their way up the broad stairs of the ferryboat and out to the forward deck. Here in the sunshine, the fresh breezes from the Bay bringing a touch of red even to yellow-tinged cheeks, the trio settled to enjoy the ever-changing scenes of a ferry trip. Like children the world over, they were full of questions. "Oh, *ma ma,* what boat is that?" and *"Ma ma,* is that big bird a sea gull?"—their childish treble rose in excitement.

On the seat opposite the group a party of tourists sat intrigued by the strange picture. Finally, one who could restrain her curiosity no longer turned to the young "mother."

"Are they really yours?" she ventured.

"I hope I may be forgiven," said Miss Cameron as she related the incident nearly a quarter-century later. "You see they were legally mine and I just said yes and let them go back to their Eastern homes with their amazing story of California local color."

Out of that incident sprang the title by which Donaldina Cameron has since been known and loved by Chinese girls the world over. They are numbered by the thousands, these girls who have been rescued from shame and slavery by her daring and understanding, a daring and understanding that have motivated her quest for human gold with the same courageous spirit that early brought seekers of the precious metal to California shores. The children on the ferry trip had been two such nuggets. A few days after the trip, one of them came to Miss Cameron with dark eyes full of understanding.

"We're not going to call you *'ma ma'* any more. It makes people look at us so. We'll have our own name for you, but it will mean the same thing."

And so it came to pass that "Lo Mo," "The Mother," was bestowed upon this gentle-born Scotslady. There had been Old World titles on both sides of her own family; but no one of them was ever more truly earned than the gracious token of affection by which this Cameron of the New World became known to those she served.

The little "daughter" who chose this name was evidently not an accomplished Cantonese grammarian. Students of Chinese will recognize that a strict interpretation of "lo mo" would be "old mother," and will sense that in its more general usage the term carries a disrepectful implication — "old woman," like our American expression, "old man." But that sentiment was farthest from the mind of little Leung T'sun Tai as she groped for a name that would not attract the unwanted attention which so often followed the use of *"ma ma,"* and yet would sound the note of filial devotion which she and all her little "sisters" felt for this altogether lovable guardian. If Leung T'sun Tai had had the benefit of a Chinese education, Miss Cameron's cognomen might have been "Wun Mo," which, with proper Cantonese inflection, pictures a charming, gracious young mother; or even Sse Mo, teacher, counselor, mother in a more general sense. But Leung T'sun Tai's schooling had been limited; and so it is that to the hundreds of girls who came under the spell of Donaldina Cameron's training in the Sacramento Street home, and to the thousands of friends and supporters scattered throughout the world, "Lo Mo" expresses all that is finest in that hallowed word "mother."

But as we have just seen, that was not the only title she had acquired with the passage of the years. Like the intrepid 'forty-niners, she sought her gold at the risk of life and limb. And in the battles with the underworld from which she unearthed her treasures, Miss Cameron won that other name by which she became known to those who feared her — "Fahn Quai, White Devil." One potent weapon which the wily slaveowners used against her was to fill the minds of their servitors with lurid tales of the tortures they would endure if they fell into the hands of Fahn Quai.

Perhaps the love of adventure, along with the indomitable faith "to remove mountains" if need required, was part of the inheritance of this "daughter of raiding border clans." She herself was not born in the land of the heather; for when the Cameron family consisted of father, mother, five girls, and one son, the head of the family decided to try to recoup the fortune lost in a great financial crash by going to far away New Zealand. The youngest of the girls at that time, Isabella, was left in Scotland to keep the grandmother from feeling the break in the clan too deeply. Never again was the family reunited, and not until 1904 did Isabella, who later married a doctor for an East India tea estate, see the new little sister, Donaldina MacKenzie, born in Clydevale on the Molyneux, July 26, 1869.

Donaldina first came through the Golden Gate as a two-year-old in the arms of William Greer Harrison, a ship's acquaintance on the long trip across the Pacific. This man, whose name is linked with the founding of many of San Francisco's historical enterprises, among them the now famous Olympic Club, and who also started the new city's first charity, a home for foundling babies, was always attracted by little children. And so this one who thus entered the city of her future labors looked up into his kindly eyes, and there began a friendship that was to guide her through perplexities then undreamed of.

Donaldina's mother, with her brood of six, was following her bearded rancher-husband, who had been lured from sparsely settled New Zealand to that land across the Pacific which ever beckoned the pioneer. Surrounded always by the retinue that served such ladies as she, both in the old Scotch home and on the great "station" where her husband had been overseer in the new land under the Southern Cross, the mother was aghast at primitive San Francisco. She had inquired the name of the best family hotel from a fellow-passenger, and upon her advice had taken her children to the American Exchange Hotel on Sansome Street instead of to the Grand Hotel where her husband, delayed in arrival from the ranch in the San Joaquin, would have expected to find her. The mistake, however, was a boon to baby Dolly, for she would stand nose flattened against the windowpane, fascinated by the stream of long-queued Chinese men pattering by in glazed black sahms under their cotton umbrellas when the pouring rain kept the children confined to their hotel room. These Chinese were the employees of a cigar factory near by. Never once did their strange appearance create aught but interest in this girl whose father had taught his children to "love all peoples."

Down in the San Joaquin Valley, where this man of the open soon took his family to an extensive sheep ranch, in the days when antelope still roamed the plans, Dolly found herself a chum of one of these same strange yellow men: she was always the pet of Jim, the old ranch cook, who tweaked her rosy cheeks as he handed her the special tart or the star-shaped cooky cut for her.

In the isolation of this ranch amid the brown rolling hills family ties were knit closer and Dolly had a privilege the older ones had missed. Her earliest cherished memories are of crooning ballads hummed to her by the mother with eyes full of wistful memories. There were no nurses with stiff starched bonnets in this lonely Western country, and the mother who had been the "party-day lady" to the older ones was Dolly's tender caretaker. Then suddenly, when the youngest was five years old, the mother died, leaving a gap in the family circle which could never be filled.

Donaldina and another sister, particularly, inherited much of the beauty of form and grace of spirit which so characterized this transplanted Old World lady; but as one the daughters all agreed, through the dim mists of years, that "no one was ever so lovely as our mother."

The ranch was home no longer, and the bereaved father soon moved his clan to The Willows, a suburb of San Jose, where they could more readily acquire their education. Here Dolly and her sisters attended the Castleman School for Girls, with its quaint atmosphere, and made lasting friendships among the daughters of Santa Clara County pioneers.

After a few years here the home was moved to Oakland, across the Bay from the great city that would later owe so much to Donaldina. Here began a friendship that was to become a guiding force not only in the life of the youngest daughter but also in the future solution of one of the most trying problems of the Pacific Coast; yet no one foresaw in the warmth of Mrs. P. D. Browne's friendship any other influence than that of a large-souled woman upon a motherless family.

By this time Annie, the oldest of the sisters, had reached the age where she could share with her father the task of bringing up the family. And through the long years she had a vital part in keeping the home spirit alive for all the busy sisters and the only brother, who went out from the hearthstone to serve in various ways in the developing history of a great state. Annie baked the birthday cakes, helped to plan the reunions, and offered encouragement in word and deed.

Oakland days were happy; but the California scene which was indelibly stamped in the affection of the Cameron family was the Southland, where the father was called to become manager for "Lucky" Baldwin on the famous old Puente Ranch in the San Gabriel Valley. This ranch home was seldom without guests, in the old hospitable way that tradition carried over from the days of the vanished California dons.

Among the school friends who came to share the long glorious summers of horseback riding over poppy-gold mesas and picnic tramps in the Sierra Madre foothills was Eleanor Olney of Oakland, whose memory treasured an episode of early 'teen-age. It was the Fourth of July. No band-playing celebration as in town, with the excitement of firecrackers, speeches, and red fire, was possible. Nothing daunted, Donaldina must give vent to her patriotism. With her chum she persuaded Allan, the popular brother, to join them in a private parade behind the barn, near the old creek. It was time for "Washington" to "cross the Delaware," but the girls were not good sailors. The boat rocked, tipped, capsized, and Allan, gallant commander, had to drag his crew to safety. It was a bedraggled group of patriots that crept stealthily in by a side door, fearing the sisterly disapproval of Annie's watchful eye, white dresses sadly stained with the red and blue of the dripping crêpe-paper decorations.

And so the years of her carefree childhood slipped away. Dolly wandered in the fields, knew each flower, roamed the plains, and loved the wild things. In the hot summer afternoons, or during the winter hours around the fire, her sister Katherine — inimitable storyteller — filled the mind of this little sister with stories from Dickens and Scott and other masters represented in the small library of books brought from the old home across the seas. Each sister contributed something to the shaping of the youngest. Helen, the sparklingly beautiful, taught her to know "the things of the spirit in everyday life." Lines of familiar hymns, verses from the family Bible, all took on added meaning as they came from the lips of this older sister.

The courage Donaldina imbibed from the Scottish chiefs of Katherine's stories never failed in case of need. One day the Brownes were visiting their former Oakland neighbors. Their daughter, Evelyn, had through the years become another devoted friend of Donaldina's — "Donald," her shortened term of affection. She missed her chum, then suddenly spied her, bronze hair flying in the wind, high up on the platform of the windmill. Evelyn ran for her father. Pulling him excitedly to the window to point out Donald's perilous position, she was nonplussed when he casually remarked that he "guessed she would take care of the situation all right." And Mr. Browne's confidence in the young Scot, whom he so affectionately admired, was shortly justified as the disabled windmill resumed its activity after Donald's successful repair.

Almost instinctive response to need has characterized Donaldina Cameron's entire life. But in those days it took outsiders to recognize the daring and bravery that go with this instinct. Dolly was the adored baby sister in a big family. As girlhood days ended she entered normal school in Los Angeles. Yet teaching held no incentive for her. She was restless, although she scarcely recognized it herself. Beauty, gaiety, freedom, the good times that normal youth craves, were hers in full measure, among the host of friends that the Camerons possessed. Throughout her long life the older sisters continued to see, instead of the firm, experience-seasoned Lo Mo, the vivid Dolly as she started off for a flower festival in Los Angeles. Her dress of cream nun's veiling only served to set off the gorgeous coloring of her cheeks, her gray-brown eyes and penciled black brows, and a tight-fitting cap holding in place the tumbled mass of hair from which two heavy braids of iridescent bronze hung down. A happy united family the Camerons were in those days, making each successive guest a part of the wholesome ranch circle. But beneath it all Dolly was restive — eager to be doing something.

Then came a hot summer day. The Brownes again were visitors at the Cameron ranch. Driving home from the little country church, Dolly listened enchanted as Mrs. Browne described her busy days in the fascinating city in the North, her active brain alert with plans for helping in many places. With glowing eyes she talked of the Chinese girls rescued by her remarkable friend, Miss Culbertson, from brothels and dens such as the sheltered Dolly had never even read about. She spoke with enthusiasm of the new branch of the Young Women's Christian Association which she had helped to found in San Francisco.

Young girls, alone in a big city, did need some wholesome recreation and religious life.

Mrs. Browne was driving the old family horse. She loved this change to country ways. Suddenly she halted the buggy in the shade of the bending pepper trees.

"Dolly" — her hand rested affectionately on that of her young companion — "don't *you* want to do something?"

"But what? I'm not prepared." Donaldina looked up, half wistful, half reluctant.

"Won't you come up and help Miss Culbertson at the Chinese home? She's getting so frail, and now that Miss Houseworth has to leave she will be so overburdened." A burden bearer! That is what Donaldina always was, with her gay and buoyant spirit. Even as a lisping baby, her sisters love to recall how during a siege of whooping cough she would come to them, the taller ones, inviting "Tome, toff on my bweast!" And so it was that her heart heard this appeal, as her imagination leaped toward adventure.

CHAPTER II

DAUGHTER TO MISS CULBERTSON

IT WAS IN A CHINATOWN which has long since passed into fanciful tradition that Donaldina Cameron came to live and work on that gray, foggy morning in 1895 — greeted unexpectedly by Eleanor Olney, who sprang up from the carved teakwood chair in Miss Culbertson's anteroom. "Just for one year," her adoring family had reluctantly consented. In her early twenties, unsophisticated and untrained, she came, overflowing with something unexpressed within that poured out freely and fully to meet the need which greeted her on every hand.

Miss Culbertson's niece, Anna, was staying with her at the time, while she attended art school. At the end of that first afternoon, Anna appeared with an armful of white roses to welcome the new assistant so near her own age — a gesture that warmed the heart of the flower-loving girl from southern California.

But not all of her introduction to 920 Sacramento Street was as reassuring. Very soon after her arrival, Miss Culbertson called Donaldina into the office.

"Are you sure you will not be afraid in this work?"

"Oh, no!" she answered quickly.

"It isn't too late to change your mind — there are dangers, you know."

Immediately her Scotch blood was aroused.

"Why?"

Without raising her voice, Miss Culbertson explained that on that very morning the girl who was cleaning the halls had found a strange-looking stick. Police were called and after a hasty investigation declared there was enough explosive in that "stick" to blow up a whole city block. This was unusual, for the Chinese seldom went this far with their bitter threats against the Home. But the latest slave girl rescued by Miss Culbertson had represented such a high purchase price that the owner had attempted to wreak direct vengeance.

Miss Culbertson turned quietly to her new helper.

"Now, are you going to stay?"

"Are you?" just as calmly returned Donaldina Cameron.

"Of course."

"Then I shall stay too."

Thus began a relationship between two women of finely tuned sensibilities which made it possible for the ideals of the older one to live on and on, transmitted through the devotion of the younger to hundreds of girls who, though of another race, are one in spirit with her. Reared in the gentle refinement of a western New York home, Miss Margaret Culbertson had come to California as governess for the small boys of a brother of that well-known pioneer and empire builder, D. O. Mills. Because of their common cultural interests a friendship had sprung up between her and Mrs. P. D. Browne.

Mrs. Browne had been early identified with a group of women who had sensed a unique need in old San Francisco. Hordes of Chinese, lured across the Pacific by the same glitter that had started covered wagons across the plains in '49, had poured into California to supply the labor needed for the development of mining camps and other industries of this pioneer land. By 1876, of the 148,000 Chinese in America, 60,000 were in California, one-half of these crowded into nine teeming, colorful blocks in San Francisco. In the year 1882, 40,000 Chinese immigrants came in. Bitter opposition began to arise. These thrifty Chinese, with their rice bowls and low standards of living, were considered a menace to white labor. Every reader of Bret Harte and Joaquin Miller is familiar with "the heathen Chinee" of those days, with his long, braided queue, and his stealthy, slippered feet, his reeking opium-den, as well as with "John," the ever-faithful servant appearing with his bowl of pungent China lilies blossoming for Chinese New Year, or with the silk-coated gentleman merchants of old Dupont Street.

But perhaps not so many know the stories of the little slave girls kept behind barred doors of the labyrinthine dwellings in back alleys in old San Francisco's Chinatown. Easily forgotten bits of humanity they were, smuggled in like the opium their owners craved, bought and sold with the shining gold that gleams through all the history of these early days.

Ordinary domestic slaves sold for from $100 to $500; the pretty creatures bartered to the keepers of houses of ill-fame brought much larger sums. In the unequal population of these colonies of Chinese workmen, the lives of these children of the dark were pitiful beyond description.

Little wonder, then, that the group of women associated with Mrs. Browne felt the appeal of those helpless beings, many of them barely in their 'teens. The pressing need was a place of shelter in which they could be guarded, under the protection of United States laws based on the Thirteenth Amendment, from their scheming owners. At just about this time church women of America were organizing for foreign mission activities. The women in San Francisco were being urged to help found an orphangage in Shanghai; but they were soon convinced that within their own gates was an opportunity uniquely their own. And thus it happened that the so-called Occidental Board was organized in 1873 to undertake the only foreign mission enterprise ever carried on within the United States.

The pioneering was made easier by the knowledge of Chinese ways and language contributed by Rev. and Mrs. I. C. Condit, who in 1870 had returned from a number of years in the Orient. The friendly relations that they were able to establish with the better type of leaders in the Chinese community laid a firm foundation for the years of useful work that were to follow.

With the help of these friends and many others, they sought to build up a haven for the stranded and friendless among the pathetic waifs, bereft of all except evil ties in this strange new land.

B. E. Lloyd, writing in 1876, says in his *Lights and Shades in San Francisco:*

"Although as a race the Chinese are characterized for their love of domestic life, few family circles have been formed among them in San Francisco. Woman, the important link in the sacred chain, is not here; or if she is here she has been forced to engage in that infamous pursuit that is the destroyer of homes. Of the whole number of Chinese women in San Francisco, there are, perhaps less than a hundred who are lawful wives, or keepers of homes."

Such slavery had been accepted without question from time immemorial in the country from which these immigrants came. In China girl children sold into domestic slavery in some instances became secondary wives or concubines; but the passage of the antipolygamy laws in May 1931 revealed a revulsion against the custom in modern China. In the early days of California, however, the transplanted system, condoned both by law and by morality in the ancient countries of the Orient, became even baser in its operation in the new environment. Girls kidnaped in China or enticed from their homes by false promises of marriage or education, brought into this country through deceptive practices, would then be sold, not to one man, but into houses of prostitution where they were forced to earn vast sums for their owners. This situation was of course not a sign of peculiar viciousness in the Chinese; indeed, in the early days of which Mr. Lloyd was writing the greed of knavish American officials willing to share in the profits through the bribes and fees that are necessary wherever unlawful practices exist made a condition such that "the Chinese were white compared to their Anglo-Saxon conspirators."

When the women of the Occidental Board first sought to provide shelter for the helpless victims of this system, they were able to secure only three or four upper rooms at 8½ Prospect Street, a small new building on the very edge of Chinatown. That their humble efforts were not wasted is evidenced by the useful records of many of the first who fled to these tiny rooms for protection. Practically all of these "pioneer" rescued girls devoted their entire subsequent lives to the work of interpreting, and of rescuing and educating their less fortunate countrywomen, some of them returning to China for this purpose.

At the time that Mrs. Browne brought her appeal to her friend, Miss Culbertson, in 1881, the work had been established in a permanent home. On the side of one of those steep San Francisco hills where the old cable cars clattered down to the Bay through the narrow thoroughfare lined with Oriental shops and queer-smelling food stalls, the Board had bought for the purpose a red brick building. Then, some years later, the more familiar Home across the street, now 920 Sacramento, was erected to house the ever-increasing family of the rescued. The cornerstone was laid by one of the early "daughters," T'sang T'sun, who was already interpreter and assistant. "With strong faith in the salvation of my countrywomen in this country and in China, I lay this cornerstone in the name of Jesus Christ."

It was to "Nine-Twenty" that young Donaldina came so blithely in 1895 to learn from the leader whose sixteen years of service had won her the title of "Mother" to Chinese girls and women.

The young daughter of a Board member described in her diary the first appearance of Miss Culbertson's protégé at an open meeting of Occidental Board. She wore, according to Vina Howland Edwards, a purple shirtwaist and a black voile skirt lined with rusty taffeta. The waist had the usual mutton-leg sleeves — "and they were mutton, not lamb, for they were very large, lined with what was called 'fiber chamois.' When a coat was put on, the sleeves were folded down to get it on."

Donaldina's hair was worn in a big soft pompadour. Although she was barely twenty-five, it was streaked with gray, adding dignity to the serious young face.

From her window, barred and guarded as were all of the outlooks of this quiet citadel on the edge of Chinatown of the 'nineties, Donaldina looked up "China Street," as Sacramento Street was known in those days, to Nob Hill, home of aristocrats, where the Hopkinses, Stanfords, Floods, and Huntingtons ruled the salons which their newly won wealth had ingrafted upon picturesque, pioneering San Francisco. Young and beautiful, with family ties that would have gained her entrée anywhere, Donaldina could easily have had her place in the functions that nightly blazed from this hilltop. The path, however, that led her into the heart of the city's night life followed another direction. Down the steep walk to Stockton and Dupont streets below, this young girl followed her courageous leader into dens that frightened the most adventurous of tourists. Here she beheld sights she had never dreamed existed.

"I'll need your help tonight," Miss Culbertson had said, as she glanced up from a tightly folded scrap of paper which had been slipped into her hands a few days after Donaldina's arrival. With three officers as guards they made their way to Spofford Alley, then one of the worst of the narrow by-passes of Chinatown. The door indicated in the note was heavily barred. No amount of pounding would bring an answer. Out came axes and sledge hammers. A shattered window, its iron gratings pried off by the powerful police, was opened, and in crept the rescue party.

They found an anxious girl nervously awaiting release. With true feminine regard for her possessions she begged the officers to help her get her jewelry and watch held in the safekeeping of her mistress.

"Not here — I get," readily responded that individual, starting out of the house. An officer stepped to her side to insure her return. What she wanted, and accomplished, was to notify the master of the house in a gambling den a few basements away. "Native son of the Golden West," he was, educated in California public schools, and ready with his subtle answer.

"Let her prove she have property, then I give"; adding, "Madam, you know what these women are — how they tell lies, tell things not true."

"Yes," said Miss Culbertson, drawing herself up with stern dignity to stab this schemer with her piercing brown eyes. "We know these women are what you men make them. You compel them to lead these wretched lives while you live off their earnings."

"Madam, you shut up. You talk too much." He turned on his slippered heel.

No amount of persuasion could produce the missing jewelry; but the rescued slave girl went off to gain, through her redirected life, treasures which neither rust nor thieves could touch.

All the drama of life unrolled before the startled eyes of the new assistant in those first breathtaking days. Less than two weeks after this first raid, Miss Culbertson was to leave for New Orleans with a bride who was to marry a prosperous Chinese merchant there. Here was a task ready-made for the romantic Donaldina. The bride must be taken to the shops for a complete American trousseau, for there were few of her race in distant New Orleans, and her future husband was very proud of his own newly acquired ways.

No sooner was the bride started for her Southern home than Donaldina was greeted by a message from a ship's officer saying that a woman, dangerously ill at the docks with two small children, was desirous of being taken to the Home. With Anna Culbertson she hastened to the dock to find the message all too true. The children were immediately drawn to the young "teacher" and readily came with her, while her friend attended to the needs of the invalid.

Despite the best of nursing and medical care the sufferer lived only a few days; but her death came in peace, for her prayer had been answered. She had survived to reach the Home, where her little ones would be assured of care and education. All her possessions were committed to these friends of her own rescued childhood, with the wish that the daughter should become a medical missionary and the boy a minister. Hong Leen, the mother, had been one of the early brides from the Home, and her Los Angeles bungalow had been one of prosperity and happiness. But her husband, Woo Hip, with true Oriental pride in ancestry had longed to take his family to the land of his forefathers. In 1893, despite the warnings of friends that war clouds and plague made this an unfavorable time for a visit, he had sailed across the Pacific. Smitten with the plague in Hong Kong, he had arrived at his home in China insane, to live only a few days. Then, added to Hong Leen's grief was the tragedy of parental blame on her as the cause of her husband's death. Persecuted and ill, she had finally determined to come back to the only home now left to her, and thus had begun that last journey.

Excitement, romance, tragedy, these made up Donaldina's strange new days, days which she described in the first report she wrote as "each interwoven with its own particular lights and shadows — the shadows neither dark nor deep, while the lights shine brightly, 'bidding our hearts look up, not down, as the cross fades before the crown.'"

The promised year was drawing to a close. Letters from the ranch were full of sunshine and freedom. Young friends were planning summer camping trips. Would she be home in time to join them? The day was cold, an early summer fog graying the close-standing walls of city buildings.

Donaldina walked down Market Street. Would that it led out to green pastures instead of to the blue-gray Bay, whence the weirdly insistent fog horns sounded intermittently! Something of the spell of this strange city was stirring within her. Yet she felt oppressed. There was so much that was sordid about it. She needed the courage that sounded in Allan's brotherly voice, Annie's wise counsel, Jessie's reading of poetry—just someone who really belonged. Miss Culbertson was very ill. More and more the daily tasks came to Donaldina. She dared not burden the invalid with too many questions. It was all very perplexing. Why had she come? Should she go back, now that the year was up?

In the midst of her reverie she quickened her steps. She sensed the presence of someone she could not see. A large hand, vibrant with friendliness, was laid on her shoulder.

"And how is Donaldina this morning?" rang out the rich Celtic tones of Dr. John Hemphill. For many years this tall black-bearded Irishman had spoken with eloquence from the pulpit of old Calvary Church, then facing on Union Square. His friendship for this young girl with a common British heritage was one of the bright spots in both of their ministries. Little did he know that this conventional greeting and the few casual remarks they exchanged as he "walked a mile" with her would have such a profound influence on this young friend's life. But she turned back to the Home that morning full of new zeal. She was ready to stay on, ready to take her share of the increasing burdens.

And then, just when her mind was at rest in her decision, came a surprise. Charlie Bailey, mining-engineer husband of sister Jessie and always a hero of the youngest Cameron, appeared unexpectedly one evening at dinner. He was gay with news from the orange-blossom valley whither, like Gwen of *The Sky-Pilot,* Dolly so often "sent her heart away." With his debonair possessiveness he persuaded Miss Culbertson to let her helper come home on a vacation of two weeks before "the year" was up.

There was an ivy wall on a lot on California Street between Kearny and Grant Avenue. "I could lead you to the exact spot," Lo Mo said many years later, recalling the excited girl she was then, "where the birds nesting in the ivy echoed the song in my heart when I almost ran down the street early the next morning to do my shopping for that trip. I bought a flat sailor hat for a dollar and a half, a few crisp, high-neck shirtwaists, and a gay muslin dress for each sister. Then I was ready to start on the *Owl* with Charlie that night."

Excitement appeared even before Donaldina and her brother-in-law reached home. The train was halted in the Tehachapi by an unusual April snowfall, and Charlie Bailey showed her how to make snowballs. Exhilarated by this novel experience, she was ready to plunge into the round of gaiety that the family had planned. Picnics, long horseback rides, jolly parties attended by old friends filled every waking hour, building energy and happy memory-pictures for the years ahead.

But by the end of these two weeks in the land of her dreams Donaldina, recognizing the tug of her new life, was ready to go back to Nine-Twenty fortified for tasks she could not foresee.

Miss Culbertson's strength ebbed fast during the next year; but she refused to leave her adopted family. Finally, letters from New York persuaded her to come home for convalescence promising new power for the tasks ahead. Her sister crossed the continent to care for her on the long trip home. The day came for her departure. The ambulance stood at the door, for she must travel without rising. As the stretcher-bearers carried their frail burden down the winding stairway at Nine-Twenty there was not a dry eye in the double row of girls who lined the stairs. Married girls with their babies in arms, school girls who had stayed home for the day, young and old, they had all gathered to wish her Godspeed. The driver was ready to start when little Yoke Lon, one of the youngest daughters of the Home, was lifted up for a final kiss.

With this baby still in her arms, Donaldina turned back up the steps to the waiting family that would now be hers. As the last sound of the wheels over the cobbles echoed back, an overwhelming sense of her unfitness came over her. Unlike Miss Culbertson, she had not been trained by travel and education to assume so much authority. She had felt no "call" to be a missionary. In fact, she had little understanding of what that meant. But her splendid father, whose sublime faith had carried him over every difficulty and disappointment in his own life, had in some way imparted to this youngest daughter the fundamental stability that she needed. She recognized that like the windmill of her childhood this damaged human property was hers to repair.

One of Miss Culbertson's favorite "daughters" was waiting for the birth of her child, and in the long days of preparation they had spent many hours together, the older woman imparting the sweetness of life's meaning to this girl who had hitherto known only the bitter. For Miss Culbertson to miss the fulfillment of these months of waiting had been almost harder than leaving the living.

But it fell to Donaldina Cameron to take the babe from the doctor's hands when the time came a few days later. She laid down her new charge, bathed with trembling hands, to answer a ring of the doorbell. The messenger handed her a telegram. Miss Culbertson had not lived to reach the home where her other sisters waited. Silently Miss Cameron climbed back up the stairs to the room where the girl mother was resting. The sun was breaking over the Berkeley hills across the Bay as she stood by the eastern windows lifting up her eyes for help.

"Dear God," she breathed, "may the mantle of that wonderful woman fall upon this little child!"

CHAPTER III

NEW RESPONSIBILITIES

AGAIN MRS. BROWNE had to choose a leader. She knew that the future head of the Home was there in her young friend. The Board, too, recognized Miss Cameron's magnetic hold on the girls, but felt that she was too young to bear the burden alone. Donaldina herself wanted to fly.

In the inner struggle of that Sabbath afternoon the youngest Cameron daughter faced life with its terrifying reality. She knew she could not undertake this responsibility alone. But unexpected help was ready.

The mother of one of her school friends was called from the Chautauqua platform to be the nominal head of the Home. Mrs. Mary H. Field's charming manner lent grace and maturity, and her gifted pen preserved much that was picturesque in the early record.

One morning Mrs. Field came to the staff breakfast with Kipling's new poem, "The White Man's Burden," in her hand.

"How like our work that is," she remarked as she read aloud the lines:

> To wait in heavy harness
> On fluttered folk and wild,
> Your new-caught sullen peoples,
> Half-devil and half-child.

Mrs. Field's report amplified this reaction. She dwelt upon the bad influence of the turbulent spirits of some of the rescued girls, their vulgar habits, concluding that in most of them there was very little to which one could appeal. She added, too, that hard as it was to deal with the ignorant and degraded of her own race, the low-grade Mongolian woman presented a harder problem — "more conscienceless, more suspicious, more fiery and voluble, more utterly bereft of reason — half-devil and half-child."

To Donaldina Cameron, on the other hand, this was not a "white man's burden." She was not dealing with a race problem. She was making friends, living naturally among these girls. To her they were individuals capable of full development into useful womanhood, when the resuscitating power of love could awaken their souls. Spring after spring she had watched wild flowers crop up on the Puente hills, urged through the sod by the warmth of the valley sunshine, and to her the release of dormant good in the stunted lives under her protection was a process just as natural. Only one must first expose them to the sunshine.

Whenever she walked up the gangplank of an incoming trans-Pacific steamer with an immigration officer there was something in her manner that inspired the confidence of the trembling Chinese girls waiting for their interview. Little Jean Ying, a fifteen-year-old Cantonese girl, was seeking admission as the "daughter" of a Chinese merchant. The officer had detected a strange incoherence in her story and he asked Donaldina to come with him while he requestioned the child.

Jean, wearied and bewildered by the long trip in steerage, the fierce threats of her guides, the innumerable official questions which she had answered as taught, looked up blankly at this new face. At first unresponsive with the hopelessness born of despair, she warmed slowly to the kindness of the very pretty lady who smiled patiently as she waited for the interpreter to relay her message. Then Jean promised to send word if all was not well after landing.

There was nothing for Donaldina to do but to wait and wonder. Weeks passed. Then one night a strange Chinese messenger appeared at Nine-Twenty — he must see Miss Cameron.

"You come help," he entreated; "very young girl, she sold to bad house — she say, you come get her."

Donaldina sent him back with her promise to help and a bright red handkerchief to be used by Jean as a token of identification.

When the blackness of night settled over Chinatown two policemen of the Chinatown squad called for Miss Cameron. Search warrant in hand, they proceeded to the address given by the mysterious messenger. The child with the red handkerchief was Jean!

Successfully rescued, the little Cantonese remained some months in the Home, pouring out her true story to Donaldina Cameron.

Only daughter of a well-to-do manufacturer in Canton, she had gone on a visit to friends. On the way she was kidnaped and quickly spirited off to the distant seaport of Hong Kong. At last a purchaser was found willing to pay $175 for this human chattel — a man who agreed to bring her across the great Pacific where her parents could not possibly find her. Like many another child lost in this darkly plotted traffic, she had been coached and browbeaten into lying about the psuedo "father" awaiting her in San Francisco, until the gentle spell of this rescuer of frightened girls, Donaldina Cameron, had touched her life.

Letters crossed the Pacific. Jean's grateful family sent money for her passage home, and friends of the Home sailing back to their station in China took her with them. Eagerly Donaldina opened the long envelope from Canton telling of the safe arrival and the reunion with Jean's anxious parents.

Not every situation unfolded with the miraculous swiftness of the rescue of Jean Ying. An older slave girl who had made her own escape was safely installed as a member of the Nine-Twenty family. But her owner, who lived in Palo Alto, a new town sprung up in the shadow of the recently established Leland Stanford Junior University, soon discovered where his property was hidden. One cold March day he appeared at the Sacramento Street Home accompanied by a burly constable holding in his hand a warrant for the arrest of Kum Quai on the charge of stealing jewelry. He showed Miss Cameron a "picture" of the girl he wanted, but unaccustomed as she then was to all the subtle tricks, new with each case, she said quite frankly:

"You have made a mistake. We have no such girl here."

"Let us see for ourselves," demanded the constable, producing his search warrant.

The brass gong was rung, lessons were stopped, sewing was dropped to the floor, and brooms were stood in corners, as the excited family quickly gathered in the large chapel room. This was always the custom when a search was to be made; but usually the guardians knew which girl was wanted and she was carefully hidden between a double folding-door or under rice sacks back of the basement gas meter.

This time, however, no one knew. Miss Cameron was quite sure the searchers were on the wrong track. With horror, then, she saw Kum Quai's face pale at the sight of her leering owner, and she was quite helpless to prevent the course of the law as the constable served the warrant on the terror-stricken girl. She pleaded with him with all her usual force; but he was there to do his duty and earn his fee. No silly woman could stop him. Miss Cameron dismissed the other weeping girls and reluctantly turned the key that opened the heavy bolted front door. The biting wind from the Bay swept up the narrow street, sending added shivers over the thinly clad little girl clinging to Lo Mo's hand.

"Come along here, we must be off," demanded the impatient officer, jerking her from her protector's arm. For one instant Miss Cameron stood hesitant. Then a voice spoke in her heart: "Go with her—she is yours." And, hatless and coatless, she ran after the retreating trio, followed by Yuen Qui, the interpreter, supplying needed outer wraps. All the way to Palo Alto she sought to calm the despairing girl, who shrank trembling from the rough constable and the triumphant Chinese owner.

Even when the cell doors of the shack they called a jail were locked on her charge, Lo Mo stayed beside her. Two boxes were all the bed provided, but sleep was not to come that night. About midnight voices were heard talking excitedly in the corridor. The jailer appeared to open the cell. Kum Quai's "friends" had arrived with bail. Lo Mo knew this trick well enough. Miss Culbertson had told her too many tales of girls thus bailed out who had completely dropped from sight, or who had been found months later in conditions unspeakably worse than those of their former servitude. She barricaded the door with a piece of scantling, but the bailiff took out his ax. When he had succeeded in battering a hole big enough for his arm, he reached through, knocked down the barricade, and grabbed the girl from Lo Mo.

The exulting Chinamen lifted their prey into a waiting buggy. Lo Mo climbed in too. But rough hands pulled her out and threw her into the tar-weed beside the road. Scarcely sensing whether she was hurt or not, the undaunted Lo Mo fled to the heart of the village for help. The only friend she could rouse was Dr. Hall, a druggist on a corner near the Circle. He introduced her to the proprietor of Larkin's Hotel, who gave her a blanket and allowed her to rest on a sofa in the lobby for the few remaining hours of the night. Dr. Hall then telephoned the San Jose sheriff to send a searching party after the fleeing Chinese.

In the meantime the Palo Alto justice of the peace, returning from a ride on the county road, had met the escaping trio. They asked as a special favor that he hold the trial then and there; and so in an improvised roadside court, at two-thirty in the morning, the frightened girl, waiving jury and counsel, pleaded guilty to the charge against her. One of her escorts acted as interpreter, while the other paid the five-dollar fine imposed by the judge, and off they galloped.

By morning the college town was thoroughly incensed by news of the outrage, which had spread among citizens and also among the Stanford University students. Local papers and San Francisco dailies carried columns of reports and cartoons, and by night a mass meeting was called to denounce the public officials who had participated in the affair. Handbills were circulated throughout the town and university, the Campus one reading:

"On to Palo Alto! Our reputation is at stake. Bring own rope. No. 3 Hall. 8:00 o'clock tonight."

"No meeting fraught with more genuine sensation has been held in the college town for years," said the *San Francisco Examiner* of April 7, 1900. "So great was the indignation that none of the alleged conspirators dared put in an appearance. Resolutions drafted by the Stanford chaplain, D. Charles Gardner, and signed by a committee of citizens and professors were adopted condemning the whole affair and all officials participating in it."

But mere resolutions failed to satisfy the students' wrath. Three hundred strong they marched down University Avenue and then along side streets to the jail, with lanterns and torches. Then, according to the news columns, "began a tumult, the like of which Palo Alto had never before heard at 10 o'clock in the night."

With cries of "Burn it up," "Tear it down," they clambered upon fences and ripped off boards. For a time it looked as if the jail would be wiped out; but finally the angry mob contented itself with carrying off the boards and the filthy blankets from the cell in which Miss Cameron and her charge had been locked. These were taken to the center of town, where an effigy of the justice of the peace was burned "amidst the shouting of hundreds of curses."

A San Jose lawyer with a large Chinese practice was openly accused of engineering the abduction plot. Because of this, San Jose also waxed indignant over the situation and secured Miss Cameron to come there on the following Tuesday evening to narrate her story before an audience of several thousand gathered at Turn Verein Hall.

A few days before this meeting Miss Cameron had been visiting at the home of some old friends, whose son, then a railroad clerk, had been fired with this opportunity to outwit the vicious political gang that held the city in its clutches. It was rumored that the gang bosses proposed to pack the meeting in defense of Attorney Herrington, and Paul Dinsmore set himself the task of countering this. With borrowed money, later raised through popular subscription, he paid five hundred dollars to charter a train from Palo Alto which transported enough Stanford students to fill the reserved center section of the great hall. What happened is best explained in the graphic report of the *San Francisco Chronicle* for April 3, 1900:

The chairman stated that the meeting had been called to denounce the perpetrators of the foul outrage that had been committed at Palo Alto and to take such action as would insure that the fair name and fame of Santa Clara county would never again be brought to shame by the perpetration of such acts in the name of the law and by officers of the law.

The storms of applause that frequently interrupted and followed the utterances of these sentiments gave no doubt as to the views of the audience. A feature of the applause was that of a large delegation of Stanford students, who sat in a body in the center of the hall. They gave three cheers for Colonel Whitton [the chairman of the evening] and three groans for the Palo Alto Justice. This caused much laughter and applause.

Seldom anywhere has a great audience made so wonderful a demonstration of enthusiasm as when Miss Cameron came forward in response to the introduction and told her simple, straightforward story of the experience she had had in attempting to protect her ward and prevent her from falling into the hands of two Chinese who were bent on her capture with the aid of the officers of the law. Although low, Miss Cameron's voice was heard in all portions of the room.

The speaker proved by her beauty and modest manner that she was a refined and cultured woman, and it seemed amazing how men could subject such a woman to such vile indignities as she related as having been perpetrated at Palo Alto, the statements being uncontradicted by anything that was urged during the evening in favor of the accused.

Chairman Brun of the Palo Alto investigation committee was then introduced and read a statement from the Justice in which he corroborated the story of Miss Cameron almost to the letter. A presentation of the case was then made by Attorney Weigle of Palo Alto, who championed the cause of Miss Cameron there.

In the midst of the meeting the accused attorney made a dramatic entrance through the excited crowd, smiling and bowing to the hissing men who were shouting for ropes and yelling "Hang him!" In an impassioned speech he described the "happy marriage" of his client on the evening following the Palo Alto affair, and not only produced the Chinese couple under heavy bodyguard but displayed a certificate of good character for the groom from a number of high officials of Tehama County, then a sparsely settled county in the northeastern corner of the state.

In spite of Herrington's speech, resolutions similar to those of the previous Palo Alto meeting were adopted uanimously and with rousing cheers by the meeting:

The citizens of San Jose in mass meeting assembled denounce the late outrage committed at Palo Alto by officers of Santa Clara county in the name of the law upon Miss Cameron of the Presbyterian Mission of San Francisco and the Chinese women in her charge.

We admire the fearless, heroic, and womanly action of Miss Cameron in her efforts to prevent the abduction of her ward, which was accomplished under the guise of law.

We most earnestly commend the action of the people of Palo Alto in their determination to bring to justice the guilty parties, and in the prosecution of such offenders we pledge to the citizens of Palo Alto our moral support and financial aid.

We rejoice at the prompt action of the Presidents of Stanford and the

University of California in their denunciation of the outrage and in their demand that the guilty parties be brought to justice.

And we now declare that the time has come when it is the duty of every man and woman within our country who has any regard for human rights and public decency to take such action as will not only secure the punishment of such offenders, but will in the future prevent the recurrence of such gross outrages within our borders.

Following its story of the San Jose meeting the *Chronicle* gave a graphic account of the marriage referred to by Herrington:

Justice of the Peace Thomas F. Dunn of this city unwittingly played a part in the Palo Alto outrage that will make it still more difficult to release the unfortunate Kum Quai from the highbinders. It appears now that the woman was married Saturday afternoon under the assumed name of Ah Guey to Chung Bow. Justice Dunn performed the ceremony in the attic of a house on the north side of Pacific Street, between Kearny and Dupont.

According to the story told by Justice Dunn, Saturday afternoon as he was about to close his day's labors, Harry K. Wolff, a clerk in the employ of Attorney H. H. Lowenthal, called upon him to perform a marriage, for which he had just obtained a license. With Wolff came two Chinese, Chung Bow, the prospective bridegroom, and his friend, Wong Fong. As there appeared to be no objection to the marriage, a carriage was secured and the party started for Chinatown.

Wong Fong, who acted as the master of ceremonies, led the party up a narrow flight of stairs, through a number of dark and circuitous passages, across an enclosed bridge and finally ushered them into a heavily curtained room. There was no furniture in the room except a few chairs. Two Chinese women, apparently awaiting the arrival of the party, were its sole occupants. As soon as the door was closed Wong Fong disappeared for a moment, but shortly returned with the unfortunate Kum Quai.

Justice Dunn thought the proceedings a little strange, but, after questioning the woman through an interpreter and finding that she was willing to plunge into the matrimonial state, he quickly performed the ceremony making her the wife of Chung Bow.

Chung Bow represented to the Justice that he was a mining man from Trinity, where he holds a number of small placer diggings. Harry Wolff says that he has known the man for some time, having often met him in his employer's office, where he was a frequent visitor. He made no pretense of knowing the woman, he says, and if there was any crooked work he was not a party to it.

In the meantime the true picture was being conveyed to Miss Cameron through those secret underground channels that only she and her close associates know. She was told that Kum Quai had been forced into this marriage under threat of death. Then, while Chinese friends were busy gathering further evidence, a wire came from B. F. Hall, telephone agent at Palo Alto. Hall had recognized one of the Chinese escorts, Wong Fong, as he passed through on the San Jose train en route to San Francisco, and had sent the message at once to Nine-Twenty. Miss Cameron hurried to the station in time to meet the incoming train, calling to her assistance Policeman O'Connor, to whom she explained the situation. Together they watched the crowd file off the train. "There he is," she called, as Wong Fong approached the gate. His face was indelibly fixed in her memory of the Palo Alto jail night, and there was no mistaking his identity. O'Connor greeted the astonished Chinese with handcuffs, and he was taken to police headquarters, where he was charged with abduction.

The trial was called at Mayfield, and here was presented the opportunity to spring the coup that Donaldina Cameron's intimate knowledge of the ways of the Chinese world made possible. She had been informed on good authority that Kum Quai was one of a large number of girls who had been brought into the country the year before, ostensibly for the Omaha Exposition but in reality for the San Francisco slave market. Accordingly she had no legal right to remain in the country.

Miss Cameron appealed to federal authorities for assistance. In those days the courtly Colonel Jackson was Collector of the Port and Immigration Commissioner for San Francisco, a man remembered by pioneer residents as a typical "gentleman of the old school." Immediately his interest was aroused and he sent John Endicott Gardner, official government interpreter, to Mayfield to represent him at the trial.

The late afternoon sun was filtering through the dusty windows of the country courthouse when Bert Herrington, attorney for the defendant, strode into the crowded room announcing that he was going to produce the Chinese girl, Kum Quai, as a witness. A path was made down the aisle as she entered, in American dress and heavily veiled, accompanied by Herrington's sister.

The Justice of the Peace recognized Dr. Gardner in the audience and invited him to act as interpreter. This was the opportunity that he and Miss Cameron had awaited.

"May I ask the witness a question?" he inquired of the Judge.

The Judge nodding assent, Dr. Gardner spoke to the girl in Cantonese.

"Have you a *Chuck-Jee* (registration card)?"

Taken utterly unawares, she shook her head: "No *Chuck-Jee.*"

"Then, in the name of the Government of the United States, I place you under arrest!"

Pandemonium reigned in the courtroom at this unexpected turn of affairs; but thankfulness welled up in Lo Mo's heart. She knew her charge was safe in federal hands.

Attorney Herrington asked to have his witness removed from the room, to be allowed to wait outside with his sister, to whom she had "become greatly attached in these trying days."

This was granted and he seated the two women in the back seat of a vehicle, of which the horses stood untied by the watering-trough.

Herrington now returned to the trial of Wong Fong. Dr. Gardner, who had followed his prisoner from the room, was also called back to his post as interpreter but he left Dr. Hall and two other friends on guard outside.

Suddenly Herrington slipped from the courtroom and sprang, hatless, into the front seat of the waiting vehicle, before the watching guards could sense his coming. He lashed the untied horses to a full gallop and dashed off along the country road.

A yell to the courtroom, and proceedings suddenly stopped. Dr. Gardner ran from the room, the tails of his frock coat flapping in the wind, and the gray-bearded Dr. Hall untied his own horse. The two jumped into his light sulky and lunged down the road in hot pursuit.

They had not gone far when they saw Herrington's vehicle stopped by an unexpected padlocked gate across a side road which he had taken by mistake. Dr. Gardner, out in an instant, grabbed the horses' heads, and placed all the occupants of Herrington's vehicle under federal arrest.

Back they drove to the courthouse, Dr. Gardner holding the reins of the Herrington equipage, with Dr. Hall following alone in his two-wheeled sulky.

Thus ended the tangled legal battle. Kum Quai was soon turned over to Miss Cameron's custody by the federal authorities, who had implicit faith in the ability of the Home to care for such girls, and she began anew the life of freedom she had so long and desperately sought.

CHAPTER IV

LIFE IN THE HOME

THE TURN of the century had brought many changes. Within five years from the time that the carefree Donaldina had come so gaily to tasks unknown, the full weight of this adventure lay on her young shoulders. Mrs. Field had found the routine too wearing, and with her resignation the official title of "Superintendent" had passed to the one who had already for some years borne the brunt of the burdens. Later the friend and counselor, Mrs. Browne, had resigned as president of the Board, after nearly twenty-five years in this office. Her successors were all women of sympathy and vision; but the break from the intimate relationship with one of Mrs. Browne's deep personal interest made the superintendent's task seem more "official."

Full responsibility for a family of fifty girls, many of them just released from years of mind- and soul-stunting slavery, was a task which would have baffled anyone trained and mature; but to one whose girlhood years had been spent in roving on California hills, it was little short of overpowering. Like many a young mother of a growing brood, Donaldina had daily to meet unforeseen difficulties, protected perhaps from the crushing weight of care by her very innocence. Then it was that she learned to rise day by day serenely conscious of a supreme source of strength, and to say with Paul of old, "I can do all things through Christ which strengtheneth me." Because she felt herself so utterly unfit for the crowding tasks, she brought to them no hampering inhibitions or theories which held in check her impulses. And so sure was she of the righteousness of her cause that she won the sobriquet of "Covenanter" from one judge, who secretly admired her disregard for such "man-made" hindrances as legal forms, even when he made her path harder by his own zeal for "the dignity of the law."

Because she did have this ingrained conviction, the lilt of her buoyant voice won the confidence of all who shared her days. Problems and perplexities which would have overwhelmed one of more cautious discernment were unraveled by her serene faith that what *had* to be *could* be done. There was a contagion in her cheer that drew sad women, timid children, weary men, to ask or give her help. Yet there was an aloofness in her Scotch reserve that served as protection and proof against intrusion.

This tall slender young woman with her constant bodyguard of solemn-faced children was a familiar sight to those who knew the Chinatown "before the fire." No matter how busy the day or how meager the reserve from the tiny salary the Board could pay, she rarely missed the chance of slipping up the hill to reward a "good girl" for tasks well done or lessons perfectly learned by a visit to the basement bakery around the corner owned by Miss Priest. Many a cream puff or lollypop bought from this kindred soul sealed a bond of devotion lasting through the years.

As in family circles bound by blood ties, it is the little events of daily routine which build the memory picture that survives major breaks in the clan, so it was with this unusual family—an International House, before such institutions were a part of American university campuses.

In those early days there were not only Chinese daughters but also Japanese, a few unwonted mixtures of Oriental and Indian blood, and some from Hawaii, that land of tangled race heritage, not to forget the faithful Hoormah, Persian matron for twelve years. These girls stayed varying lengths of time, but each carried away a new conception of home life and individual responsibility. The young superintendent set them an example by her willingness to attempt any task, no matter how lowly, which could make for the betterment of the home that sheltered them.

In addition to the matron, who supervised the household duties shared equally by all of the girls, her staff consisted of a teacher of English and a Chinese assistant and interpreter. For a few congenial years the teacher of English had been vivacious Evelyn Browne. This pleasant arrangement had come about one day when Donaldina, still in the position of Assistant, had come downstairs after a particularly trying morning with a group of younger children to find her chum resplendent in ostrich plumes and London-bought clothes, just home from a trip to Europe.

"Why, Donald!" Evelyn had exclaimed. "Who would have thought of finding you here. Just wait till I talk to mother. She'll have to find me a job, too."

And thus it was that Evelyn's boundless energy, her musical talent, and her keen sense of humor had all been thrown wholeheartedly into brightening the lives of the children she taught, while her exuberant friendship had cheered the really burdened Donaldina. Then, when tasks were done, and there were no thrilling night adventures to draw them from the homey fireside, the presence of Evelyn Browne with her host of acquaintances brought to Nine-Twenty some of the normal social evenings which Dolly had so missed in her first year there.

But it was upon Mae Cheng, one of Miss Culbertson's girls who was acting as interpreter in those first years, that Donaldina Cameron came to look as her main support. Mae's tactful suggestions, "Do you think we should do it this way?" and, "I remember how Miss Culbertson did that," helped many times to perpetuate the technique of the pioneer leader.

When Mae Cheng married and left Nine-Twenty, her place was taken by one of the most beautiful of the "daughters" harbored there. Yuen Qui had been brought to its shelter in the innocence of early childhood by cousins who felt that this lonely orphan would there be assured of safe girlhood. She had previously been sold to liquidate an old debt; and while she had not been actually misused, her cousins had doubted the sincerity of the "foster parents." Apparently they were the proprietors of a Wooey Association, a sort of insurance scheme popular in old Chinatown. A group of people would agree to pay a certain sum a month into this association for a definite period of years. The president was then responsible for loaning it out at a high rate of interest. Any member might borrow from it by paying this interest. Then at the end of the time specified everyone was paid back his money plus the interest earned. Yuen Qui's foster parents used the little girl as a "bank messenger." When she was brought to the Home by her cousin, she had several hundred dollars on her person, and refused to have anything to do with the strangers there until the proper persons could be found to receive the money with which she had been intrusted.

Once made a part of the family circle, Yuen Qui had become an apt pupil in learning the simple household duties through which normal home life was taught these girls. She became expert with her needle, and learned to read with the avidity of a born scholar. But beyond that she was ever sensitive to that intangible deeper motive that underlay all this material effort. As her own girlhood blossomed she was one of those guiding spirits among the older girls who made Lo Mo's task of interpreting simpler.

Yuen Qui responded, too, to a droll situation in a way that strengthened the bond between her and the Scotch Lo Mo, whose own sense of humor saved her many a bitter moment.

On one of her first days as assistant, Miss Cameron called Yuen Qui to act as interpreter during a call from a rotund Chinese official. He was seated on a hard overstuffed horsehair chair. His slippered feet, with baggy black trousers tied in around immaculate white-socked ankles, barely touched the floor. As he bowed his short body in respectful salutation he lost his balance. His tight-fitting skull cap flew across the room, the chair came on top of him, and he landed on his knees. Lo Mo looked around in vain for Yuen Qui, then set herself to the task of putting her caller at ease by quickly replacing the black cap which custom decreed should never come off in company. When the short visit was over, Yuen Qui was discovered on the lower step of the winding stairway so overcome with laughter that she could scarcely speak; but Lo Mo understood the courtesy that had sent her flying from the room.

Another Chinese assistant, Leung Kum Ching, had come to the Home, a nine-year-old, sobbing out the story of a dying sister. As was the persistent pagan custom, when death seemed certain, the afflicted child had been removed from the family circle of relatives with whom these orphans lived to go out of this world alone. Kum Ching had somehow glimpsed the contrasting tenderness with which the strange women on China Street treated the sick. The sight of her playmate and sister suffering death agonies alone on the cold pavement of the entryway had been too much for her child soul. She had run for help.

This was a time when Chinatown was under strict quarantine owing to an alarm of bubonic plague. No one was allowed to cross its borders, in or out, without permission from the Board of Health. But fleet Kum Ching had sped past the warning shots of the officer on guard and before he could catch up with her had dodged through byways and alleys into the arms of Miss Cameron.

Then came Donaldina's problem. How could she go herself to the house with its doomed sufferer? Yet she could not disappoint this trusting child. There was an old herb doctor on Kearny Street, just outside the boundaries of Chinatown, whose third wife had once come under Miss Cameron's protecting care. For various reasons he had a debt of gratitude to the Home at Nine-Twenty. She sped to his shop with her tale of distress. In his eagerness to help, he put her through a skylight, whence she climbed over roofs to an address on Commercial Street, where she knew of another skylight that would let her down again into the heart of Chinatown. Disguised and hidden under a cotton umbrella, she slipped through the street into the tenement where

Kum Ching's sister was still faintly breathing. Assured of conditions, she returned to Nine-Twenty by the same devious path, and telephoned the Board of Health. A kind doctor answered her call at once with an ambulance authorized to take both past the quarantine lines to the house on Jackson Street. His skillful examination revealed that the child was dying, not from bubonic plague, but from acute appendicitis. Tenderly she was lifted into the ambulance and taken to the clean white bed waiting at Nine-Twenty. She was too far gone for surgery; but her last breath was drawn under the soothing care of those with whom she left her orphaned sister.

Guardianship papers were not hard to obtain for Kum Ching, who then grew up through the varying phases of girlhood until she herself was going out with Lo Mo to rescue other helpless children. When she finally went back to China, the first kindergarten teacher to be sent to that great central city of Chansha, she took with her years of priceless experience in molding little lives with patient tenderness.

Calls from varied sources frequently brought the young superintendent and one or another of these native helpers to places other than the dens and tenements already described. Before the establishment of an adequate immigration station at Angel Island there was no place except a forlorn shack at the Mail Dock where Chinese could be held in detention during the searching of their landing papers. Government officials soon came to realize the value of the Home at Nine-Twenty as a place to which girls and women could be safely sent in this period of uncertainty. Among these transient guests there came one day a tiny babe purchased in Hong Kong for ten dollars by an old woman who had tried to pass her as a grandchild. To the young superintendent, who always loved babies, this one was a special charge. Then to her utter consternation came a peremptory order from Washington to "deport said Chinese person on the next steamer sailing for China." With her usual directness, Donaldina Cameron put on her hat, took the babe in her arms, and fled to Colonel Jackson himself.

"Take the child home," were his reassuring words; "I will see that the matter is forgotten."

Another agency which turned for co-operation to the Home was the Society for the Prevention of Cruelty to Children, whose secretary, Mr. Hunter, had brought many of his forlorn discoveries to Miss Culbertson in the early days. One morning a representative of this Society called for Miss Cameron to go with him to a tenement house crowded into one of the malodorous alleys between Stockton and Dupont streets. A wraith of a child was found preparing the family breakfast. She was ten, but her roughened hands were like those of a charwoman of fifty. Pinched face and bleared eyes told all too plainly their tale of abuse and suffering. Tenderly the strong arms of her rescuer carried Yute Ying down the steep stairs to the narrow street. Encouraged by the smiling eyes of the one who had helped so many little girls, she looked up appealingly at Miss Cameron, then tightly clasped her extended hand and walked with her to the Home. A legal battle ensued. In the words of the yearly report, "Many affectionate Chinese 'relatives' sprang into existence in a day; but a kind and honorable judge and the child's own testimony and appearance won the case for us."

After a year in the Home Yute Ying was called upon to face an ordeal requiring real courage. The grand jury of San Francisco was reviewing the evils of this asserted slave trade. Little Yute Ying stood fearlessly before them testifying to the astounding fact that even tiny children were brought into this country as slaves. Her quick, intelligent answers to the lengthy questioning, her devoted allegiance to her foster-mother, her neat, well-kept appearance, all aroused the curiosity of the august body who sat in judgment. They would visit the Home and see for themselves the tangible evidence of this rescue work. Thus new friends became aware of the increasing usefulness of this fight. And if these same men could have looked down the years they would have seen a white-capped nurse moving efficiently among the patients in the wards of a metropolitan hospital—Yute Ying's daughter!

Of course there were many whose moral courage would not stand the test of defying the cruel masters whom they had obeyed so long. Such a one was Yoke Hay. Her sad face could be seen as Miss Cameron walked pust the entrance to a basement where she was splitting wood. Her master was a sour old Chinese doctor. She must keep the fires burning to boil the herbs for his medicines. Chinese friends told the Home that an older servant girl in the same family had been sold to a keeper of a house of ill fame in Fresno. To protect Yoke Hay from a similar fate Miss Cameron secured a warrant and brought the child before the judge. As the rescue party drove to court, Yoke Hay told her story through an interpreter. The doctor and his wife were not her parents. It was true that the other servant had been sold. But when she stood trembling on the witness stand facing her angry master and a group of Chinese friends, her courage failed. She refused to repeat the story told on the way. The judge felt convinced that Miss Cameron had the truth; but "because of lack of evidence" Yoke Hay was turned back to her weeping "father" despite the fact that there was sufficient "hearsay" to make those who cared quite sure that he was negotiating to sell her that very week.

Yoke Hay's neighbor, Kum Yong, fared better in court. This child was another of those "parentless" waifs who, passed from one owner and place to another, finally found herself washing clothes and cooking meals with a baby strapped to her back—doing work of all kinds for a small-footed mistress in the heart of San Francisco's Chinatown. When the day's work was done she was kept busy sewing till midnight, for in those days, before child labor laws, many of the overall factories of the Coast were just such households as this. If Kum Yong fell asleep from utter weariness she was roused with heated irons or other instruments of torture. From head to foot she bore scars of cruel treatment when her plight was finally discovered and she found refuge at Nine-Twenty.

Attorney Monroe, representing the Home, applied for letters of guardianship; but her owner was a merchant of high position, and the case was bitterly contested.

Even the Chinese Consul was summoned to testify as to the law-abiding character of her owner. He certified to that part, but amazed the Chinese, when drawn out by a question from the judge, by paying a glowing tribute to the work of the Home. Kum Yong herself was a witness worth hearing, always sure of her point, and ever eager to show her appreciation of these new friends. The Chinese owner had engaged a needle-witted attorney, who sought constantly to prick the truth of her assertions.

"And how did you know you had been sold?" he demanded abruptly, interrupting Kum Yong's testimony.

"Because I saw the money."

"How much was it? and what kind of money?"

"Twenty-dollar gold pieces—twenty of them," answered the girl without hesitation.

Then began a bantering crossfire between the two attorneys as to whether she knew whereof she spoke.

"The only way to settle this is to test her with coins," interposed the judge. "Possibly one of the gifted legal advisers can do this for the court."

Henry Monroe reached into his pockets, drawing forth an assortment of coins of smaller denominations—this was in days before paper currency was common in California.

"I guess we'll have to look to our worthy opponent for such wealth," he concluded.

After a few minutes more of word-play that individual produced the required gold piece, and the judge held the assorted coins before Kum Yong's keen eyes.

"There were twenty of these," she reasserted, picking out the double-eagle at once.

The courtroom full of spectators cheered. In the course of the trial Kum Yong had won their sympathy when she had been ordered to exhibit to the court the deep scars burned by her mistress as punishment for brief moments of rest. Public interest in the case grew; the city papers printed lengthy stories. At last the day came when Judge Coffey read his decision awarding Kum Yong to the custody of the Home. Attorney Monroe walked out of the crowded courtroom to the group of reporters gathered in the corridor.

"Well, boys," he greeted them, "now is the time to toss up your hats!"

This they did with real vim, as spectators, witnesses, and friends gathered round to congratulate the jubilant Kum Yong.

And so it was that more and more of these burdened girls and children were brought out of dark corners into the normal family atmosphere of the friendly brick Home, often with secret co-operation from sympathetic Chinese friends. But many times the technicality of the law prevented others from sharing its benefits. Mr. Monroe worked incessantly for a new statute that was finally passed in 1904 by the state of California. Lo Mo summarized the effect of the new law in her annual report:

In years past it was necessary in each case in a way to break the *letter* though not the *spirit* of the law when we rescued a Chinese child, for there was no written law to uphold us in entering a house and carrying off a child. Then, too, before it was possible to carry out guardianship proceedings, the ever available writ of habeas corpus would in many cases deliver the child back into the custody of the Chinese until the matter could be settled in the Superior Court. In such cases we seldom or never won. Our attorney saw wherein the difficulty lay and proposed an amendment to the law of the State in the matter of the guardianship of minor children, which would give power to a presiding judge to sign an order to the sheriff commanding him immediately to take into custody the child whose name appeared on the warrant and place her in the care of those applying for guardianship, until such time as the hearing could be had. Our Board here, and representatives of our work at Sacramento took the matter up last spring. Those who had friends in the Senate or Legislature used all their influence to have the bill passed and it went through with flying colors, but it had done that the year before and then been vetoed by the Governor—he considered it unnecessary. A member of the Board knew the State Controller, whose duty it is to bring many bills and documents personally to the Governor for his signature. The good offices of this friend were besought; he agreed to lay the matter before Governor Pardee personally. Many letters, telegrams and telephone messages passed back and forth between the Home and the Capitol of the State, for we all felt that much was at stake. Our friend appeared before the Governor with our bill and prepared to use all his influence to get it signed, but he was too late. Governor Pardee had already signed the bill and it had become a State law! So that is how we can now go boldly into any house where we believe a slave child is, and take her away.

Thus the official recognition of the California state government was added to the unofficial sanction which the Home had for many years enjoyed from the federal authorities. In addition to utilizing the quarters at Nine-Twenty for temporary detention of would-be Oriental immigrants, the government agents had more than once made use of the large chapel room as a corral in which to round up the half-wild creatures herded together in the periodic raids in search of those illegally in this country.

One of the largest and best-known round-ups took place following the Omaha Exposition. All the dark corners of Chinatown had been searched; and finally about thirty girls and women were gathered into the chapel at Nine-Twenty.

"What pandemonium reigned for a time when these half-frenzied creatures found themselves prisoners!" wrote Miss Cameron. "They shrieked and beat themselves with their hands; they spat upon the furniture and clean floors, and cursed in English and Chinese. The scene was one of horror and yet of pathos. Some were liberated that day; but a number were left in our care until further investigation could be made. They neither ate nor slept for the first day and night. Among the number was a noted procuress who was positively identified by one of the girls in the Home. This woman, Fong Suey Wan, was kept locked in a room by herself. After several days her case was brought into court, but alas, she slipped through their hands and made her escape, much to the grief of all who knew her history. Great efforts were made to find her again, but no trace of her whereabouts could be discovered. The others were liberated one after another, the evidence being insufficient to deport them."

What a contrast! All this official "fuss and feathers" and nothing permanent to show for it. But whenever the friendly magnetic hands of Lo Mo and her Chinese assistants opened the doors of the dark, squalid dens, the frightened, oppressed creatures within sensed the sunshine streaming through and came instinctively into its redeeming light. No wonder Will Irwin, in telling of San Francisco's Chinatown as he found it in 1907, said: "From a woman, and she a pretty, fair-spoken Scotch maiden, this slave trade took its hardest blow—playing her desperate lone hand (in a warfare of ten years), she reduced the traffic by about one-half."

CHAPTER V

"EVERY ROOF IN CHINATOWN"

THIS MUCH-FEARED Fahn Quai could not and did not play a lone hand. But the sincerity of her purposeful life and of the influential Board women backing her drew into the fray many able assistants from official and professional circles. In the early days they had to fight not only highbinder and tong but also avaricious Americans whose fees were earned from the profits of the nefarious trade, as well as a public opinion which scorned "uplift work" among a politically despised race. It took real courage for men and women to join in the crusade led by such as Margaret Culbertson and Donaldina Cameron.

Many a gold piece was passed by secret messenger to officials in and out of court who could help in keeping the lucrative traffic going; and it took the combined persistence of the strongest personalities on police and detective squads to back this modest Scotch "mother" in her desperate attack on brothel and gaming den. More than one former head of the Chinatown Squad spoke in praise of these women who day and night stood ready to risk all for the sake of the helpless girls they sought to protect. Duncan Matheson, a former chief who later became city treasurer, explained the transformation of Chinatown into "one of the most orderly sections of the city through the gradual education of the Chinese people and the force of character-building institutions such as the Home at 920 Sacramento Street."

What he called "intuition" on the part of Miss Cameron was largely responsible for the successful location of the skillfully hidden evil houses that harbored the prey of the slave-owner. "She was never wrong in her information," according to another of the group of detectives who, like Duncan Matheson, "knew every roof in Chinatown in those days." "We knew we could rely on the leads she brought us," added Lieutenant Richard, "and she was never afraid to go herself to help in the raids."

Her help was valuable, too, for she would not give up till the last panel was torn loose, and the last basement searched. She developed an expert touch in detecting trapdoors, loose floor boards, hidden caches.

"This velly good house," many a wily Chinaman would say when she and her police escorts would suddenly appear at an alley door; but in she would go past clotheslines and hanging towels, carefully feeling for that one loose nail that indicated a panel door. The loose board out, the rescue party would squeeze through into a tiny dark room with its fan-tan layout spread on the teakwood table. From here into another room, thence downstairs into a vacant store, out by a secret passage—and they would know their girl had been spirited out to another street.

But even then Miss Cameron would not give up the quest. With two officers and an interpreter she crossed the Bay in answer to a call from a girl recently sold. On the way they had stopped at a store at the foot of Sacramento Street hill where axes, sledge hammers, and crowbars were stored ready for action at a call from Nine-Twenty. Armed here for any emergency, they made their way to the Oakland address whence the note had come. There was need for the hammers before the doors were opened; but no girls were in sight, in spite of every evidence of the recent occupation of the room. These houses, with their gambling and other evil practices, were invariably protected by a store, used as a blind, below; and there the interpreter and one of the officers had been left on guard. When the search of the upper rooms revealed nothing, Lo Mo returned to see what they had discovered. She found Kum Ching excited.

"Something is wrong, Lo Mo," she whispered. "These people keep insisting 'no one here.' The officer has been trying to make me go on upstairs to you. He says we're mistaken; but I'm afraid he may stand in with them. You said to stay here and I stayed; but I heard queer noises up there," pointing to the ceiling above the back room.

"We'll all go up, then," decided Lo Mo, urging the dubious police to follow her. These men were new to this detail and did not know her ways.

Again they searched the upstairs room, to no avail. Then Lo Mo suggested turning back the linoleum in search of a trap door.

"She was right! Here it is!" exclaimed one of the officers as his foot touched a loose board. The door was quickly pried open, to reveal a large square box between the floor and the false ceiling below. In this were huddled two comely young girls and a shriveled old woman, their caretaker. All three were taken into custody and brought to San Francisco, pending investigation of their legal rights to be in the country. The old woman was released on technicalities; but the two girls, who had been smuggled in, were ordered deported, a process carried out safely under the guiding hand of Donaldina Cameron and her associates.

In ways that were strange and devious, word would come telling of girls who sought release from plights such as that of the smuggled Oakland prey. The sixteen years of Miss Culbertson's work had produced enough results to convince the better elements in the Chinese population of the desirability of the Home on the hill. But it required daring to bring messages to "the White Devil." Suppose a rival tong were robbed of its valued slave. The life of the messenger would be forfeit.

Foon Hing paid with his life when he brought his cousin to the Home. No sooner was the girl safe in the haven he had found for her when a highbinder bullet laid him gasping on the sidewalk at its very door.

Then there was Lew Yick. His life was saved in the nick of time; but not until he had despaired of his last hope. Yick had succeeded in bringing about the rescue of a girl then in the seclusion of Nine-Twenty. The secret of his part in the plot leaked out, and he found himself held prisoner in the upper room of a Clay Street house near Grant Avenue. For thirty hours he was kept awake by prods of heated irons in the hands of changing guards from the rival tong who owned the girl. Eight o'clock of the second day of torture was approaching, the hour set for his death should he fail to raise the seven-hundred-dollar ransom demanded. He had no access to friends or bankers. He was nearly dead from fright and anguish when in came John Robinson, immigration official, and life-long friend of the Chinese, as well as of the work on the Sacramento Street hill. Accompanied by a posse of police this man had arrived in time to prevent the threatened tragedy, and the incredulous Lew Yick was removed to a place of safety across the Bay.

With tales such as this current in the underworld, it was indeed a terrified Chinese who called at Nine-Twenty one busy Saturday. Furtively glancing about, he asked to see Miss Cameron. In rapid breaths he whispered his story. He had met a girl in a slave house on Mah Fong Alley; "boardinghouse," he called it. She had confided her troubles to him. Here she must earn enough to pay for all her food and clothing and clear three hundred dollars a month besides.

She could stand it no longer. His sympathy had turned to love; he would take care of her if she would run away. So one dark night she had slipped away to a lodging-house on Dupont Street where her befriender lived. Thither her owner had traced her. Discovering that the new friend belonged to a rival tong, her owner dared not drag her forcibly away lest the six-shooters should start barking death in a "tong war" which would almost inevitably follow such an act of violence. But under the tong code of honor he could, and did, demand that her rescuer produce one thousand dollars with which to purchase her. Meanwhile she would be held hostage at the headquarters of her owner's tong.

Seeking frantically to raise the price in the short time allowed him. Sin Kee thought of Miss Cameron—and here he was: "Please, you help quick. No can get money; you come rescue her from tong!"

Kum Ching, the interpreter, was washing windows.

"Take off your apron quickly," Miss Cameron called. "We must go on another rescue."

At the corner they spied an Irish policeman, old and fat.

"Come with us," called Miss Cameron, and he followed as she and Kum Ching hastened with their frantic friend to the address in Ross Alley where the girl was being held hostage. Fleet-footed Kum Ching dashed upstairs and into the entrance of the tong headquarters before the sleepy old doorkeeper realized what had happened. As Miss Cameron hurried past, he came to and put down his pipe in a rage. He had let in Fahn Quai! He sought to slam the heavy barred entrance door, but little Kum Ching stuck her foot in the opening, screaming *"Fi dee* (hurry)," to the puffing policeman. He arrived in time to terrify the guard, while, all unprotected, Miss Cameron flew down the hall, drawn by muffled screams at the end. She turned a right angle just as a huge oak door banged in her face.

Breathless, the old policeman came up at this moment. The door refused to yield. He would get assistance. Alone with Kum Ching, Miss Cameron waited twenty minutes, frantically listening to sounds of moving, smashing, banging, behind the impenetrable oak. What was happening to the captive girl? Sick with apprehension, she followed quickly when a trio of police returned and battered open the door. Inside all was calm and quiet, every bit of furniture in place, an official tong meeting apparently in progress. Thirteen Chinamen sat around the table placidly smoking long water-pipes, seemingly oblivious to their disconcerted visitors. In disgust the police searched everywhere. Nothing unusual was to be seen. They were about to give up. Miss Cameron had been deceived this time. Then she stepped out on the fire escape for a breath of air. A muffled call attracted her. A painter, an American, was working on a swinging scaffold across the alley.

"They took her up through the skylight, across the roof next door," he called.

Telling Kum Ching and two police to continue their search, Miss Cameron motioned one officer to follow as she slipped quietly out of the room. Down the long flight of stairs and up another just as steep they climbed.

"Velly good house—my daughter only girl here—fine Clistian home," protested the black-coated owner as he recognized his callers.

But the skylight was open. A ladder was in evidence. Still, no girl. They were about to give up when Miss Cameron noticed a dresser slightly out of line with the wall. A black head peeked out. At the magic words, "Mission Home?," the girl allowed herself to be dragged out.

In some way the news of the discovery now flashed to the imperturbable tong meeting. Kum Ching's quick ears caught a word of the whispered conversation and with the other officers she hastened to help. As they brought the terrified newly rescued girl down the stairs a touring party was passing. Their guide sensed the meaning of the strange group, and halted his party to watch the proceedings. A shout of triumph went up from the waiting visitors as they shared the victory expressed in the upturned face of Kum Ching, who was guiding the trembling slave girl walking with downcast head and lagging feet, while the defeated owners who had taken her to the hiding-place slunk quickly out of sight, struck with terror themselves at the sound of this unexpected demonstration.

In general, police protection was essential on these raids, as Miss Cameron found on one occasion when she did try a lone hand. A telephone repairman, working at the Home, slipped her a note previously handed him by a Chinese cook. Would she come at five o'clock to an address on Jackson Street? She recognized this as the "City of Pekin," a place long notorious as a rendezvous for the men and women who lived on the illicit earnings of the slave girls kept there. It was almost five when, coming in from a conference at the Juvenile Court, she had received this note from the repairman. There was no time to call for police escort. Anyway, the plan outlined in the note did not call for entering the house. The girl had sent half a handkerchief as a token and had agreed to come to the door herself at the appointed hour.

Miss Cameron called her housekeeper and Kum Ching to go with her and proceed at once to the given number. The door was opened by an old woman! A young girl cowered behind her, but as her eyes caught sight of Fahn Quai she fled in terror down the hall, her soft silk sahm flapping like the wings of a canary. Many times these girls would pretend they did not want to go, in order to escape suspicion if the raid failed. If it ever became known that they had sought help, their fate would be worse than before, perhaps sold into distant mining-camps where there was not one other woman. Knowing this, Miss Cameron's suspicions were not aroused by the actions of this girl. She hastened after her frightened bird. The girl put her hand on a panel and disappeared. Miss Cameron touched the same place. There was the girl, cowering, terrified. She was in truth the wrong one. And here was Lo Mo deep in one of San Francisco's worst dens, without police protection! As she rushed on up this hall she saw the other half of the handkerchief in the hands of another girl. Kum Ching blew a police whistle, but before help could come, they saw men drag this girl past a trap door that would not work, through another panel. Then, in the nick of time an officer appeared.

"Through that panel, quickly!" said Lo Mo.

The officer darted in just as the last black coat disappeared around a sharp right angle into the hidden alley; but the furtive eye of the Chinese had caught sight of his pursuer. He shouted in Cantonese to the man ahead with the girl and the two dropped their prey and fled into the gathering dusk.

The girl looked half in fear at the strong-armed officer who lifted her, quaking and breathless; then turned with thankful heart to follow Lo Mo and Kum Ching, who stood just inside the panel. The men had gone. The girl was the all-important object of their quest. It was better for the officer to guide them safely back to Nine-Twenty than to waste time searching out the refugee owners in their basement gambling dens.

Thus, where three impatient women had rung the bell of the notorious house, four walked out, their way secured by the policeman escort who climbed back with them up the steep "China Street" hill.

As Lo Mo looked from the graceful Suey Wah (Water Bird), now describing to Kum Ching her sinking fears when the men had dragged her past her would-be rescuers, to the retreating figure of the potent officer who had just turned their seeming defeat to victory, she thought back to the days when she had known not whom to trust. In the first years, coached by the ever-vigilant Miss Culbertson, she had been wary of every untried aide, in uniform or out. So bitter had been the anti-Chinese feeling of those rough-and-ready pioneer days, and so enticing the bribe-money freely offered, that these purposeful women had learned to rely on their own resources many times rather than chance the double-crossing of their aims and plans.

Then, in Sacramento, the state capital, she had actually accomplished the rescue of one girl by her own unaided efforts. Warning had been given to Miss Cameron not to let her whereabouts be known even to the police. The note brought her by secret messenger had said the girl she sought would be watching for her at an address on I Street at nine o'clock in the evening. Until the appointed hour Miss Cameron stayed in hiding in a room at the old United States Hotel. Then she hired a carriage and drove to the heart of Chinatown. Telling the driver to wait with the hack door open, she ran into the ground-floor room indicated in her note. Here sat a pretty Chinese girl, a bundle wrapped in a scarf under the stool on which she was waiting. Hand in hand, they dashed from the room, into the waiting carriage, while Donaldina shouted to the driver to whip his horses to their greatest speed.

Safely locked in her hotel room, her next problem was how to get her charge to San Francisco. There was no train that night. Then the night clerk, a mere lad, came to the door to warn her that the police had come to him asking for a white woman and a Chinese girl. He had evaded their questionings, but urged her to be on her way, offering himself to row her across the river, in the dark of the moon. That seemed the only way of escape. Then caution awoke in her heart. What if this kindly appearing boy were an accomplice? There was a milk train in the early morning hours. Perhaps it was safer to wait for that, and she trusted again to her "intuition," which prompted her to lie low, confiding her plans to no one. Then as the morning mists were rising from the river, she roused her sleeping charge and slipped quietly down the back stairs of the old hostelry, out the service entrance, and through the deserted streets to the station just in time to astonish the brakeman unaccustomed to women travelers on this train. Fortunately they reached San Francisco unharmed; but as she realized the serious danger to which she and her charge had been exposed during this unguarded expedition, she vowed never again to forego the protection that her friends on the police and detective squads were so ready to give.

For in spite of the fears and suspicions of the early years there were always those whose integrity she could trust. Jesse B. Cook, later Chief of Police and then Police Commissioner, was a sergeant of the Chinatown Squad in the 'nineties. Candle in hand, he often accompanied Miss Culbertson and Donaldina in their searches through opium-filled basements to free hidden girls. Stepping about the stupefied smokers, they hunted relentlessly for cached human treasure. In the days when Chinese laundries flourished on every corner, it was not unusual to find girls secreted under tables and beneath the flapping sheets of the many ironing-boards.

In those days respectable Chinese "family girls" were never allowed to set foot on the public street. If an outing or shopping trip took them out of the upstairs room they called home they were always driven in hacks carefully guarded by their parents. Thus, any girl seen up and down the alleys of old Chinatown was known to be a "slave girl." They too walked under guard. In the daytime they were kept behind the barred windows of the overhanging balconies of the houses which lined these city lanes. Then toward evening they could be seen about the streets; but an old woman, the mistress, would usually pad along close behind while the owner kept a few paces away, his eyes alert for hands ready to seize his valued chattel.

It was difficult to gain access to suspected houses, for much of the property was owned by American landlords, often high in the official life of the city, who protected their handsome incomes by every means known to the double-faced. Many were the deceptions practiced by those who would sidetrack men and women bent on rescuing the hidden girls. One place attempted to prove its status as a "family house" by hiring small Wong Foon to play with his blocks in the front hall. Several times when John Robinson of the Immigration Service and Miss Cameron sought an entrance they were rebuffed by their police escorts with the report: "That is a family house—Mrs. Wong's little boy is always there playing"; but Robinson had Chinese friends who could provide him with information on any subject, and he soon discovered that Mrs. Wong was receiving a dollar a day to let her child play there as a decoy.

But whence the owners of four girls sought from another so-called "family house" produced four babies on short notice was a never-solved riddle. The rescue party had climbed to an address to which a mysterious note had directed them, only to find the rooms empty. Sounds of scurrying across the flat roof above them led the intrepid Lo Mo and her party to force their way in next door. Here all they could find were four crooning mothers—astonishingly young "mothers," to be sure—each rocking a sleeping infant with all the airs of possessiveness. There was no means of proving that these pseudo-mothers were the slave girls who had just fled the brothel which they had raided; for, as Robinson explained, "the custom was for these girls to flee from one roof to another, pulling their gangplanks after them."

There is one house on Commercial Street where Lo Mo herself tried the skylight route. She and John Robinson, with their alert Chinese interpreter, had reconnoitered from the rear, entering a steep narrow stairway on Clay Street, while the police stayed in front to watch the Commercial Street front door. At the head of the stairs she told Robinson to stand guard, while she and Tien Wu walked across the roof on a scouting tour. The block was so closely built that no planks were necessary for stepping from one roof to the next, and Robinson was suddenly alarmed to see the two women disappear down an opening in the roof of a distant dwelling. But it was not long before Lo Mo was opening the front door of the house where the girls they sought were guarded, to admit the police, who soon battered open doors, disclosing and releasing several girls.

Among the changing heads of this police force was another upon whose loyalty Donaldina Cameron could always count. Dan J. O'Brien, that genial host who headed many a hospitality parade in his later years as San Francisco Chief of Police, served once as chief of the Chinatown Squad. Many were the calls from Nine-Twenty which he answered with his strongest men. One night their quest led them to a Stockton Street dive. Sergeant O'Brien and his aide, Detective Barron, stepped to the rear door to make sure that all exits were closed before starting the raid. There, against the dingy brick of the adjoining wall, stood a terror-stricken Japanese, while two highbinders, revolvers in hand, were robbing him of his watch and money. The officers first seized this unexpected prey, handcuffed them, and started them in the patrol wagon on the route that eventually led to the penitentiary, then undertook the real business of the evening—the search of the house for the girl for whom they had brought a warrant.

Seven girls and their keepers were the results of their ferreting. When they were all gathered into one room, Sergeant O'Brien looked at Miss Cameron.

"Now, which do you want to take?"

Lo Mo's eyes had caught the mute appeal of a dainty maid in a blue silk sahm.

"I certainly want that childlike one in the rocking chair," she answered, indicating the one who looked so longingly at her.

"I'll tell you what we'll do. You say the word, and we'll take them all," offered the six-foot sergeant, adding, as he saw Lo Mo glance at the one warrant they held: "I'll stand good for it—Barron, call the patrol."

CHAPTER VI

FRIENDS AT COURT

THE inevitable results of these captures were legal tangles of real complexity. There were attorneys then as now who fatten on the fees of the wicked, and the highbinder tongs were rich and powerful. Outraged owners offered every inducement to ingenious minds to use the law to drive out the "Fahn Quai" who stole their highly valued property.

Here again the appeal of sincere purpose woke response in the hearts of the high-minded. Fearless men appeared, inspired by the unique efforts of the women who were fighting for the honor of their sisters of another race, and gladly offered their skill to combat the well-paid chicanery of the unscrupulous agents of the slaveowners.

One of the earliest legal battles was reported by Miss Culbertson in 1882. In the dead of night a fifteen-year-old girl had fled, trembling with fear, to the doors of the older home at 933 Sacramento Street. Her owner, a cruel pawnbroker, had beat her severely, and at the risk of her life she had made her escape while he was out at a gambling den.

Yute Ho's story, as it was sobbingly told through the lips of Chun Fah, the sympathetic interpreter, pictured her in a famine-swept village of old China, the ten-year-old child of a poor widow. Into their lives there had come a traveled Chinese woman from faraway California. With fabulous tales of chances for girls in that wonderful land this woman had bought her from her mother and carried her away into the midst of strangers and hard work. After many vicissitudes she had finally become the property of the pawnbroker at a price of $300.

When this man had discovered the whereabouts of his fleeing property, he at once made overtures to those who guarded her. The president of Occidental Board, Mrs. Browne, lived in Oakland at that time, and the wily pawnbroker wrapped up a gorgeous suit of silk to present to her as he crossed the Bay to pay his respects at her home. When this strategy failed, he sought an interview with the entire Board at their monthly meeting. Accompanied by Colonel Bee, a prominent lawyer of that day, and a group of Chinese friends, he made an impressive entrance, dressed in his silken robes. The hush that fell when Yute Ho, pale and shrinking, was brought in to face her late master was tense. Bland and serene, he promised to treat her kindly if she would but come with him. Her refusal was resolute. Then Mrs. Barstow, wife of Judge George Barstow, a leading figure in the judicial life of early San Francisco, and president of the Board just before Mrs. Browne, spoke:

"If this girl elects to become an American citizen, that privilege should be accorded her, and there is no law in the land to compel her to a life of servitude."

His efforts at conciliation proving vain, the displeased pawnbroker withdrew to his attorney's office. Then came a summons to Miss Culbertson to appear with Yute Ho, said to be held as a prisoner, at the Law Library on Saturday night. Accompanied by Mr. Kerr, then pastor of the Chinese Church, Miss Culbertson went at the appointed hour.

"Where is the girl?" threateningly asked the drunken lawyer waiting with the pawnbroker at this impromptu court.

Told that she had been left at the Home, his invectives knew no limit. He turned to the judge with a demand for their arrest for "contempt of court."

"But your Honor," explained Miss Culbertson, drawing herself up with dignity, "this summons came at such an unusual hour that we hastened off without fully comprehending its meaning."

"Your explanation is accepted. Go back and place the girl with the Chinese Consul-General pending court hearing."

It almost took force to drag the weeping Yute Ho to this house. Then, as there were no women in the Consul's establishment, the Vice-Consul was sent for and took her across the street to his home. While Yute Ho was talking with some children, Miss Culbertson slipped quietly away, only to hear wails of despair as the door shut behind her.

When the case was called on the following Tuesday, Yute Ho was not brought, and the hearing was continued for a week. Meanwhile gorgeous presents were pouring in upon the "prisoner" in the Vice-Consul's home, and friends, both Chinese and American, were rallying around the pawnbroker to testify to his good character. A document bearing hundreds of signatures conveying this testimony was presented to Miss Culbertson with the expectation that such a formidable list would overawe the Board.

Miss Culbertson went to Mr. Hunter of the Society for the Prevention of Cruelty to Children, who had insisted that she apply for letters of guardianship. He was discouraging.

"I fear we shall lose this case. You have *only* the girl's testimony against hundreds of witnesses for the pawnbroker."

And it did seem hopeless. Wearily Miss Culbertson climbed the steep hill to the Home and sat thinking what step to take next, when a voice seemed to say in her heart, "and having done all, to stand."

Ten days passed, and again they went to court. This time the Home had a distinguished advocate. Judge Barstow himself appeared to plead their case, stipulating that all the women of Occidental Board should be present, "for," he said, "we will let them see that your cause is supported by the best ladies of the land. All these things will have an influnce." T'sang T'sun and two other girls from the Home were taken along to prove what care was provided for girls released from bondage.

Two o'clock, and the bailiff called the court to order. Neither the pawnbroker nor Yute Ho was present. The prosecuting attorney, still half-drunk, asked for another continuance.

Judge Barstow was on his feet in an instant.

"Your Honor, I demand that this court issue an order at once remanding Yute Ho to Miss Culbertson's care. There is no doubt in my mind but what there is a deep-laid purpose in the continued non-appearance of this child." He argued with such effectiveness that his plea was granted, and Mr. Hunter went with Miss Culbertson to bring Yute Ho to the Home till there should be another hearing on Friday. On that day the defense was promptly in court again, but, strange to say, the pawnbroker and his attorney were both absent. A Chinese friend appeared with the message that he would abandon the case. Letters of guardianship were promptly issued, and Yute Ho, free at last, came to spend five happy years before another enemy, the dread white plague, ended her life.

It was not long until the kind Judge Barstow's career of helpfulness came to an end. His death was mourned as sincerely in the Occidental Home as in any other place in the great city he had served.

The Judge's valued assistance had been placed at the disposal of the Home quite naturally as the result of Mrs. Barstow's deep interest; but the next one to proffer help was a man who could hardly have been expected to have any concern for this work. Miss Culbertson, with her usual independence, had gone to court one morning, entirely unassisted. The judge had heard the prosecution. Then he turned to ask:

"Who pleads for the defendant?"

"If it please your Honor," the unperturbed Miss Culbertson had begun, "I will state our own case. We have no attorney—"

At this point a young Jewish lawyer arose from an inconspicuous back seat.

"I will be glad to plead the lady's case if she will permit," and the brilliant mind of Abe Ruef came to bear on the side of right and order.

His help during the thrilling days of pioneering was invaluable. Not only did he give of his time in office and courtroom, but his resourcefulness was placed at Miss Culbertson's command during some of their most exciting hunts for girls. One seventeen-year-old rescued girl was kidnaped from her San Francisco protectors. Miss Culbertson had secret information that she was in San Diego. Mr. Ruef and two armed constables accompanied Miss Culbertson to this seaport on the border line of California and Mexico, then a hamlet of about fifteen hundred people. Chinatown there was a most forbidding place; but these rescuers were indefatigable. They traced their girl to one of the back halls of a gambling den. After forcing their way through one secret passage after another, they followed the fragrance of burning incense to still another room. Here on a couch lay an effigy of the girl they sought, a dagger through its heart, a red banner pinned above the head. Translated, the Chinese characters read, "Death to anyone who seeks further for this girl!"

No more clues were available and the quartet returned to their hotel, where two further death threats awaited them. This was late at night and they needed rest. They were awakened next morning by a dazzling sunrise which filled them with fresh zeal. As they sat at breakfast, young Mr. Ruef looked at Miss Culbertson:

"I am prepared to meet my Maker on a morning like this. How about you?"

"Certainly, I am always ready. Shall we renew our search?"

So on they went, to the utter amazement of the Chinese who with their traditional fear of death could not understand the point of view of these strange foreigners.

Persistence and the armed officers finally won. Then began a week of legal struggle for the girl, and at last they stood on the platform of the little wooden station hoping the train would arrive before the threatening bullets of the lurking highbinders turned their success to failure. A price of $2,500 was set on this particular girl, and the owners were desperate. It was necessary to change trains in Los Angeles, then also a village of about three thousand inhabitants. Warning came that tong allies of the owners were waiting there in a final effort to regain their lost property. At a junction just outside the town the rescuing party got off, secured a carriage, drove rapidly through the outskirts, and succeeded in boarding the northbound train at another station across the town. Thus was another girl brought to freedom through the indefatigable and courageous efforts of these two who so effectively pooled their energies and intellects for the benefit of this human property often overlooked in a preoccupied world.

The pages of the Supreme Court records of the state of California contain a minute history of the difficulties encountered by Miss Culbertson and Mr. Ruef in another San Diego raid. The girl they rescued there in 1887 from conditions of squalid despair became a leader in the Chinese community, bringing up a family typical of that enterprising second-generation group being educated side by side with other young Americans.

When Miss Culbertson found this child of ten, she told her rescuer that she had been brought from China to San Francisco, sold three times, and finally held against her will in a disreputable house in the southern town. With the help of the San Diego chief of police and other interested friends, the child was taken from her owners and brought to San Francisco, where letters of guardianship were issued to "Maggie Culbertson" on September 28, 1888.

But peace was not so easily had. There soon appeared an indignant woman demanding her child back. "She is my own daughter," she insisted, with violent weeping, backing up her claims with a court petition to have the letters of guardianship set aside. Affidavits from white men in both Bakersfield and San Diego, purporting to be old neighbors of this woman, Ah Yow, testified as to her "respectable character," as well as to the presence of the little "daughter" in the home. A photograph was introduced as evidence of the fond relationship of "mother and daughter." The case dragged slowly through the lower courts; but Attorney Ruef was sure of his ground. He knew too well the type of white men who would perjure themselves for bribes in such cases; he could easily discredit their testimony. And he had authentic information from San Diego that Ah Yow had paid five hundred dollars for the child and had been negotiating, at the time of the rescue, to sell her for seven hundred dollars, as she was approaching the age when her earnings would count. With these facts he convinced the Supreme Court that Miss Culbertson was the only proper guardian for the girl, whom they at last won doubly.

Many times the children sought by Miss Culbertson would be spirited away to carefully covered hiding places after court proceedings for their guardianship had been begun. Miss Culbertson and Abe Ruef traced one such child to the basement below a tenement building adjoining the Chinese theater on Jackson Street. Here the ground quaked with dampness as they made their way through a veritable open sewer, where fleas, bugs, and other vermin crawled about in the half-lighted halls. The stupefying fumes of opium were overpowering.

No wonder the appeal to rescue the tiny human beings hidden away amidst such squalor took these early helpers of the Home away from private interests and gain. Mr. Ruef's aid was particularly appreciated by both court and Home, for he spoke many languages and he was not easily deceived by the subterfuges of clever opponents. As time wore on, however, his varied business and political interests made it necessary for him to relinquish his gratuitious services for these friends so strangely differing in race and creed.

At about this time a young attorney, just out of Hastings Law School, was rooming at the house of a member of the Occidental Board. Mrs. Chown's descriptions of the rescues made by the heroic Miss Culbertson and of the difficulties she faced in her legal battles fired his imagination and awoke his sympathy.

When Donaldina Cameron came to share the burdens, she found in Henry E. Monroe, this friend who had brought his talents to the aid of her predecessor, one on whose counsel and advice she could lean heavily in all her perplexities. For more than thirty years this man gave of time and ability, sometimes days on end, to guide the work past dangers and problems that threatened its very life.

As years brought recognition and honor in many spheres, Henry E. Monroe never neglected this work to which he had pledged his youthful enthusiasm. And he gave to it more than the free use of time and talent, for it was his respected position in the community that won others of high standing to support his claims in court and out. Head of the Bar Association for many years, his word had authority, and men of such high reputation as Judges W. W. Morrow, William C. Van Fleet, and Edwin H. Heacock paid their respects to a work guaranteed by a colleague of Henry Monroe's integrity.

It was he who found the way out when the slaveowners came armed with their favorite pretext, warrants for arrest on minor charges, such as that presented in the Palo Alto case. When confronted with these warrants the authorities at the Home were powerless to keep their charge. That was when expert advice was needed. There was a day long remembered when an officer arrived from Stockton with a demand similar to that of the Palo Alto constable. This time Lo Mo refused to be bullied. Her attorney was out of his office. Calmly she turned the key in the door and kept her caller prisoner for two hours until Mr. Monroe could be reached and could secure bonds. The trial was called in Stockton. A talk with the District Attorney obtained his promise of a fair deal and acquiescence in Attorney Monroe's demand for "a jury and a change of venue."

When all the facts were presented it was not long before Bow Yoke was allowed to return to San Francisco in custody of these friends who had twice rescued her from her enemies. She knew only a few words of English; but probably no amount of money could have more amply repaid Mr. Monroe than did the gratitude in the broken words spoken as they stood on the deck of the river boat returning to San Francisco and shelter. Her hand was laid timidly on his sleeve as she faltered, "Mr. Monroe, I think you *very* good man."

All her life, spent partly in America and partly back in China, this gratitude remained fresh. Never a year went by as long as Henry Monroe lived without a visit or a simple offering to this man who found the way to freedom for her. Always self-supporting after she graduated from the shelter of the Home, Bow Yoke consistently won respect wherever her employment took her. When middle age found her broken in health and alone, she came back to the only home she had ever known. She had money saved with which to pay her board and room. Care and congenial surroundings wrought wonders for her. Gradually strength returned until she could take over the supervision of the staff kitchen. There she ministered daily to the bodily needs of Lo Mo's large family, teaching the younger girls the art of wholesome cooking. But it was in her room at night that she was Lo Mo's secret aid. Exhausted from her day's labor she would sit propped up in bed talking earnestly far into the night with some bewildered new girl, explaining in simple, easily understood language the meaning of life at Nine-Twenty.

It was seldom that even the skill of her lawyers gained the speedy results which earned Bow Yoke's lifetime gratitude. Forty-seven times in a weary contest lasting over a year and a half did the faithful Lo Mo and her legal supporters appear in court to aid Yoke Wan in her futile effort to regain a baby daughter. As a young child Yoke Wan herself had been one of the slaves brought here from China and placed in a dive by her owner. A baby girl was born to her, only to be snatched away and sold to a woman slaver and divekeeper. Two years later Yoke Wan became the second wife of a Chinese who redeemed her from her owner. Still, she had never seen her lost baby since the day of its birth. She could telephone the owner regarding its welfare, but that was her only approach. The first wife now resented the newcomer. Conditions became desperate. Yoke Wan tried the only escape known to these ignorant slave women. With her bright silk scarf about her throat she attemped to end her pitiful existence, but others found her before her breathing ceased. She was resuscitated. Then her husband took her to an inland town. Life was harder than ever, until finally the day came when kind hands guided her to the Home on Sacramento Street. Here she learned of One who had commanded that little children be brought to His arms—could these friends who looked to Him for strength find the way to rescue her child?

Then began the weary round of court procedure. Attorney Monroe threw himself heart and soul into the struggle for justice, pouring into his pleas more fervor than he had ever before expended; but the technicalities of the law stood in the way. Unfortunately Miss Cameron had taken the case to the Juvenile Court before she had referred to him for advice. Mah Shee, the owner of the child, brought proceedings to adopt her; but Mr. Monroe was able to show that she and the Chinese man who sought to claim the infant were not legally married. This obstacle was quickly removed by a hasty marriage ceremony and the adoption application renewed. In the meantime the case had been removed from the Juvenile Court to that of Judge Sargent in the Superior Court and an order for the custody of the child had been issued to Miss Cameron. Before the order could be put into effect, however, a call came to Attorney Monroe asking that it be deferred.

By the next day the case was returned to Judge Murasky's court; and so it see-sawed from one court to another, finally coming up before a third judge, who, quite unfamiliar with the background, concluded that Yoke Wan—a former inmate of a house of ill fame—was not "a fit and proper person" for the custody of the child and so awarded it to Mah Shee for adoption, a decision later upheld by the Supreme Court, thus making it irrevocable.

One incident of the anxious months of trial brought the only ray of hope the heartsick mother had. The court had issued a temporary order giving the child to Miss Cameron, and this time it was tall Captain Goff, then Chief of the Chinatown Squad, who saw to it that the order was enforced. With Lo Mo, Yoke Wan, and the Chinese interpreter, he had gone to Mah Shee's apartment with the order. No sooner had that wicked old woman answered the peremptory ring on her bell than she recognized her callers and slammed the heavy door in their faces, but not before the commanding sergeant had thrust his foot in the way and literally flung himself across the room to snatch the bewildered babe from its toys in the far corner. Yoke Wan seemed to have a presentiment that the precious minutes with her child would not last, and insisted that they should go at once, under police protection, to the photographers, where she could at least have a picture to cherish should the child be snatched away. To Yoke Wan in her sad and lonely years across the sea in China, where she later went to study, this became her only consolation for the pains of motherhood.

Disappointments and delays in cases like this were compensated for by the sense of achievement when the quick mind of the legal adviser found the weakness in some of the hasty plots that thwarted Lo Mo's plan. One such time came when Henry Monroe answered a long-distance call from Fresno. Miss Cameron and her charge, a girl rescued in Los Angeles, had been taken off the northbound train and detained by a writ of habeas corpus demanding their return to the southern city. Quick as a flash, Mr. Monroe detected an error in the formal serving of the papers as she described the details over the miles of taut wire.

"Come on with all speed to San Francisco," was the advice she knew she was safe in following.

This time the mistake was evident; but often the law seemed to be on the side of the offender. And not everyone showed understanding when the letter of the law seemed to be violated in the interest of possible future good. A girl vigorously sought by her highbinder former owners was bound for Chicago to be married to a man highly approved by her new guardians. It was almost train time when an officer appeared with a special order "to produce the girl." Utterly ignoring his threats, Miss Cameron put her on the train in charge of her Chinese assistant, Choy Gay, only to find herself cited for contempt of court. The presiding judge was vicious in his decision to prosecute the case. He ordered Miss Cameron to proceed to Chicago and bring back the girl. She went, but returned alone. In the contempt proceedings which followed, two of the three judges stood by the courageous Lo Mo and the case was dismissed. As for the girl she befriended, married and settled in her own home, the wife of a Chicago citizen, she was safely beyond the jurisdiction of California warrants. And there she stayed, a wholesome influence in the Chinese community of that city by the Great Lakes, her home a place of refuge and inspiration to many of her younger countrywomen.

There was another time when Lo Mo was caught within the meshes of the law. The judge who issued a bench warrant for this gentle protector of helpless girls in the days long past later used all his influence as a member of the Superior Court of California to atone for that act. At the time there was a hard-fought contest in his court and Miss Cameron was carefully avoiding being at home to receive the papers demanding the appearance of the girl in question. Late in the afternoon she came cautiously down the steep hill to the Home watching to see that no men with long envelopes were hiding near her door. There was no one in sight, and she went in, only to receive both the habeas corpus issued for the girl and a bench warrant for her own arrest because she had ignored the former. Chagrined beyond words, she hastened to her lawyer's office, where the indignation of both partners over this unjust use of the law was mingled with hearty amusement at Miss Cameron's tearful fear of jail. She who dared anything to protect or rescue her girls shrank from this unnecessary outrage with all the tremor of a truly feminine soul. Their teasing over, the two lawyers accompanied her to the chambers of justice in time to furnish bail until the case should be called next day. When the hearing was held Lo Mo was heartened by the presence of not only several Board women but also their indignant husbands, and the case proceeded to a successful finish. In the process of the trial Attorney Monroe had opportunity to prove that the writ of habeas corpus was unjustified and thus win the girl. He also convinced the court that the bench warrant had been an unnecessary indignity; but it was years later when the Judge came to acknowledge the worth of this particular decision. This assurance came when Lo Mo slipped into his chambers one day on other business and incidentally showed him a picture she had just received from China. The portrait of two small children came from Canton, where the girl she had won in that case of long ago was the wife of the owner of an efficient modern factory run on Golden Rule principles.

Attorney Monroe, to whom Lo Mo went so often with these puzzling legal problems, occasionally had callers of quite a different type. One busy afternoon a wily old Chinaman appeared at his office.

"You know when Miss Cameron make raid?"

"Yes."

"I give you two hundred fifty dollar month. You tell me. See. No one else know. Don't you think that nice scheme?"

"Yes—but it won't work!"

There were others, though, to whom such money was too alluring. Many are the signed checks used as evidence of the collusion between certain officials, both Chinese and American, who engaged in the opium trade some years ago and as a consequence succeeded in smuggling in human property as well as the coveted drug. Department of Justice agents investigating a bonded actress, who had infatuated a Chinese interpreter at Angel Island, brought word of the case to the superintendent of Nine-Twenty. Immediately Lo Mo set out to help the interpreter's deserted family. In the legal proceedings that followed, the American accomplice of the Chinese interpreter lost his job, and the young Oriental returned to his native land. He had been receiving a salary of $125 a month, yet checks in the amount of over $50,000 were signed by him in the course of six months, apparently part of the returns from the opium traffic.

As time went on, more and more of the Chinese work in the law office was handled by a young Stanford graduate, Robert Borland. Then when Mr. Monroe felt he could no longer carry the perplexities, his associate came to Miss Cameron, saying:

"If you think I can take care of the work, I shall be glad to attempt it."

Borland stood by the Home with the same energetic determination that started his former associate to face the evil forces undermining Chinatown. His files contained numerous letters testifying to amazing lack of understanding among outsiders of the tricks employed by defenders of slaveowners. One indignant note came to Miss Cameron from Harry K. Thaw when an American immigration official lost his job. She was urged to intercede in behalf of justice. To Borland's explanation that if the man got what was coming to him he would be behind the bars of San Quentin came the cryptic answer:

"Excuse me! I did not know!"

Such was the excuse behind which many an American judge or attorney hid when an indignant and seemingly honest Chinese appealed to the law to regain his stolen "daughter."

It was not, however, a case of bribes or "excuses," but of honest misunderstanding, that led one highly respected judge of the Superior Court to issue a warrant releasing a girl to her supposed father. A few days before, in the gray dawn of a February morning, Miss Ethel Higgins, acting for Lo Mo, who was in the East, had led a rescue party through silent streets to seek for Suey Ching in a house opposite the park where Robert Louis Stevenson used to write his seafaring romances. Police had smashed the panel of the door with its many bolts and fastenings in order to break into the room where she was held in bondage. Then the would-be rescuers had been baffled when the girl refused to admit the name of Suey Ching. Finally, it had been necessary to produce a bench warrant from the Juvenile Court before the girl, her mind poisoned by tales of fear of the Home told her by her owner, would leave her barred room.

Then the would-be "father," friend of the one who had paid $3,000 gold for Suey Ching, had appeared from Stockton and demanded her custody. This seemingly respectable merchant, who had deceived immigration officials into landing her as his daughter, was in reality the agent for a professional slaveowner. But now he was seeking the custody of the girl on the ground that she had been "visiting friends" in San Francisco and he did not know the character of the place where she was found when arrested. Judge Parker, of Mono County, sitting for Judge Murasky of the Juvenile Court, ordered the "father" to produce written guaranties of his own respectability from Juvenile Court officials in his own city, and left Suey Ching in the Home until such affidavits should be forthcoming. Then had come the strategy through which Suey Ching was lost to those who had risked their lives for her.

Miss Higgins had called up the court in the morning to ask if the case were to come up that day, and had been assured that it was not on the docket. With amazement, then, she received word from the court in the afternoon to the effect that in response to a telephone message purporting to come from Judge Parker a substitute judge presiding temporarily had signed the paper which returned Suey Ching to the custody of the supposed father. In despair she telephoned her lawyers. Mr. Monroe himself had been in court on another case when the bailiff had handed the telephone message to the judge.

"It was all done legally," he assured her; "our hands are tied."

But Attorney Borland, who was an intimate friend of Judge Parker, hastened to inquire the reason for the sudden change of mind. Assured that Judge Parker had had nothing to do with the fictitious telephone message, he immediately communicated with the substitute judge. The order of the previous day was rescinded, and Suey Ching was once more a ward of the Home—provided they could find her!

Judge Parker was furious, and promised every assistance in his power.

"Since my name has come into this, I will stay by you till that girl is found, if I never do another thing," he had promised, and in the following weeks of fruitless search, he made good his pledge. Whenever Miss Higgins appeared with a clue to discuss or advice to ask, he would set aside other business, declare a recess in court, and go into an anteroom, generous with his legal talent.

Before the false order was issued, he had refused to look at the affidavits brought by the "father" until the representatives of the Home also should be there to see them. In the weeks of searching he had advised Miss Higgins to go to Stockton and check the validity of the affidavits presented. It was through the help of the Juvenile Court officials of that city that she had been able to sift the pretended "respectability" to the point where she found this "merchant" had served a term for violating the narcotic laws. Further interviews with the men who had signed the affidavits revealed the fact that they had never even been in the place of business run by the Chinese.

In the meantime fears for Suey Ching increased. Then a call from Oroville took Miss Higgins and her associate, Miss Bankes, to help another girl in that mining town in the northeastern part of the state. On the return trip the conductor's "Wait forty minutes for connections in Sacramento" was the last straw to the weary couple. It was late afternoon on one of those sultry April days that occasionally give to the interior valley towns a hint of the coming summer. The two women had been awake all the night before in a futile raid. They were too tired to be hungry, but Miss Bankes's suggestion that she "knew a drugstore near the station" promised a refreshing dish of ice cream. They walked listlessly up the elm-shaded street. There was a saloon on every corner but no drugstore in sight.

"This is a fine town you know so well," sighed Miss Higgins. Then her voice changed, electrified, as they rounded a corner.

"Suey Ching!" she screamed, as they almost bumped into the long-sought girl intently watching a passing Knights Templar parade. Miss Higgins grabbed her tightly by the arm; but Suey Ching sat stubbornly on the sidewalk, as her two escorts, one of them her owner, slunk quickly into the milling crowd. Miss Bankes ran for a police officer near by who looked at the excited women as if he thought them escaped inmates from the Stockton Asylum. It took earnest persuasion to induce him to escort the girl to the police court until Miss Higgins could communicate with San Francisco and produce evidence of her right to Suey Ching's custody. Grudgingly he accompanied the strange party, while the terrified girl still clung to the toy balloon she had waved so gaily a few minutes before.

It was nine o'clock before the long-distance wires brought confirmation of Miss Higgins' claims, and every minute she feared the authorities would lose patience with her. Once her claims were verified, however, she was treated with a courtesy that was in marked contrast to the jail experience related so often by Lo Mo of her own early days. On the pretext of keeping the lonely girl company because of her own ability to speak a few words of Chinese, she insisted upon spending the night in the jail. The matron was out of town. Miss Higgins was given her room. Adjoining that was one reserved for inmates en route to Stockton. Here Suey Ching was assured of a clean bed, at least. In the early morning hours a police officer arrived with the usual "habeas corpus"; but Miss Higgins held her ground and kept the girl near her until time for court to convene.

A stranger in Sacramento, she racked her brain for the name of a lawyer Miss Cameron had given her should she ever need help in this city. Then she remembered a notebook where these emergency helpers were listed under the names of cities. This was in a drawer at home; another long-distance call brought back the name of L. T. Hatfield. It was early, but she telephoned him immediately. "I'll be right over," came his reassuring answer, and in a few minutes this elderly friend of Miss Cameron appeared with his calm "Don't worry."

The Chinese had engaged a lawyer of convenient conscience who tried to have the trial set for the following Monday and thus keep the whole party stranded over the weekend. But a police officer arrived with Yoke Lon, interpreter from Nine-Twenty, on the morning train. When they produced the warrant bearing the seal of the court, which made it good anywhere in the state, there was no argument against Miss Higgins' right to return with Suey Ching that same day.

The rescuer's first thought when her charge was safely landed was to telephone Judge Parker: "We have found Suey Ching!"

"Good for you!"

By the time the case was finally called in the San Francisco court, Judge Murasky had returned and Henry Monroe presented the facts to him. Suey Ching confessed that she had been expected to earn one thousand dollars to pay the lawyer who had engineered the plot imposed on the substitute judge; but this lawyer failed to appear. The new lawyer argued for an hour and a half, filling most of his plea with jibes at Henry Monroe, whom he accused of "getting rich on fees from the Presbyterian Missions." This modest gentleman, who not only had never received a fee for his years of service to the Home but had actually, like his predecessor, paid many court expenses out of his own pocket, paced rapidly back and forth, his only way of showing annoyance at the long delay. The prosecuting lawyer insisted that Judge Parker, being from another county, had had no right to give Suey Ching to the custody of the Home. If this claim had been allowed, it would have invalidated every decision made while Judge Parker had sat for Judge Murasky. When his long harangue was over, Henry Monroe stepped quietly forward to cite a Supreme Court decision covering exactly this point and showing that when one judge sat for another by invitation he was vested with the proper authority.

The following day the prosecuting attorney dropped dead on the street, and there was another long delay; but when weeks later Judge Murasky rendered the final decision appointing Miss Cameron guardian for Suey Ching, the girl had been so completely won by the cheerful life in the Home that she chose voluntarily to remain and repudiated all of her former associations.

It is to this same late Judge Murasky, pioneer of Juvenile Court work who brought about Suey Ching's ultimate freedom, that much of the credit for the successful rehabilitation of young Chinese womanhood on the Coast is due. From their first contacts, he and Miss Cameron found a common interest in the plight of these helpless slave girls. Never did he try a case without an interpreter, never did his interest become mechanical. Each child who came to his court was an individual who should be given a chance to realize its capabilities under the most favorable circumstances the law would provide. And even when he turned a guardianship case over to Judge Coffey of the Probate Court, another real champion of this struggle to bring freedom to these victims of a degraded social system, he always followed the course of action with an interest that was broader than the merely professional.

Judge Murasky gave unstintedly of his time and thought to the problems presented by Donaldina Cameron. Through lunch hours and recesses after court they sat together pondering the future of the little bruised bodies that had come under their jurisdiction.

These children, white, black, or yellow, were the personal pride of this man, whose kindness, patience, and sympathy were monumental. How he rejoiced with Miss Cameron over the successes of any of her family. But his interest was not in hers alone. Lo Mo overheard a telephone conversation before a crowded courtroom:

"Her curls *must* be cut?—Is it really necessary?—Well, if it must be; too bad!" Closing the circuit, he turned to Miss Cameron with a laugh: "Just one of my little girls at the Detention Home."

CHAPTER VII

" 'MID PLEASURES AND PALACES"

THOSE legal problems and other perplexities which Donaldina faced in her early days at the Home proved so engrossing that before she realized it, the "promised year" had stretched into eight. By that time the family would no longer be denied. Dolly must at least have a vacation from the responsibilities that were making such incessant demands on her strength and sympathy. Occidental Board women were also anxious to hasten the fulfillment of Donaldina Cameron's long-cherished dream of seeing China, that land so strangely interwoven into her own life fabric. Friends and former neighbors who had returned from San Francisco to old Canton were eagerly offering hospitality.

But another whole year elapsed before suitable plans could be worked out to relieve Lo Mo of her pressing obligations. Typical of the calls which could not be ignored was that which came one day from an excited Chinese neighbor telling of the attempted suicide of an abused little "mooie-jai" (household slave), Chow Hay by name. This child, in a desperate effort to escape her life of drudgery, had drunk a poisonous herb solution used for hair dye. The dose had not been fatal, but her condition was serious enough to demand immediate action. Miss Cameron called police headquarters, and Detective Reynolds, a man who had often helped in raids, answered. Together they climbed to the third floor of a "family house" on Stockton Street.

This time it seemed impossible to locate anything out of the way, but at the end of the third-floor hallway Miss Cameron came upon a securely barred door. Just as Detective Reynolds was getting out his crowbars in order to force the door, a child unlocked it and ran quickly down the hall. In the two walked, searching everywhere for Chow Hay. They were almost in despair, when a shabby curtain moved and a black head peeked out cautiously. There was their quarry hidden among the pots and pans! The interpreter spoke gently, but the child was terrified out of her wits by the unexpected appearance of this Fahn Quai. She fought with vehemence born of fear until the big detective picked her up and slung her over his shoulders. Then she kicked his back with her heels and beat his face with her fists. It was necessary to take her to the police court for detention until a proper warrant could be made out; and it was a strange procession that made its way down Stockton to Washington Street, the short Chinese interpreter reaching up to hold Chow Hay's hands, while Lo Mo walked behind the tall detective, firmly grasping the child's struggling heels.

Their burden safely landed in the police court, Miss Cameron hastened to Attorney Monroe, leaving Chow Hay in charge of her interpreter. She was back in about half an hour, to find this older girl cuddling the little stranger in arms that have harbored many such. In a torrent of tears and convulsive words Chow Hay was pouring out her story to one who had assured her that she too had once been a helpless mooie-jai.

Almost as soon as Chow Hay was made a part of the family on the hill, she began to tell of another mooie-jai with whom she had often talked on their midnight errands for "sieu-yea" (supper) for their mistresses. She did not even know where this other girl lived; but how she longed to help her to this friendly home.

Day after day went by with no clue to follow. Then Chinese New Year came with all its festive activity. Firecrackers popped in the gutters all day. Parades headed by fire-spitting dragons wound through the streets by night. Small-footed women left their guarded homes to display their gorgeous headdresses in the nightly throngs which roamed the sidewalks of Chinatown.

Even the doors of Nine-Twenty were open in the general spirit of holiday. Guarded, of course, by Lo Mo and her Chinese helpers, the family were sitting on the steps to enjoy the mildness of the early February evening. A bevy of Chinese women and children came up the hill, laughing and chatting in high spirits, on their way to make New Year's calls on the then closely populated Joice Street, at the corner of which Nine-Twenty stands. Suddenly Chow Hay became rigid. She grasped the arm of her older friend, the interpreter:

"There she is—there—the mooie-jai," pointing to a small household slave walking a little apart from the others.

"Keep perfectly still—don't speak to her. We'll watch where they go and trace her later," replied the experienced interpreter.

Then Chow Hay, who in later years became a clever assistant to Lo Mo in other rescue cases, quick as a flash hugged up to Miss Cameron, calling *"Ma ma, ma ma"* in loud tones of endearment. She had caught the look of recognition in her friend's eyes and so staged a clear invitation to share her happiness.

That very evening, just at midnight, before Lo Mo had even worked out plans to trace her, this mooie-jai, Quai Fah, appeared at the door of Nine-Twenty, with all her worldly possessions wrapped in a silk handkerchief. Sensing the happy freedom which Chow Hay had won, she had slipped away when her mistress had started her on the usual nightly errand—and here she was to join her friends in the household which Chow Hay had embraced with such obvious content.

These two young "daughters" seemed to have a special claim on Lo Mo's sympathies. Her tender care was such a complete contrast to the abuse and beatings to which they had become accustomed that they could not bear the thought of her leaving them. But the young Superintendent, who now for nearly nine years had let the interests of her large and varied family always come ahead of any care or thought for herself, was exhausted almost to the point of a physical break. Finally, with a substitute leader on hand and trained in at least the fundamentals of caring for her large cosmopolitan group, she acceded to the insistent urging of family, friends, and Board members, who by now had planned to send her to China via Scotland.

Even with trunks packed and sent, it looked almost as if the trip might still fall through when the moment of parting came. The older girls had joined enthusiastically in the plans and preparations for this much-needed vacation. But the youngsters could see in her going only the loss of the best friend and protector they had ever known, and there were many tears as she came down the stairs to say good-bye. The wailing of Chow Hay and Quai Fah, especially, was almost more than she could bear; but with the assurance of the acting superintendent and the loyal older girls that these "babies" of the family would be kept happy all the while she was away, she at last found herself on a cablecar bumping down the hill to the ferry.

The ever-present obstacle of a slender purse had been one of the complications in planning this long-deferred trip. Then her good Scotch friend, James Horsborough, passenger traffic manager of the Southern Pacific Company, had helped with a pass which spanned the continent without cost. A stopover had been arranged at Minneapolis, to help one of the daughters of Nine-Twenty over some temporary family troubles. But while this stop, like everything else in Miss Cameron's life, was for the purpose of helping others, she herself found an unexpected welcome from one who truly proved a friend in need. The stifling August trip across desert and prairies had drained the small reserve of strength remaining after busy weeks of preparation. It was a mere shadow of the buoyant Donaldina Cameron whom Miss Emma Page, old friend of Chinese work, literally kidnaped and took to her Lake Minnetonka lodge for a week of enforced rest spent under the trees beside the swishing waters, instead of to the parching heat of New York which her itinerary had provided.

Greatly refreshed, she met in New York a shipping man who had been interested in her trip through Mrs. Lyman Kelley, one of the Board members. He sifted the possibilities of every line down to a Red Star freighter sailing direct from Philadelphia to Liverpool, loaded with fresh beef for the London market, and taking a select few paying passengers.

"The intimate companionship of a few kindred spirits traveling with like purposes is one of the compensations of trips like this, without the luxury and formality of more expensive tours," is the way Lo Mo introduced the memories of that happy voyage. The first friend she made on shipboard was one whose loyal interest has continued through the years, Miss Lucy Minnegorod, who later became head of the public health work of the American Red Cross in Washington. She too was making her first trip across the Atlantic to visit sisters in England. With a keen mind herself, she was immediately drawn to the young Scotch Californian. These two, with such similar backgrounds and ideals, would day by day take their tin boxes filled with sweet crackers from the dining room, two bottles of ginger pop, and their steamer rugs to a place they called their own away forward on the deck. Here they would talk themselves to sleep in the warm autum sunshine, and wake up, refreshed, to eat their simple repast while they continued the interrupted daydreams of this wonderful respite from care.

Three months in Scotland, that land of tradition and deep-seated inheritances, was a period of thrilling adventure for Donaldina. And that she herself was an object of curiosity was evidenced by the remark of her stately Great-aunt Jess, who turned to the other relatives after the first words of greeting to remark, "She really speaks quite decent English," thus summing up the family expectations of this descendant of the MacKenzie-Cameron clans born in the wilds of New Zealand, brought up in the woolly West of cowboy California, and now spending her life among "singsong Chinamen."

Aunt Jess herself was typical of the mid-Victorian period, a woman, dashingly beautiful in her early youth, who had given up all personal plans to keep the old home open for the children of her brother, Sir William MacKenzie, of the old British East India Company.

Donaldina’s time in Scotland was divided between the home of her Aunt Annie at Nairn, famed watering-place of the Highlands, and the quaint village of Beauly in Invernessshire with its crumbling old monastery, said to have been often the refuge of the ill-fated Queen Mary. Here Donaldina stayed with her mother’s sister, her own Aunt Catherine, a Highland lady, who drew her household consisting of two faithful Scotch maids around her every morning for devotions and a careful survey of the *Inverness Gazette,* from which she herself gleaned the world news that was fit for the others to hear.

To this home came the sister whom Dolly had never known, then living in Aberdeenshire. What a lifetime of romance was crowded into the conversations of these two closely related “strangers”! And what secret amusement the practical Isabella had at the expense of her sister’s sentimental insistence on seeing every nook and cranny which had figured in the traditions told her by the older ones whose memories carried them back to Scotland.

Together they roamed the glens and countryside so pregnant with inherited memories. Then, into the midst of this family reunion came two friends from the official life of the American sister. A telegram from Edinburgh one day announced the presence of Dr. and Mrs. Abraham Woodruff Halsey en route to Africa. Dr. Halsey, secretarv of the Foreign Missions Board in New York, and a lifetime friend of Woodrow Wilson, whose classmate he had been in the Princeton ’79 group, had met Donaldina Cameron the year before in Los Angeles, and had shown a profound interest in her career in San Francisco’s Chinatown. Wires were kept hot, and it was finally arranged that these two distinguished friends should visit the moors and Druid stones of the Highlands as guests of Donaldina’s aunt.

But in spite of all the ties to this land of her ancestry, and the pleasant days with old and new friends, half of Donaldina’s heart was on the other side of the globe, and she must press on to the still more ancient country which was her goal. Through a nephew of Aunt Jess’s, one of the owners of the British East India Company, arrangements were made for her to sail on the steamer “Mombasa” of that line, under the personal care of Captain Stephenson. This sturdy seafarer, a member of the Royal Navy Reserve, had been a personal friend of Queen Victoria. He knew each Chinese official in every port. On the voyage, when his port duties were all attended to, he would send for his jaunty captain’s gig and take his young charge ashore to call on these fascinating and cultured Oriental officials and merchants. Lifelong friend of the MacKenzies, there was nothing he would not do to make this voyage of their American cousin rich with memories.

Donaldina understood Captain Stephenson's strict, yet silent, control of all that happened on shipboard. He joined in the life of his shipload of young people returning to their homes in India after school days in England; but she, like all the rest, recognized that when he walked the deck at ten o'clock in his immaculate gold-braided white flannels, the faint aroma of his cigar announcing his approach, that it was time for parties to break up.

She enjoyed, too, the captain's dignified Church of England Sunday morning services, never forgetting the time he announced a familiar hymn, saying: "We will omit the third stanza, for the words, 'imperiled on the sea' are an insult to the intelligence of the captain."

One morning he came at dawn to rouse his young friend as they were quietly moving across the languorous Red Sea.

"If you want to look where Mount Sinai stands, come on deck now," he invited, adding, "but you probably will not see it. It is always veiled in cloud."

With thoughtful courtesy, he escorted her to a place from which he pointed the direction in which she should look. The decks were cleared and washed. No other person was in sight.

"I'll leave you alone," said Captain Stephenson and quietly withdrew.

Donaldina stood transfixed as the desert sunrise flooded earth and sky, its message sinking deep into her subconscious mind to be later shared with friends at the Home. Clouds rose as if a wand had brushed them aside. Rugged, pure gold, the majestic peak stood out in bold relief against the sky. Then the mantle of cloud dropped again, as if the sight were too much for human eyes. "He shall bear them and carry them away on eagles' wings"—the voice of the Psalmist seemed to explain all the mystery and wonder of her trip in those brief ten minutes.

The voyage was nearing its end when Donaldina made another discovery which forever endeared her memory of the stately captain. She was seated at his table for dinner when the conversation turned to California and its writers.

"No one has quite caught the spirit of our early days like Bret Harte," she said as she explained the real disappointment of her London visit, her failure to lay a "sprig of Western pine" on the grave of this interpreter of California pioneering.

"I brought this from the Sierra home of my sister where I stopped for a brief good-bye before I left. We have read his 'Dickens in Camp' so often there that I felt it a duty to follow the request of his last lines—but," she added ruefully, "I had to burn the sprig in the fireplace the night I left London."

The captain had listened with a quizzical smile as she related this incident. By way of answer he turned to open a cabinet at his side.

"Here is all the Bret Harte you can want," he told her. "I think every word he ever wrote is included in the volumes on these shelves."

Donaldina said good-bye to this friend in Calcutta, where she stopped over to visit a cousin on the Cameron side. This relative, who had literally been "reared among the Western Isles," was the son of her father's favorite brother, Patrick Cameron, for fifty years pastor of the little white kirk in the Baedeker town of Oban on the west coast of Scotland. In Calcutta she saw Kitchener riding down the Mall, but she left the city disappointed, for convention stood in the way of a promised trip to Agra. Another cousin, a bachelor, had taken a long trip on elephant-back with the express purpose of taking her to see the Taj Mahal; but women in those days did not go on such adventures. And so she who had faced highbinder and desperate tongmen in her daily pursuit of duty was forced to humor the conventional fears of her careful cousins.

From Calcutta these cousins arranged passage for her on a slow freighter, placing her in the hands of their captain friend and his Scotch wife. For two weeks this vessel ploughed "the slumbrous summer seas," stopping at every port, where a homesick American fellow-passenger knew and guided her to each point of interest. More cousins met her at Singapore; and at last they dropped anchor in Hong Kong. She was in the land of her dreams!

Here she was met by an acquaintance from San Francisco, the American secretary of the former Chinese consul-general in her home city. This secretary, whom she always called the "man of mystery," had met the cultured and highly educated Ho Yow, a graduate of the University of Edinburgh, in Europe and had attached himself to his retinue. Ho Yow, a brother-in-law of the Chinese minister to the United States, Wu Ting Fang, had been a staunch friend of the Home at Nine-Twenty. On one occasion he had brought his own wife with her nurse and servant there for convalescence following a long illness. And by an odd coincidence she had occupied the room furnished by his predecessor, the former consul-general, Owyang King, as a tribute to Miss Culbertson.

Another friendly greeting in Hong Kong came from a lad who had grown up under Lo Mo's eyes in San Francisco while he was a pupil of her friend, Miss Baskin, in the old Occidental Day School. Returned to China to study his native tongue, he took Miss Cameron to call upon his mother in one of those exquisite homes so redolent of ancient Oriental culture.

But perhaps the outstanding memory of the days in this city was that of her visit to the Berlin Foundling Home. Here German Protestant nuns mothered what seemed like myriads of Chinese babies. The sister in charge had been retired and sent home three times, but each time the heart tug of her babies had called her back. Here they were sleeping in what looked like wooden troughs, row upon row of them partitioned off, each in a section large enough for its wee occupant. Every night the coverlets were turned back, wooden tubs were wheeled down the aisles, and older girls lifted the little ones into the cool water, bathed them, and slipped on each a clean cotton tunic in preparation for refreshing sleep after the tropical day. Then the beloved "sister," passing up and down, would stop by each partition for a good-night kiss.

Hong Kong had been interesting, but Canton was her real goal. The boat docked there early, and her friends were not yet down to greet her. Hundreds of Chinese swarmed on shipboard, offering by signs to help her off with her baggage. But she sat determinedly on her English portmanteau, firmly grasping suitcase and bag. Then an English officer arrived, much amused as she smiled off the coolies who tried to tip her from her seat. He sent along a sailor to escort her to her friends, and at last she stood on the soil of old Canton, with a feeling second only to the thrill of scenting the Highland moors. The afternoon was lovely; but it seemed that they passed through endless byways, narrow streets, and alleys before they stood in front of a gate emblazoned with the English words "Canton Christian Hospital," and she knew she had reached the compound where her friends awaited her.

Her hostess here was Evelyn Burlingame, a former neighbor and teacher in the old Stockton Street Chinese Church in San Francisco. Called "Mein Bow Jai" by the little children she used to take on picnics to North Beach, this teacher had her name from the tight roll of hair gathered in at the back of her neck like a hard-crusted bun. "Mein Bow Jai" was living with Dr. Mary Niles, founder of a great work for the blind in South China, and an artist-missionary who also had spent years in San Francisco; and together they conspired to make each moment of Lo Mo's stay in Canton vivid.

In the old city of Sz Pai Low, Miss Burlingame taught in a school where one of her pupils, recently married, said his wife had known Lo Mo and wanted to meet her again. Accordingly Miss Cameron accompanied her friend on the next teaching day. No sooner had they reached the school than the door opened to admit the radiant bride, gorgeously dressed in embroidered silks. Whom should Lo Mo recognize but Leen

Howe, rescued three years before in a thrilling raid on a gambling den in Isleton, an asparagus-cannery village on the Sacramento River! She had been kept in the Home but a short time when it was necessary to send her back to her own land, from which she had been brought illegally. But Lo Mo realized that the friends in whose care she had sailed had been faithful to their charge when she saw into what happy paths Leen How's feet had traveled. As the caller rose to go, she handed Lo Mo seven scrolls, pale blue silk lettered with Chinese poetry.

"How did you know this was my favorite color?" asked the astonished Lo Mo.

"Oh, I remember your room was blue."

A houseboat up the Chue Hoh (Pearl River) to visit a former daughter of the Home was the next event. This trip gave Donaldina an insight into the home life of native villagers such as few travelers can have. Her artist friend, Miss Durham, had lived so long in this part of China that she had the friendly confidence of all classes. For this trip she engaged a boatman, long known to her, who brought his whole ménage along—wife, children, chickens, dog.

Each evening as the long twilight invited to calm, this river-going group would rest on the well-scrubbed deck. Miss Durham would read aloud in native tongue to the old boatman, placidly smoking his long pipe; while Donaldina, glad of a chance to be alone with her thoughts, would gaze off over the low-lying hills of South China, her heart back in the brown Puente Hills. One evening as they sat longer than usual in this reverie, watching the myriad lanterns of the quaint villages which dot the river shore, Donaldina was almost tipped from her chair by a monster rising through the loose deck boards under her feet. She barely escaped falling backward into the river as the other sprang to her rescue, only to stand looking upon the pink-and-white, beautifully scrubbed, family pig, whose presence she had never detected by sound or smell during the three previous days on board.

"And where is he kept?" she demanded when fear and laughter had subsided.

Her answer came on the following morning when the boatman took her below to view the immaculate pig pen which his wife and little boy had cleaned while he had taken Master Jü into the river for his daily scrubbing.

"But never will I forget the punishment administered to his poor pink snout that night when he had merely stuck his head up to remind us that it was past his feeding hour," laughed Donaldina Cameron.

The river boat pursued its leisurely way and at last they found moorings near the village of Chek-Hahm, where they eagerly awaited the meeting with N'Gun Ho. In the gathering evening dusk they were somewhat alarmed to see a strange Chinaman pacing back and forth upon the lonely shore. Bandits were common in those days, and this man in his rough peasant clothes seemed determined to hail their boat. As a protection from possible danger they were flying the American colors, and he appeared to be attracted by that very fact.

"Any passengers aboard?" he shouted to the boatman.

"Why do you want to know?" came back the answer.

"I have a friend from California coming here."

Knowing that Miss Cameron had several acquaintances in this part of China, Miss Durham ordered the boatman to take his long bamboo pole and push his boat nearer shore that they might identify this man. But the eager eyes on the shore were keen with anticipation and the old man had recognized his friend. Bending down, he rolled up his cotton trousers knee high and started wading into the muddy water with outstretched hands.

"Missy Dolly, Missy Dolly!"

"Why! It's the Unruhs' 'Sing'!" almost wept Donaldina Cameron, her quick mind flashing back to girlhood days in the San Gabriel Valley. She saw again young Joe Unruh driving up with the shiny family buggy to take her into Los Angeles on one of her frequent visits to these old family friends and heard again the cordial greetings from all—Grandfather Dunn to Sing, the faithful cook for years.

The boatman speeded his poling and Sing clambered aboard to explain that the Unruhs had written him of Miss Dolly's plan to come to China and he had learned through N'Gun Ho's pastor that she was coming up this river. Not waiting for the promised word of arrival he had tramped through miles of rice fields to be the first to greet her.

His plans were laid to have them travel next day to the interior village whither he had returned to his ancestral home. True to his word, the following morning three sedan chairs stood ready with their waiting coolies. Miss Durham climbed into one, Donaldina into the next, and Sing, with all the airs of a proud mandarin, into the third. The coolies lifted their burdens and Dolly viewed the rice fields from her swaying carriage of state. As they neared the thatch-roofed village, Sing's old wife came out with nearly the whole population to form a guard of welcome to this visitor from afar. Once inside the simple home came the most touching tribute of all. With the pride of Sarah of old, the wrinkled mother brought forth her precious son. He may have been twelve as she claimed, but shrinking and overwhelmed by the strange women he looked far younger. Through Miss Durham the mother explained that Sing had talked and talked of Missy Dolly and all she was doing for his countrywomen in America. Would she take this son of theirs home to her school in San Francisco? There was no chance for education in this faraway village and they did so want him to grow up to be a great man. Gently Donaldina had to explain that her work was for girls alone, that so far no one had built a Home for Chinese boys, and that she could not take this lad to the far country.

This unplanned side trip over, the river-boat party proceeded to the village which had been their original goal. Here they were greeted by N'Gun Ho, who had been one of the two special charges among newly rescued girls turned over by Miss Culbertson to her young successor. As a child of fourteen, N'Gun Ho had been brought into the Home just a few months before Miss Culbertson's death. In spite of the difficulty with which her rescue had been effected and her own reluctance to stay, two days among these new friends had been enough to lead her to choose voluntarily in court to remain in their custody. "All the past with its sin and contamination seemed to fall from her like a mantle" as she entered into the wholesome atmosphere of this new life, and by the time she was nineteen she was married to a young Chinese going back to his native land. "Mein Bow Jai's" friend had found her in a faraway village, the only Christian woman there, an outcast for her belief. She was anxious to come to Canton to study more. All this had been described in a letter to Miss Cameron a year before, and of course she wanted to make her own plea with the mother-in-law. In the meantime the husband had returned to California and his immigration papers would not permit him to bring his wife back. Life for N'Gun Ho with unsympathetic relatives in the village of Chek-Hahm had been hard indeed.

Miles from this village was a chapel built with money sent by Chinese Christians in faraway California. Week after week the faithful girl had tramped through the rice fields for an hour of the teaching she had learned to love in old Nine-Twenty. Thither she took Lo Mo on the bright June Sunday following her arrival. The Chinese pastor, a man of evident inborn culture and scholarly attainments, had years before dropped from his high position to the lowest depths of a gambler and then had risen out of that degradation into the new light of Christianity. As he walked out of the church with his visitors, he asked them to wait while he brought something to show them.

He returned with a wooden ancestral tablet, the cherished possession of N'Gun Ho's mother-in-law, which she had turned over to him when the gentle influence of this girl from over the seas had finally won her from her native worship. A rose vine bearing a single bloom grew by the chapel door. Stooping, he plucked the fragrant bud, and stuck it in a crack of the tablet.

"Here, take these both back to America. Show them to your women and say, 'Herein lies the difference between the dead old religion and the living new faith.' "

After the Canton visit Lo Mo stopped over in Shanghai, reviving childhood memories of strange gifts of silk and tea, carved ivories, and pictured fans, which had been brought from this city to the old Puente Ranch by her cousin, Sir Ewen Cameron. This member of the clan had always held the awed interest of his American cousins when he had stopped off to visit on his frequent trips between England and China. Donaldina remembered the excitement in the family circle when he had not only been knighted but had been the first foreigner to be made a mandarin by the Imperial Chinese Government. In his position of president of the Hong Kong–Shanghai Bank, he had negotiated with Li Hung Chang, great statesman of the old Empire, what was then the largest loan ever made to a foreign power by this bank, and his services had been rewarded in both the country of his birth and the land of his adoption.

In spite of all her years of picturing a possible visit with her distinguished cousin, Donaldina arrived at last in Shanghai after Sir Ewen had returned to England. Her days, however, had been so brimful of other pleasures that she would not let this disappointment blunt her enjoyment. By the time she reached Shanghai, homeward passage had been engaged on the "China Mail." This vessel allowed her one more glimpse of Hong Kong; some fleeting hours in Japan, where children in bright kimonos pattered about in their slippered feet, budding chrysanthemums with their tiny scissors, and sweeping up with whisk brooms the least debris which would have spoiled their exquisite little gardens; a sight of Honolulu; and then steamed across the miles of ocean bringing her home.

In the harbor inside the Golden Gate the tugboat bearing port officials chugged alongside the great steamer. Passengers crowding to the rail for the first welcome to the land of their destination wondered for whom the basket of gorgeous pink roses on the forward deck of the tug was meant. Donaldina, like the others, joined in the mild curiosity. Then she watched John Endicott Gardner, government interpreter, her helper of the Mayfield courtroom, pick it up and climb carefully up the swinging Jacob's ladder let down from the deck of the "China Mail." He came directly to her through the crowd of envious passengers, greeting her with cordial welcome:

"I am the envoy of your family, but these speak their language better than I."

Donaldina, who knew too well what sacrifice had gone into the purchase of this offering from girls and staff at Nine-Twenty, buried her face in the flowers; and then lifted her eyes to sweep with caressing sight the vista of hills across the Bay, which meant return to what she called "my own brown California."

On the dock a group composed of her own family, some of her adopted ones, and members of the staff waited to greet her. As soon as necessary details of baggage were attended to, she hastened to the "one spot beloved over all." There on the steps of the Home all the rest of the "family" were gathered to welcome Lo Mo. Among them were two small girls proudly offering gifts they had made in the months they had longed for her return, Chow Hay and Quai Fah, freshly clad in their pink cotton foos and sahms. They were very different little girls from the two wailing children she had left on the steps almost a year before. Her roses handed to Yoke Lon, Lo Mo gathered the two into her arms and answered their first excited questions about the long journey. She told them how she had slid down the hill on a huge banana leaf in Penang, where the crowd of children amusing themselves with this sport had intrigued her into joining them; how the "little gray monkeys" had so fascinated her that she had nearly missed her boat in the Malays; how she had loved the babies in the Hong Kong foundling home; "but," she added, "there are no babies in the world quite like my own."

CHAPTER VIII

THE OLD HOME PASSES

DONALDINA came back to Nine-Twenty more fully prepared not only to understand her girls, but also to impress the increasingly large audiences which thronged the monthly meetings of the Occidental Board. As those whom she had met in her travels or who had come to know the girls sent out from the Home spread the word among their circles of friends, more and more visitors were attracted to these meetings in Culbertson Hall. And always when the hour for Miss Cameron's report came there were still others who had dropped in out of curiosity and who remained in admiration.

One visitor caught her enthusiasm over bright little Choie Seem. Lo Mo contrasted with dramatic brevity the conditions from which this child had been rescued with the cheerful homes she had visited. She told of the eagerness of the little girl to learn, of the inadequate budget of the Home, only able to provide bare fundamentals. When she finished speaking she introduced a group of children, dressed in gay embroidered native costumes. Choie Seem was among the singers, her sparkling dark eyes meeting response in the heart of the Eastern visitor. No sooner was the meeting over than this guest was making plans with Lo Mo to let her adopt a foster child.

Among the visitors in those years following Donaldina's year of travels was one of the most distinguished of her fellow-countrymen, a man who, like herself, had employed the best of his heritage in the affairs of his adopted land. Andrew Carnegie's brief glimpse of some of the Nine-Twenty family produced results, not for one child alone, but for all whose days in the Home have followed that time. His opportunity to meet this Scotch guardian of Chinese girls was arranged by Judge Morrow, whose own concern for the Home had been aroused by Attorney Henry Monroe. Judge Morrow's reasons for planning a meeting of these two who had so much in common are explained in the story told by the *Examiner* reporter in a front-page feature story with a picture of Margaret Carnegie receiving flowers from the hands of Chinese babies.

"Without in the least disparaging either the official or the social receptions which had been planned for the entertainment of Mr. and Mrs. Andrew Carnegie and their little daughter Margaret, doubtless the happiest memories that these visitors will take away with them are those of a merry half-hour reception which had no place on yesterday's calendar.

"This was the visit of three dainty Chinese maids who called on the Carnegies at the Hotel St. Francis under the chaperonage of Miss Donaldina Cameron, president of the Presbyterian Foreign Mission Home on Sacramento Street.

"As perhaps the most distinguished Scotchwoman in San Francisco, and certainly one whose splendid altruistic services have glorified the field of woman's endeavor, irrespective of all nationality, it was only fitting that Miss Cameron should meet the man who, of all her former countrymen, was most representative of those admirable traits of character and ability which are the heritage of Scotch ideals.

"Miss Cameron, therefore, believing that the most convincing evidence of her work in San Francisco were the little Chinese maids themselves, children who had been rescued often from lives of slavery and degradation, took three of these charges with her, and their presence was an eloquent plea for the things for which the big brick home at Sacramento and Powell streets stood.

"The girls were Miss Ching Leung, a soft-voiced gentle-mannered young girl who has been trained under Miss Cameron to be a teacher of the children of the home; little Ah Que, looking like nothing so much as a big Chinese doll; and Ah Yoke, another diminutive maiden, her black satiny dress tied with gay bows, wearing a dainty sahm of blue, the handiwork of one of the older girls of the school. The trio formed as picturesque a group as one could wish to see.

"They brought an armful of yellow daffodils to Mrs. Carnegie and Miss Margaret Carnegie, and when baby Ah Que saw Mr. Carnegie, something in his benignant smile encouraged her to fly to him with extended arms. Judging by his effusive gladness, such a welcome from the flower-like little miss was more than he had counted on. But he enjoyed it hugely.

"Little Margaret Carnegie, with the affectionate frankness of a child, responded to the advance of her visitors in the same spirit, apparently as delighted with this unexpected meeting as they were. The Chinese girls, dressed in the most approved native style, but speaking the most perfect English, were frankly admired by the daughter of the steel king, who had probably never before heard such rosy-cheeked, bright-eyed lassies from China, well-bred as the most fastidiously educated children of fine families, speaking her own language so prettily.

"The visitors remained for half an hour or so, chatting gaily, Mr. Carnegie questioning their young teacher about the school and their environments. When they left, they each had big pieces of gold coin held tightly in their hands, and as they bowed out, the Carnegies seemed loath to have them go."

On the day following this visit Lo Mo and a few of her children were scheduled to start for Riverside to appear at a meeting in the Mission Inn. At the Third and Townsend depot they had just walked through the gate to board the train for the south when they saw the Carnegie party going to their special car attached to the rear of the same train. Kum Ching, the interpreter, and the same two children who had made the previous afternoon so colorful for the kind Scotchman, were with Lo Mo. No sooner were they settled on the plush cushions of the Pullman than a note was handed Miss Cameron by the friendly porter, who had already been attracted by her picturesque charges.

"We will be glad to see you and your party in our car," Mr. Carnegie's note had read, and so another pleasurable and unexpected visit was enjoyed. The children sang again, and were shown about the luxurious car, wonder shining in their polite dark eyes. Then, when it was time to say good-bye, Mr. Carnegie pressed an envelope containing a generous check into the hands of the overwhelmed Lo Mo, adding the words, "This is to do with as you please."

Even as she guided her gay charges down the swaying aisles of the long train, Donaldina Cameron's mind was leaping across the Pacific. Especially since her visit in the homes at Canton and her glimpses of the Old World culture of the educated Chinese she had met in her travels, Lo Mo had yearned to give her foster daughters some of this education which should have been theirs by inheritance. But funds to bring a native teacher from Canton could not be asked from a Board hard pressed to provide daily necessities. Now the means were in the envelope she clutched so tightly, and Lo Mo could scarcely wait to begin negotiations across the great ocean to bring to her Home the very one she had longed to engage when she herself had been in Canton. And how much the transplanted children of China really did need knowledge of their native tongue was proved by the very term of endearment by which Donaldina Cameron is known to household and friends. How little she or they understood of the musical Cantonese!

This had been borne in upon her as she realized that the words of the street spoken by many of her uneducated children gave a connotation entirely different from that of terms familiar in the dialect of the home province of South China.

As soon as the Riverside meeting was over, Miss Cameron returned to her desk at Nine-Twenty enthusiastic over plans for the coming of Mrs. Yung, first teacher of Chinese, from Canton. And many years later when this delightful scholarly Chinese woman was on an Eastern visit, she was entertained by the Carnegies in their New York home. Margaret Carnegie was presented with a sahm embroidered by one of the girls who had sung for her in the San Francisco hotel.

In those years when world visitors were coming so frequently to the meetings in old Culbertson Hall, there was one special Annual scheduled for April 18, 1906. The girls had put in days of scrubbing and polishing, for the Home must look its best on this day when a new president of the Occidental Board was to be installed. One of the staff workers had an engagement for five o'clock in the morning with a University of California student to pick wild flowers on the Berkeley hills in order to bring some of the springtime freshness so loved by Donaldina Cameron into the well-ordered halls.

That early morning flower-picking date was not kept nor was the meeting itself ever held. What happened instead was recorded by Donaldina Cameron:

The strange, mysterious old Chinatown of San Francisco is gone and never more will be.

But amidst surrounding ruin, on one consecrated spot stands a solid brick wall, unshattered by earthquake shock and unblackened by the breath of flame. Within that wall an unmarred archway still bears in stone letters the legend "Occidental Board of Foreign Missions." . . . .

Busy preparations for annual meeting had gone on cheerfully and vigorously. Our girls had scoured, swept, and dusted up to the evening of April seventeenth when final touches were given, curtains hung, and a beautiful fish net (the gift of a rescued Chinese girl) draped in the chapel room. All was ready for the events of the coming day. The last good nights were said, and the family sank into quiet rest.

The terrible earthquake shock that in one instant roused a sleeping city, spared not in its rude awakening the peacefully sleeping house at 920 Sacramento Street. During the never-to-be-forgotten moments the solid earth took on the motions of an angry ocean while chimneys crashed on to our roof, while plaster and ornaments strewed the floors. There was terror and consternation among the fifty Chinese and Japanese girls and children in the Home; but not one symptom of panic, or of cowardice. Older girls forgot their own fears in anxiety to care for and soothe the little ones. Not one attempted to seek safety alone. All stood to their duty like little soldiers—a miniature performance of the Birkenhead Drill, for everyone believed her last moment had come. How that five-story brick building on the side of a steep sand hill stood firm while walls of brick and wood around caved and crumbled is little short of marvelous. The first great shock over, we thanked God for having spared our lives, and looked forth to see how others had fared. Already columns of smoke were rising like signals of alarm; but so great was the relief of present deliverance no dread of another form of danger troubled us at that early hour.

To calm the frightened children and see that they were dressed, to reduce in some measure the chaos of our Home again to a semblance of order, were our first cares. Then the problem of breakfast for so large a family in a chimneyless house had to be faced. This last perplexity was promptly solved by our efficient matron, Miss Ferree, who almost before the bricks stopped falling had managed to secure from a nearby bakery a large basket of bread. This, with some apples and a kettle of tea sent in by our neighbor, Mrs. Ng Poon Chew, was the last meal eaten in the hospitable dining-room of "920." Our girls gathered round the little white tables, sang as usual the morning hymn, then repeated the Twenty-third Psalm with more feeling and a deeper realization of its unfailing promises than ever before. The simple meal was not finished when another severe shock startled all from their places. We hurried to the upper floor. Opening an eastern window and looking across the city, our anxiety became a certainty of approaching danger. The small wreaths of smoke had rapidly changed into dark ominous clouds, hiding in places the bright waters of the bay. As we gazed with feelings of indefinable dread over the blocks below, there passed at full gallop a company of United States cavalry. The city was under martial law.

Turning from our post of outlook to the group of anxious, questioning faces near us, we realized that the problems of the day were hourly growing more serious. . . . .

A consultation was held with Mrs. P. D. Browne (who had passed the night in our Home, having arrived the evening before to attend the annual meeting), Mrs. C. S. Wright, Mrs. Robbins, and Mrs. L. A. Kelley, the latter of whom had walked several miles to come to us. One plan after another was suggested. At length the First Presbyterian Church at the corner of Van Ness Avenue and Sacramento Street was decided upon as a safe place, as it had stood the earthquake well and was far removed at that time from the burning districts.

The streets in the neighborhood of the Home were fast filling with refugees from the lower parts of town who sought safety or a better view of the fires from our high hillsides. Chinatown also had begun pouring forth its hordes and even in the midst of the general calamity the ever vigilant highbinder was on the watch for his prey.

To have our Chinese girls on the streets among these crowds after nightfall was a danger too great to risk. As hastily, therefore, as we could work amidst the confusion and excitement, we gathered some bedding, a little food, and a few garments together and the last of the girls left the Mission Home. They tramped the long distance to Van Ness Avenue, carrying what they could. On the way the children joined the party, and the entire family was at last established for the night in the Presbyterian Church. . . . .

For the last time in the early hours of Thursday morning we sought again that spot best loved by us for a final farewell. Martial law had cleared the desolate streets of all living things for many blocks. But, thanks to one soldier's sympathetic heart we passed the closely guarded lines and were permitted, with many warnings to make haste, to enter our Home. The red glare from without lit up each familiar object in every room. The awful events occurring without were almost forgotten for the moment, while we stood in the room that used to be dear Miss Culbertson's and recalled the happy hours spent there with her, and the Chinese children whom she so loved. There was little time for sentiment. On the block below a terrific blast of dynamite was set off. The soldier on duty outside imperatively ordered us to make haste. We gathered a few more papers and valuables from our desk, then hurried through the hall strewn with many of our personal belongings—treasures which the Chinese girls had tried to save, but at the last had to abandon. We took a final look through the dim shadows of the large chapel room into the executive meeting rooms, sacred to memories of many an earnest and inspiring meeting. Then a last good-night to old "920." By dawn, two hours later, the flames had wrapped it round.

At break of day the little band were hurriedly preparing for another march, the shelter of the night being no longer secure. Fire menaced from three directions. What tragedy, what pathos, and what comedy too, were crowded into our lives these two days! Never shall we forget the hasty preparations made that Thursday morning for the long march to the Ferry. Many things carried so far must be left behind; much must be carried. Which to take, what to leave, and how to carry what we could not abandon, these and many more were the problems to be solved. Sheets were torn up for ropes and broom handles served for bamboo poles. Laughing in spite of their distress, the girls tried the vegetable pedlar's scheme with their bundles, and it worked well, for two bundles could thus be carried by one person. All had a load, not even little five-year-old Hung Mooie being exempt. She tearfully consented to carry two dozen eggs in the hope of having some to eat by and by. An older maiden, whose name I forebear to mention, added not a little to her own load by carrying in her bundle a large box containing the voluminous correspondence of a devoted suitor! Her look of genuine distress when advised to abandon the precious box was so appealing we had to save it. Poor old Sing Ho just out of the City and County Hospital, who had recently lost the sight of one eye, staggered bravely along under a huge bundle of bedding and all her earthly possessions, which she cheerfully rolled down steep hills, and dragged up others. Two young mothers tied their tiny babies on their backs while others helped carry their bedding. As tears would not avail (the hour for weeping had not yet come), laughter was the tonic which stimulated that weary, unwashed, and uncombed procession on the long tramp through stifling, crowded streets near where the fire raged, and through the desolate district already burned, where fires of yesterday still smouldered.

But to all things there is an end, and so the long walk to the Ferry at the foot of Market Street ended. A boat was about to cross the bay to Sausalito. Our desired haven was the Seminary at San Anselmo. We lost no time going on board. It was a thankful though a completely exhausted company that sank down amid bundles and babies on the lower deck of the steamer, too weary to walk to the saloon. But tired and homeless, knowing not where that night we were to lay our heads, our only feeling was one of gratitude for deliverance as we looked over the group of more than sixty young faces and realized how God had cared for His children.

Safely arrived at San Anselmo, the only available place of shelter for us there was an empty barn and of this we gladly took possession. Life in an empty barn, with very scanty bedding, insufficient food, one tin dipper and a dozen teaspoons and plates for a family of sixty is not comfortable; yet all made the best of the situation and shared unselfishly the few necessaries available.

To mention the names of all the good and generous friends who have helped by sympathy, by gifts, and with money, would require the writing of another story. But in due time and place each one of these good people will be "honorably mentioned." Our tale would not be complete without the usual touch of romance that should go with every true story.

Long before the eighteenth of April the cards were out for a wedding at the Home. Yuen Kum, a dear, bright girl who had been with us several years, was to be the bride of Mr. Henry Lai of Cleveland, Ohio. The date set for the wedding was April twenty-first. And to prove the truth of the old adage "Love will find a way" let me tell you that the wedding did take place on that very date! The ceremony was performed by Dr. Landon in the beautiful, ivy-covered chapel at San Anselmo, and notwithstanding all the difficulties the young man had gone through in finding his fiancée, on his arrival from the East the day of the earthquake, and all the trying experiences through which Yuen Kum had passed, they were a happy couple as they received the congratulations of those present. Just after the wedding Mr. and Mrs. Henry Lai started for their home in Cleveland amidst showers of California roses and the best wishes of their many friends. So romance with its magic touch helped us for a time to forget our great loss.

CHAPTER IX

BARN DOORS TO NEW "NINE-TWENTY"

THE SAN ANSELMO barn was hardly a place to stay in, even in the balmy days of Marin County springtime. Conditions in Lo Mo's homeless family were becoming serious after a week of fruitless search for shelter. In all the communities surrounding San Francisco during those post-earthquake days one of the major problems of the relief committees was to crowd the hundreds of refugee families into available spare rooms. Even boats floating about the Bay sheltered some stranded and helpless households. Little wonder, then, that it seemed almost impossible to find a place spacious enough to house a family of sixty—ranging in age and needs from blind old Sing Ho to tiny Jun Ping.

Lo Mo, however, continued her quest, serene in her faith that if she looked far enough she would find what she sought. That her buoyant spirit did not fail her even in the perplexities of these trying times can be read between the lines of the report which records the San Rafael home that finally offered suitable shelter.

An odd procession started for the new home. Upkempt and rumpled, they gathered up their few bundles of ragged bedding, the gift of the neighboring orphanage, and the three babies, Jun Ping, aged one month, the three-months-old daughter of a Japanese girl, and eighteen-months-old Oi Ching. With a few cheap saucepans and tin dishes they were ready for a new adventure. But word of their plight met responses from many sources. Mr. Gail Borden of Los Angeles soon arrived laden with gifts. Boxes of clothing, bolts of materials, warm bedding, a new sewing-machine, a big tent, and school desks that lessons might go on—many and varied were the daily surprises.

How the tasks heaped upon the Superintendent! Trips to distant cities where the scattered tongs had spirited their slave girls took her away for days at a time. The Chinese community was finally located in Oakland pending the rebuilding of San Francisco. Four hours were required for the double ferry trip from San Rafael to Oakland, a trip which it was often her lot to make. It was a strain too great for any constitution. A permanent location must be secured before winter. Thus by October they had moved again, this time to Oakland, while funds were already being pledged throughout the country for the rebuilding of Nine-Twenty.

Among the calls for help which took Lo Mo from her dependent clan at that time, one had come from Marysville, where a pitiful domestic slave was rescued from a cruel mistress. On this visit Miss Cameron met another girl who told of unhappy family conditions—but apparently there was nothing serious enough to justify a "rescue" at that time. A few weeks later the long-distance operator called from Marysville again. Would Miss Cameron come back to rescue Yoke Jun, the girl she had met on her previous trip? No time was lost. Lo Mo hastened back to this town about a hundred and twenty-five miles north, where the remnants of early mining days still left picturesque relics in the suburban Chinatown. Yoke Jun was waiting at the police station, to which she had escaped at dawn on the morning when she was to be sold as second wife to a Chinaman old enough to be her grandfather. She had pleaded with her father against this fate, but with senses dulled by opium and the glitter of six hundred gold dollars before his greedy eyes the father had sealed the bargain. Then she thought of the beautiful lady who had helped her friend, Ho Choy. The police would surely send for her, and they did. The case was called before Judge McDaniel, who immediately issued letters of guardianship.

Many years later, after these two girls had both shared the family life of Lo Mo's increasing household, as Miss Cameron was addressing a meeting in this city of Marysville a distinguished looking man entered and sat quietly in the rear of the room. As she finished her talk, he rose from his seat to say:

"When I heard what was going on here this afternoon, nothing in the world could have kept me away. Among the memories that stand out as I look back over the years, I count very precious those times that it was my privilege to aid Donaldina Cameron in some of her difficult cases. Words would fail me were I to try to express my admiration for her womanliness, her devotion, and her bravery.

"I recall amusing incidents, too, such as that told me by a wiry young Irish police friend of mine. He had been assigned to go with Miss Cameron on a midnight raid. They found the girl they were seeking in a shack on the edge of town. She was seated in a dark corner at the end of a narrow passage. As soon as she recognized Miss Cameron she sprang up and slipped out—gone before the astonished group of fan-tan players realized what was happening. It was a bitter cold winter night, but it was not till the end of their frenzied dash to the hotel that Miss Cameron realized that the girl was attired in only flimsy silk garments. Miss Cameron had no extra wraps with her and they were taking the milk train back to San Francisco. Her charge explained that in the excitement of leaving she had left her bundle of clothes in a corner of the room where they had found her.

"It was a case of desperate need and as usual, our friend acted spontaneously. She turned the key in the hotel bedroom door and commanded her charge to answer no knocks. Then she herself hastened to the police court where the young officer was still on duty. He demurred when she made her wild suggestion of returning for the clothes; but she insistently urged the possible consequences if the girl were taken farther so flimsily clad.

"'All right, we'll go!' he said and they retraced their steps to the shack from which they had so triumphantly emerged but a short time before. The sagging door stood ajar, and the two slipped quietly into the dark hallway. Sure enough the bundle was exactly where the girl had said. Miss Cameron seized it and was just turning when she almost bumped into a burly highbinder blocking the doorway. He had only then discovered his loss, and was in no mood to tolerate any more interference. In spite of his loud demands for the girl they had taken, my policeman friend thrust him aside to allow Miss Cameron to pass. Before he could follow her the highbinder, taller than the Irishman, was upon him. The sound of scuffle called her back. In less time than it takes to tell it, she had rushed into the fray, the revolver had changed from the Chinaman's hands to those of the officer, and handcuffs were clamped on the assailant's wrists. At his breathless command to 'blow my whistle,' Miss Cameron had blown the signal that brought another officer to the rescue. Then she picked up the bundle of clothing and followed the two officers with their subdued but wrathy highbinder to the city prison.

"Old Sam had such a lesson that night that within the next few years he had abandoned all his illicit business and came to my office to ask if I thought Miss Cameron would interfere if he brought his legitimate wife back from China. I assured him that she was only interested in rescuing abused slave girls, and that she would have no claim on his lawful wife. Convinced of that, he had me make out his return papers, and started off for San Francisco. But, would you believe it, he would not sail for China until he had made a friendly farewell call at Nine-Twenty, and made certain from her own lips that she would let his wife alone."

The speaker who had evidently enjoyed this reminiscent storytelling was Richard Belcher, an attorney whose invaluable aid rescued many a Marysville Chinese girl from the disgraceful shacks along the reedy river bank. His volunteer work in these unremunerative cases had been in reality but an inheritance from his father, Judge Belcher of the California Supreme Court, who in early days had been one of Miss Culbertson's staunch helpers.

Back in Oakland, the police were quick to realize that they had an ally of utmost value in their efforts to keep law and order in the new community which had sprung mushroomlike out of the debris of earthquake days. In January 1907 Captain Peterson planned an investigating trip through the new Chinatown, taking with him Miss Cameron and her interpreter. Two slave girls were rescued and turned over to the custody of the Home. One of them was called immediately to act as a government witness in the prosecution of her former owner, Woon Ho. This woman with fourteen others had been arrested in a recent raid made by a United States Secret Service Agent who had come to the Coast to investigate and try to check the slave traffic; but as at other times when such wholesale cleanups had been attempted in San Francisco, all this official effort seemed almost futile. There was such constant fear of highbinder retaliations in the minds of law-abiding Chinese that the government had serious difficulty in securing enough facts to carry through the prosecution of those they placed under arrest.

One incident of these hectic Oakland days brought forth an unexpected and perhaps not fully appreciated ally. A note had come asking Lo Mo to meet two slave girls anxious for rescue at a given rendezvous near midnight. For some reason no police were included in this plan. Instead, Lo Mo started forth accompanied by three of her older girls, Yoke Lon, Suey Leen, and T'sun Tai, escorted by Edward Eccleston, who had often shared in the exciting raids in San Francisco. The party divided to watch two opposite street corners, with a prearranged plan for a soft warning whistle should either of them see the group they sought approaching. They did not have to wait long. T'sun Tai's bright eyes saw the strange girls coming down the street, followed by the inevitable fat old guardian. At Tai's signal all of Lo Mo's party rushed to the spot, closing around the girls, whose terror knew no bounds when, at a shout from the old woman, Chinese gathered from every direction. Leaving Mr. Eccleston to guard her own three girls and hold the crowd at bay, Lo Mo grabbed the new girls, one by each hand, and raced down Harrison Street to Seventh. Here, almost stepping under the wheels of a passing taxi, she shouted to the startled driver:

"Please stop! I'm trying to rescue two slave girls. Just take me anywhere!"

"But, Madam, I have a passenger," he demurred, only to be interrupted by a disheveled youth who lunged out of the back seat, with profuse bows, demanding, "What's wanted?"

With a Sir Walter Raleigh air, he stepped aside, holding the door open, "Madam, this *was* my taxi—now it is yours."

Lo Mo did not stop for ceremony but shoved the girls in, springing up beside them herself, while the gallant youth let down a folding seat and sat facing his court ladies with a beaming smile.

The taxi-driver, however, was not so adventurous.

"Where d'you want to go?" he asked in surly tones.

"Take us to the police station," said Lo Mo firmly; but when she reached that destination her usual problem of soothing her frightened Chinese girls was further complicated by her efforts to rid herself of her drunken escort, who insisted upon seeing all three safely into the guardianship of the night clerk.

In the meantime her true knight-errant, Mr. Eccleston, had succeeded in extricating the three excited helpers from the surging crowd on Harrison Street and was waiting at the temporary Home when Lo Mo appeared, escorted by two big men with stars and clubs, bringing with her at last the girls just retrieved.

The Oakland Home also enjoyed touches of romance. Shortly after the group was settled there two of the older girls were married and left to make homes, one in Tucson, the other in Chicago. Another wedding took courage to consummate. The couple was cut off from their Chinatown friends because the highbinder society to which the bride's former owner belonged had offered several hundred dollars to anyone who would shoot the bridegroom. The young man had refused to pay a three-thousand-dollar ransom for his bride.

The days in Oakland were further complicated, for Superintendent and Board members alike, by the necessary plans for rebuilding Nine-Twenty. Scarcely were the ashes cold before a check for one thousand dollars had come from the Board of the North Pacific with headquarters in Portland. Then followed gifts from all over the United States, proof that the work had won recognition from thoughtful men and women in many places. A Philadelphia group sent eleven thousand dollars; and individual givers such as Miss Grace Dodge of New York, Mr. Cyrus McCormick of Chicago, Mr. Lyman Stewart of Los Angeles, and many others well known in financial and philanthropic circles throughout the country swelled the total to an amount sufficient to justify orders for brick and mortar for new protecting walls.

This unexpected avalanche of pledges followed a meeting of General Assembly at which Dr. Henry van Dyke had raised his voice to plead for the "flower garden of Oriental children on the Pacific Coast." His own enthusiasm for the work had dated from a previous meeting in Los Angeles at which he had presided as moderator. Donaldina Cameron had been present at this gathering with the quartet of almond-eyed singers who often accompanied her on her speaking tours. Few were there who would forget the plaintive sweetness of one of these singers, who had walked to the platform to sing, unaccompanied, at the close of a stirring address by Miss Cameron's good friend, Dr. Halsey. And now this child's song was re-echoed in the recollections with which Dr. van Dyke awoke responses from his generous-hearted auditors.

The cornerstone was laid in August 1907, put in place again by Mrs. Wing, the faithful T'sang T'sun, who had officiated at the first ceremony in 1893. A poem in Chinese, written and read by a representative of the Imperial Chinese Consul-General in San Francisco, was translated by J. H. Laughlin, director of Oriental work on the Coast:

> We lay for women's rapid education
> This cornerstone of everlasting foundation;
> For our religious widening and civilization progressing
> And peace of East and West we pray.

By March 1908 Miss Cameron brought her flock back to the new brick Home, and less than two years after its destruction—on April 14, 1908—a distinguished company gathered for the dedication. Among those taking part were Dr. I. M. Condit, who with his wife had done so much to lay the foundations for this work back in 1873; the Mayor of the city, Edward Robeson Taylor; the Chinese Consul-General; Mr. Robert Dollar; Dr. Ng Poon Chew, the celebrated editor of the Chinese daily, *Sai Yut Po,* who in his columns and his personal relationships had consistently stood by this work for the women of his race; Mrs. P. D. Browne, still looked upon as Honorary President of Occidental Board; and many others active in the religious and social work of the community.

The Mayor expressed in earnest words what he considered the value of such institutions, as he said "in the rebuilding of our city, it is not the material but the spiritual uplift that will make this city and its institutions what true citizens would wish them to become."

But there was no relaxation even when the last detail of settling had been accomplished. The scattering of the Chinese population had greatly complicated the tasks of rescuers, and many were the calls upon the willing Superintendent.

More and more the government, represented now in San Francisco by the Honorable Hart North, first Commissioner of Immigration, turned to Nine-Twenty for aid in its questionable cases of immigrants. During this year alone thirteen "United States prisoners" were brought to the Occidental Board for protection pending the lengthy and technical deportation trials. The pleas of these girls to be kept in the Home, after they had been tricked into their attempted entrance to this country only to discover that the promised "rich merchant husband" was a professional slaveowner, were heartrending. They knew that deportation to China would mean a worse fate than that which awaited them on this Coast. Once back in their native land, they would be seized again and sold into hopeless slavery in Hong Kong or the Straits Settlements where no Miss Camerons were inspired to risk peace and safety for their rescue. As the truth of this situation became more widely known, officials showed their humanity and co-operative spirit whenever possible by allowing these girls to remain for lengthy periods under the influence of Nine-Twenty or until safe passage could be assured them in the personal care of traveling friends of Occidental Board.

The steamer "Korea" dropped anchor for quarantine inspection one bright sunny morning when the waters of San Francisco Bay danced a welcome to ship-weary travelers. Two attractive Oriental maids caught the attention of the inspector as he made his rounds among the alien passengers. One of them claimed to be "a native of California"; and her old "father," a San Francisco merchant, produced a birth certificate and a host of witnesses to prove the contention. But a representative of Nine-Twenty was with the inspector. As T'sun Tai, the interpreter, talked with Yoke Leen her doubts were aroused. The girl had made the long voyage alone, coming "home" to the waiting "father." On the trip she had made friends with a sad-faced girl of fourteen, traveling under the escort of an evil-looking man who claimed her as his daughter. Suspicion turned to sympathy, and officials were persuaded to send these girls ashore for detention at the Home.

But to the voyagers the Home suggested only a dungeon full of horrors. They had been warned repeatedly against the "agents of a great foreign slave-market" who would come aboard ship to beguile innocent Chinese girls to become household slaves to the old witch "she-devil" who lived on a hill above Chinatown. With shrieks of terror

Yoke Leen and Ho Yoke drew away as Miss Cameron and her aides came to take them from the ship. Strong arms subdued them, and despite protests and fighting they were safely landed behind the bolted doors of Nine-Twenty. As tame elephants are used in the jungle to help capture and subjugate the wild ones, so the sight of other girls of their own age and race, apparently content and happy in this strange place, gradually won submission to the ministry of love and kindness which surrounded the two distraught girls. It was in reality Ho Yoke's earnest request to be delivered to the custody of the Home that some weeks later won her the sympathy of the crowded courtroom before which Judge Graham read his decision making Lo Mo her guardian. Yoke Leen, on the other hand, was deported within a year.

Official eyes sometimes failed to find all the human freight on these great liners, as the tale of one of Lo Mo's new daughters disclosed. Mae Sien had slipped by the scrutiny of ship's crew and immigration inspectors when she had ridden across the Pacific, smuggled into the coal bunkers with a group of other terrorized girls. Landed in the dark of the moon by means of a coal bucket in which she was swung over the side of the ship into a waiting barge, she was transferred to a boat and rowed over to the Alameda mud flats. For some months she was kept in hiding in Oakland until she was sold to a woman well known among dealers in human merchandise. But the "guardian angel" of little children was working through the medium of a good Chinese woman who learned Mae's fate as she was about to be resold and sent to a lonely town in the interior. A trusted messenger was now dispatched to Nine-Twenty.

The rescue party, quickly formed, followed directions leading up a narrow stairway in a Chinatown tenement. In an inner room they came upon the child sleeping on a pallet. True, there was a guard, an accomplice of her owner; but the police ejected him. Wakened suddenly, the frightened child sprang up in terror. Then her eyes caught the look of sympathy on the kind face smiling down on her. Some weeks before a friend had whispered to her of the "teacher" who might come to get her. Eagerly Mae listened to the invitation spoken through the interpreter.

"Would she go with the 'teacher'?"

"Yes, yes——" then a look of abject terror interrupted her eagerness.

If Dow Pai Tai, her cruel owner, ever got her back, she would surely kill her. No, it was not worth the risk to run away. But the interpreter assured her of absolute safety. She looked again at Lo Mo. There was something in those calm eyes that drew out the assurance which words could not bring. She gathered up her meager possessions and followed her protectors from the house, and it was not many days before Judge Murasky's juvenile court order released her "from restraint in Chinatown."

Lo Mo's family grew constantly, and from unexpected sources. Soon Mae found companions among others new to the strange household on the hill. In fact, on the very day on which the kind judge placed her there another bright child was brought before him. Moie Jun was the property of rich owners who used every subterfuge in their power to defeat Attorney Monroe's firm determination to set her free. At the end of many weeks of contentious legal fighting, however, Moie Jun, too, was awarded to Lo Mo, whose group of "new girls" had just been enlarged by three orphans rescued from the domestic slavery into which they had been sold in China. One of these, only eight years old, had been the possession of a seemingly respectable Chinese hairdresser, who did not scruple to add to her income by occasionally importing a slave girl. Calling the child "eleven," she had offered her for sale for seven hundred and fifty dollars. At this point word had come to Nine-Twenty; and then followed an exciting period of plotting and counterplotting. It looked for a time as if Oriental cunning would win against Occidental wit. Then, when the suburban Chinatown of a distant city to which Lo Mo had been brought by secret information had been thoroughly combed, the child was found in custody of an old woman where she had been hidden to elude search in San Francisco.

Lo Mo was beset with tasks on every side—the new home to settle, these half-won girls to integrate, other cases pending. But a message came from a city in the northern part of the state. Would she come at once to search for the daughter of one of the early members of the Nine-Twenty family? The girl had been kidnaped by highbinders and taken across the border into Oregon. Her parents were afraid of their lives should they follow. Lo Mo was the only one who could possibly help.

Even as she read the letter, she was planning what train she could catch and which of her helpers should carry on this and that pressing duty. There were good reasons why Donaldina Cameron could have refused this request; but it was not in her heart to remember past ingratitude. A few years previously the mother had brought Mui Fong to the Home for a period of the training which had meant so much in her own life. The girl, brought up in a small-town environment, had been inclined to be wayward; and it had taken infinite patience on the part of Miss Cameron and her Chinese assistants to win Mui Fong's confidence. Then, just as they began to sense some progress in her relationship with them, the mother had reappeared to take her daughter out for Sunday-afternoon visits among Chinese friends. Apparently home ties had called and the pair had lacked the courage to report their intentions to their friends at Nine-Twenty. In the long search for the missing girl, two of Lo Mo's assistants had traveled to the northern part of the state. When they found that Mui Fong's mother had taken her child back to the home in the country, Miss Cameron's helpers had left her under the parental roof. Now it seemed that this decision had been a mistake. The girl's stay at Nine-Twenty had been too short. She had not imbibed enough of the spirit of filial loyalty which is part of the training of these "daughters" of Lo Mo. Now that she had strayed again the mother forgot her former breach of confidence and poured her troubles out to the one whose sympathy was always sure.

With no thought of her former thankless task, Lo Mo hurried northward to hear the frantic mother's story. A young clansman had been attentive to the pretty Mui Fong, and in an attempt to evade parental objections the two had run away. Then after he had married her—only sixteen, she had sworn to being of age—his courage had failed at the thought of the wrath of her father, his fellow tongman, and he had left her stranded. She had been kidnaped by highbinders of another tong and taken to their den in the Portland Chinatown.

Miss Cameron listened to the earnest pleas of the parents. She could not refuse to help, and so she again boarded a northbound train and arrived in the Oregon metropolis, then more or less an untried field for her. She knew only one dependable friend to whom she could turn with her problem—Rafael Bonham, United States Commissioner of Immigration, son of an American consul in Calcutta, a man of unlimited judgment and daring. At once he set in motion certain unfailing underground sources of information and located Mui Fong, held prisoner in a gambling den. With the aid of federal officers, her rescue was effected; and Donaldina Cameron slipped quietly out of the city at dawn, spiriting Mui Fong across the border into the state of Washington. Thus she had frustrated the attempt of the Portland Hop Sing tongmen to procure the release of the girl from the custody of the Juvenile Court on habeas corpus proceedings. Once across the border, Miss Cameron and her charge boarded a fast train for Seattle and went at once to the Y.W.C.A. for protection . In the lobby she looked up, surprised and relieved, to greet a San Francisco friend. Dr. Hugh Gilchrist had been addressing a meeting and came forward with outstretched hands to inquire what new adventure had brought her to this northern city. When she had poured out her tale, he was quick to offer assistance. He commandeered passage on a boat sailing that day. They knew that once the boat carried them three miles from shore, they would be free from the legal documents of the pursuing tongmen. It took real vigilance, however, to get Mui Fong on the boat. Disguised in American clothes, she boarded the gang plank on the arm of stately Dr. Gilchrist; while Miss Cameron, who had stretched her Scotch conscience enough to drop her last name in booking passage, traveled back to her San Francisco duties as a sophisticated world jaunter under the nom de plume of "D. MacKenzie."

CHAPTER X

STRENGTH FOR THE TASK

THROUGH all these busy years there were brief periods when Donaldina Cameron could drop all prefixes and become just plain Dolly again. Those who would understand how she could continue to meet the stress and strain of her many topsy-turvy days must follow her to some of the havens where her mental and spiritual composure could be regained in seclusion with her intimate friends and kin.

Her brother's home in the San Benito Valley was, in the words of the sister who loved to visit there: "Just an oak-covered hill, not a ranch. To approach it toward sunset with its crown of trees silhouetted against the soft colors of the evening sky was like entering another world after the crowded streets of the city I had left."

Here she often found Annie, the oldest sister. Now that the duties of mothering her immediate family were over, this devoted aunt found for herself new responsibilities in the second generation. In fact, the three nephews in Allan's home were the special pride of all the aunts, and in their companionship Aunt Dolly renewed much of her own country-loving youth.

It was not often, however, that she could go so far for relaxation and she welcomed the later establishment of a quiet cottage in Oakland, across the street from Helen's cozy flat, where Annie and Katherine kept a glowing fireside. In this refuge across the Bay, Donaldina could find one of her own who understood the complex cares which active contact with the throbbing life of a great city brought to both. Katherine's interests and hers were both bound up with gripping human problems, for Dolly was not the only Cameron led into social service by the versatile Mrs. Browne.

The orphanage at San Anselmo, which had offered so much help to Donaldina's wandering family after the 1906 disaster, was another child of Mrs. Browne's active brain; and she had drawn Katherine Cameron to its staff many years before.

In the days when Dolly sought her sister's companionship in Oakland, Katherine had moved into another field where her official path more often crossed that of her busy sister. As the representative of the Travelers' Aid Society at the Oakland Mole it became her duty to direct many a forlorn and homeless girl. Sometimes when Oriental wanderers came her way her duties and Donaldina's would intertwine, although this was not as frequent as might be expected. The gatekeeper used to enjoy remarking, because he knew Miss Katherine Cameron's interest in Orientals, "The people who give us the least trouble are the Chinese. They always know where they are going and always have their money ready."

There was an exception to this one day when the porter brought a frightened Chinese girl to the Travelers' Aid representative. All she had was tied up in a gay silk scarf, and in every way she answered the descriptions Donaldina had given her of the timid mooie-jais who came to her for protection. The girl could speak no English. Miss Cameron knew no Chinese. The ferry boat was whistling its last warning. Katherine Cameron ran back to "the man in gray."

"Please telephone my sister at Kearny 4768 and ask her to send someone who speaks Chinese to meet this boat," she called and hurried her charge across the gangplank held by impatient deck hands.

The man in gray knew the Cameron sisters. Many times they had passed back and forth from ferry to train, and he had enjoyed the sight of Miss Donaldina and the wide-awake little Oriental girls who clung to her hands.

But when the message came to Nine-Twenty there was confusion. Lo Mo and the regular interpreter were out at court. Who could meet the boat? There was no time to be lost, for highbinders might be lurking near the ferry and Miss Katherine was not well versed in the technique of rescues. Then Yoke Lon, who was now one of the trusted older girls, volunteered her services. She hastened to the ferry just in time to take the bewildered mooie-jai from the hands of Lo Mo's sister, and another wanderer was led to the shelter from which years later she was prepared to step out, independent and equipped to make a home, another credit to the foresight of those who keep such girls from the degradation ahead of most mooie-jais.

The San Benito Ranch and the Oakland cottage were not the only homes that beckoned Dolly when life became too complicated. In "The Canyon of the Little Greenhorn," high up in the "Mother Lode" country of the mighty Sierra, lived Jessie Cameron Bailey and her engineer husband and the daughter so devoted to Aunt Dolly. As she stepped off the dusty train at a flag stop above the old mining town of Grass Valley, Donaldina became a new person, a spirit released from care, full of anticipation of these days when she could be herself, away from watching eyes and nerve-wracking excitement.

With a hearty word of welcome Charlie Bailey would escort his sister-in-law to the waiting buggy. Behind his magnificent black horses —he was the polo enthusiast who first introduced this sport to Maui in his early youth—they would drive rapidly up the mountain road, Dolly dropping off her cares and burdens with every breath of the pine-laden air. At the summit she must always linger just long enough to feast her eyes on the rolling panorama of ridges and valleys, and other ridges beyond, purple in the gathering evening shadows. Then she would turn to Charlie with the questions tumbling out in anxious eagerness.

What of Jessie—reading new books on her couch under the giant pines? And Caroline? Would there be any new traces of the "Little Greenhorn" down in the old canyon? Could she expect to find Shasta lilies yet?

Darkness would catch up with them before they would reach the cabin where Jessie and Caroline were waiting with straining ears for the clatter of the horse's hoofs on the hard mountain road. At last the journey was ended and these four, so deeply united yet so often separated, could gather around the dinner table before the blazing log fire, shutting themselves apart from the demanding world.

Night, and Dolly could be alone under the mountain stars. By the door of the guest cabin a pine sentinel stood guard. In the morning she would lie on the pine needles and think through her many problems. Tonight there was just rest and contentment, a quiet assurance that all she believed in was true.

Through the years the very knowledge that this refuge was hers was a tonic when crowded pavements bore in too heavily. And the letters that came down to Nine-Twenty with such regular frequency were filled with pine needles and lines of poetry. For Jessie Bailey in the seclusion of her quiet life had the vision to understand and prepare the spiritual sustenance that she gleaned from the literature which her busier sister had not time to read. And there was romance, too, in "The Canyon of the Little Greenhorn" which was different from the vicarious experiences of the many weddings Lo Mo had helped to plan at Nine-Twenty. Adored and beloved all through her life, Donaldina seemed destined to realize the fulfillment of her heart dreams only in the lives of others. In the perfect devotion of this home in the mountains she found the satisfaction of her dreams come true, and she was fortified against cynic and jester.

Yet even the Canyon was haunted by visions of her work, for here, as on the ranch of her childhood, she became the confidante of the Chinese cook, and ere long he was beseiging her on each successive visit to bring him a wife!

There was one vacation trip, however, when the daughter of this mountain household thought to have her adored aunt all to herself, away from work and speechmaking. This plan was made to celebrate Caroline's graduation from the Seminary that later grew into Mills College. Just the two of them were to sail away to that playground of Hawaii where Charlie Bailey had spent his youth and where Jessie Cameron had gone, through arrangements made by Mrs. Browne, to teach in the Maui Seminary.

A few days before the sailing date Lo Mo was plunged into a court contest over a slave girl who had taken refuge in the Home. Entirely unknown to Caroline, plans were evolving in the mind of her aunt to push forward slow-moving legal machinery that the slave girl's desire to return to China should be gratified, by including her in the happy party sailing on the trans-Pacific liner. It was due only to the strenuous efforts of the attorneys for the Home that the contest terminated satisfactorily just a few hours before the "Mongolia" was to sail.

There was no time to make ordinary arrangements for her charge, but Donaldina Cameron had the full confidence of ship's officers and immigration officials. The girl was brought on board in disguise and carefully concealed to elude the highbinders who might be watching the dock to spring an eleventh-hour hindrance in the form of another warrant. In the bustle and excitement of farewells from friends and family there was still no time to tell Caroline of this latest intrusion of official duties. The stateroom was full of friends and flowers. Eleanor Olney Babcock, Evelyn Browne Keck, staff members from Nine-Twenty, the Cameron sisters, and Charlie Bailey were all there; but no one of the merry party ever guessed that safely tucked in behind the curtains of the lower berth was a yellow-cheeked slave girl trembling with relief and fear.

It was time for visitors to go ashore. Caroline accompanied her aunt to the upper deck. The gang plank was raised and the last gay serpentines flung ashore. Handkerchiefs were waved till the disappearing faces on the dock became a blur. Then, "Let's go below and open our packages," and Caroline ran lightly down the stairs ahead of her aunt only to jump back in terrified alarm as a black head peeped cautiously out from the dark green curtains drawn across the lower berth. Aunt Dolly was close behind her, however, and the explanation was shortly made, followed, to Caroline's great relief, by an immediate trip to the purser's office to arrange passage for this "stowaway" among her own countrywomen in another part of the ship.

From then on Caroline did at last have Aunt Dolly for her own, except for the occasional visits made to their grateful protégé on the lower deck and the time it took for cabled messages to arrange for safe hands to welcome the returning slave girl in the China port for which she was destined.

The days in the Islands were a gala procession of really carefree hours, where Caroline's return as the granddaughter of early pioneers furnished the setting for many a welcoming gathering at which her aunt was the gratified onlooker. All the Islands opened their arms to this delightful pair, but one of the outstanding events was the annual "Cousins' Reunion." At this there were men and women "from the seven seas" answering the roll call of the old Hawaiian families. As Caroline rose to answer the call of "Bailey," the heart of her aunt was full to overflowing. It was interesting that they should have come this year, for the presiding hostess was the music teacher from old Makawao Seminary where Caroline's mother had taught.

On the mid-Pacific island Donaldina Cameron found some of her best-loved daughters participating in the life of this community where racial differences were disappearing in respect for achievement. She talked out problems of international significance in homes of educated Orientals whose wives and mothers called Nine-Twenty "home," and she felt that she had seen "all fulfilled the vision" of which Bret Harte wrote when he prophesied that out of early bitterness would come solutions that "we who watch and wait shall never see."

She found new strength for her tasks in satisfaction experienced through the potent lives of these faraway daughters; and these lives also won for her the approbation of one whose cheering counsel always awoke her own buoyancy. Although in the years when she had first undertaken her lifework, Charlie Bailey had been among the strongest in opposition to Mrs. Browne's proposal, now the tales she brought back from his favorite land of Hawaii swung him wholeheartedly to her cause. With this new enthusiasm he became her strong shield and counselor. Even the postman came to recognize his bold clear handwriting and the Grass Valley postmark, as he would come waving a long envelope: "He hasn't forgotten you!" His look of disappointment when Miss Cameron finally remarked that her correspondent was only her brother-in-law showed how hopefully this daily visitor to Nine-Twenty was looking for the release of this beautiful woman from what seemed to him a grinding task.

But if Donaldina Cameron slowly and surely shut romance out of her own life plans, no one ever entered more sympathetically than she into the dreams of others. There is not a report but includes as an antithesis to its harrowing tales of rescue some happy account of weddings at the Home. Strange romances these—a combination of Oriental and Occidental customs. Fortunately for the successful outcome of the work at the Home, there is that tolerance in the mind of many a Christian Chinese which wipes out past experiences and makes him judge a girl by her revitalized present, not by what her past may have been. Literal indeed has been the fulfillment of the Biblical prophecy, "Though your sins be as scarlet, they shall be as white as snow." Though their "sins" have been involuntary, the result of ignorance and evil forces, nevertheless no contrast could be more dramatic than that between the sad girls rescued from dark corners, and the smiling white-clad brides who yearly went forth from the broad steps of Nine-Twenty.

Lo Mo always insisted that part of the fundamental teaching of the Home be that of good housekeeping. Under her sympathetic guidance one matron after another made it her business to train the changing households in the principles of real homemaking. She knew that when her girls became wives, they would be efficient; but her interest was not one-sided. The suitors who came to Nine-Twenty were many, and all of them had to pass before Lo Mo's discriminating eyes. Gilt-edged credentials were required before the longing swain was permitted to call upon or correspond with the lady of his choice.

Her interest and concern did not cease when she gave away the bride in those weddings carried out with such exacting detail at Nine-Twenty. From the letters that filled her daily mail or the respite of a visit to a married daughter when her travels took her near these homes, Lo Mo followed the happy results. Deep in her heart she knew, too, that there were reasons far beyond household training that prepared these girls for life. Their souls had been fed with a manna that could nourish spirit as well as body.

No one could consistently give out to others the inspiration which Donaldina Cameron poured into the lives around her without finding springs of refreshment at times. Even the seclusion of her own room was not sacred. Night after night she would take some tearful girl to the couch beside her bed for comfort because the days were too busy or the Home too full. Thus she came to depend upon the occasional break from routine and the new point of view gained from kin or friends.

When General Assembly met in Los Angeles she was introduced to the Tooker family of East Orange, New Jersey, people of world vision whose friendship came to have a lasting impact not only on her personal life but on the expansion of the work itself. Soon after they had visited San Francisco and learned of the Home at Nine-Twenty, Donaldina had to cross the continent on official business. The invitation to stop over at the Tooker home, "Evergreen Place," gave her opportunity to meet and discuss her Pacific Coast problems with such other guests as Dr. James C. R. Ewing, president of Forman College in India, Dr. Wilfred Grenfell, John R. Mott, Sherwood Eddy, Dr. Samuel Zwemer, who had spent so many years among the Moslems, Dr. Walter Lowrey of China, and many other men and women of wide sympathies and broad experience.

In the course of this visit she attended a formal banquet in New York City as the guest of the Misses Tooker and their father, who were proud to introduce their Pacific Coast visitor. Donaldina was reveling in the conversation of a child-welfare worker, her left-hand dinner partner, when a sudden silence fell upon the group.

"What are they waiting for?" she asked her right-hand partner.

"For you to speak," he replied, as he offered his arm to escort her to the speaker's table. In the engrossing conversation she had not heard the toastmaster's introduction of herself as a surprise guest.

"But I can't—I'm not prepared," protested the usually calm Lo Mo.

Then her mind leaped back to some lines Jessie Bailey had often quoted:

> I looked back far into other years,
> The scene was changed—

she began; and soon the gathering was living in scenes so foreign to their conventional surroundings that they scarcely seemed real.

The impression she left upon her audience that night was due to Jessie Bailey in more ways than in the lines of poetry. For before her departure for the East her practical sister had insisted that the busy Donaldina purchase from a leading style shop a dinner gown of the soft blue which has so become her at every age. Its graceful lines and her own vivid coloring only served to accentuate the zeal of the message she poured forth as she forgot self and audience, making the struggling lives on the Pacific Coast and in faraway Canton real for these distinguished auditors who had heard so little of her type of work.

Mary Tooker looked at her friend with new warmth. In this speech Donaldina Cameron had unconsciously revealed more of her real self than she had ever shown in the more reserved conversation of their intimate fireside groups. And even as they left the banquet hall to journey back across the River, the Tooker sisters were planning in what ways they could share in this quest for souls which had swept all other interests from the life of their radiant guest.

As their winter travels were planned, it was the Pacific Coast and the hilltop above San Francisco's Chinatown which drew these sisters to enter more fully into the life their friend found so gripping. In one of those apartments every window of which frames a view of Bay and Gate they established a headquarters where Donaldina Cameron could come for the strength that friendship gives; and they poured not only their means but their very selves into the support of her work.

The apartment was near enough so that minutes between duties could be spent in its relaxing atmosphere. These new friends, with their wide vision of service, often helped to give her broader outlook on perplexing problems, and Donaldina found their sympathetic interest a daily boon. One day she came with a tale which gripped Mary Tooker's heart in a deeply personal way. A young Chinese university student had come to the Home that morning. Standing with his hands behind his back, facing the sunlit window, he had said to this protector of his countrywomen:

"I hate to have to tell you these things about my people, but they are so, and we know you can help. My mother does not speak English, so she asked me to come and tell you of a little mooie-jai only fifteen. Just last week she became a mother. Could you rescue her?"

Miss Tooker shared in the satisfaction over this rescue, and in the feeling of relief when kind American friends took the girl mother and her baby into their secluded household.

A few winters passed, and this visitor from the East returned each fall to the apartment on Nob Hill, ever full of her generous interest in the Chinese work. But always the girl-mother was her favorite protégé. A true love story was in the making in the little town to which the girl had gone. One of the Chinese workers at Nine-Twenty had introduced a young merchant to the pretty Suey Moie. His frequent visits to the home which sheltered her won more and more of the respect of the friends who appreciated this bright, ambitious girl. At last the time seemed ripe to ask Lo Mo for Suey Moie's hand in marriage. He was willing to adopt the little boy. Miss Tooker insisted upon holding the wedding in her own spacious apartment. No mother or sister could have given closer attention to the details of this ceremony.

The tall Episcopalian rector sensed the underlying spirit of her interest when, gazing out across the docks that line the San Francisco waterfront, he mused:

"There would be no problems of international misunderstanding in our country if scenes like this could be repeated."

CHAPTER XI

NEW INTERESTS AND ASSOCIATES

IN THESE minutes snatched from the whirl of Nine-Twenty duties Donaldina discussed with her New Jersey friends in their winter apartment on the hill many an enigma of her complicated life. But one problem overshadowed all others—that of the proper shielding of the innocent children from the daily tragedies of rescue work. One of her own earliest shocks in the Home had been learning from the lips of baby Yoke Lon what were "swear words" in Cantonese, and from that day on her constant dream had been that sometime there should be a separate Home where the younger girls could grow up unsullied. In her two Eastern friends Donaldina found ready understanding of this need. She had a small nest-egg of money given by friends long interested in the work to keep for this purpose dear to her heart, and now it seemed as if the time had come to expand it into an amount equal to the demand.

Lo Mo had another ally prodding her on toward the accomplishment of this project. In 1911 Tien Fuh Wu, one of the children of the Home in her earliest days, returned to take her place on the staff. Tien had actually come into the Nine-Twenty family a year and three months before Donaldina had answered Mrs. Browne's plea for assistance for Miss Culbertson—discovered, in fact, as a tiny motherless child by the current assistant, Miss Houseworth, while Margaret Culbertson was on a speaking tour in the East. Miss Houseworth's letter with its description of the attractive little girl had been woven into a talk in Norristown, Pennsylvania, after which the superintendent of the Sunday School, Mr. Horace Coleman, approached Miss Culbertson.

"I should like to provide a scholarship for that child in your Home," he volunteered.

Tien was a tomboyish child, full of surplus energy, but also highly sensitive to beauty and refinement. As she grew up two secret affections absorbed her—admiration for the gracious young assistant who came to take Miss Houseworth's place, and adoration of the beautiful Yuen Qui.

She was still very young when that combined loyalty set the pattern for her life of service. As was her custom, Lo Mo had taken Yuen Qui with her on a winter rescue trip to Los Angeles. They were returning with the girl they sought when the train pulled into the deserted station of a small valley town around midnight. A rough constable boarded the train, woke them from a sound sleep by flashing a writ for the rescued girl, and ruthlessly pulled the three off the train into the chill of the night. Gentle Yuen Qui never recovered from the shock and exposure, falling victim to tuberculosis, enemy of so many frail Oriental girls.

Tien often begged the privilege of sitting by the bed of the invalid while Lo Mo attended to her pressing duties. One night while Lo Mo was at dinner the little girl saw the eyes she loved droop; something told her child mind this was not sleep. She ran, terrified, to bring Lo Mo to the room. Then seeing the agony of the older woman's grief, she rose quietly, put a protecting arm around her: "Don't cry, I'll grow up and help you."

From that night on there had been a determination in Tien's straightforward eyes, a purpose in her heart. Her benefactor, Mr. Coleman, recognized something in his ward that set her apart, a seriousness beyond her evident superior mental equipment. He determined that she should be given opportunities commensurate with her ability.

That promise had been fulfilled. Now in 1911 she had returned to Lo Mo, a radiant young woman, ready and prepared to make good her old childhood vow. She had had six years in the East, years crowded with privileges generously provided by the Colemans. She had graduated from Stevens Academy in Germantown, Pennsylvania, had made lasting friends among her classmates, whose cultured homes held perpetual welcome; her wit had made her a favorite companion of a distinguished group of her own countrymen then students at Eastern universities preparing for future roles in the government of modern China. In two years' study at the Toronto Bible College she had added international contacts that greatly broadened her horizon.

There were many doors open to her now, but she would enter only one. Nine-Twenty needed a housekeeper—hardly the position for a girl with her recent training; but Tien accepted its menial tasks and meager salary as a matter of course, working early and late so that she could always be ready to do the extra thing that would bring her closer to Lo Mo.

Even before she left for the East—from the age of fifteen—she had acted as court interpreter in Chinese cases up and down the Pacific Coast. Her ready tongue, her sure logic, her intelligent command of every situation were invaluable as Lo Mo pursued her quest for increasing number of girls. No matter what the demands, Tien was always ready to accompany her on the most difficult missions, as well as to stand by in every court battle. Fearless and well poised, Tien turned her onslaught of words on many a surprised American lawyer in time to save injustice and to bring some new girl into the regenerative atmosphere of Nine-Twenty.

But like Lo Mo her heart was always touched deepest by the innocent children. Her own memory was poignant with scenes from her childhood in the Home. Thus, with the enlarged vision resulting from her Eastern years, she entered insistently into the plans to separate the younger girls from the sin-drenched older ones.

The Tooker sisters listened attentively to her stories. When they left for their New Jersey home they were keenly aware of the necessity for an annex to the work of Nine-Twenty. And they urged Donaldina to visit them again should the Board decide to send her East to raise money for this project.

The women of the Board, with all their loyal interest, could not sense an internal situation with the same intensity as those who were part of the household, and for some time they were reluctant to enter upon this larger responsibility. The day came, however, when the Tooker home welcomed Donaldina Cameron, resolute and earnest, ready to start on this new quest with the high, merry heart that continually carried her through hard places.

But this was in the difficult year of 1914 when the world was torn with war cries. A Home for Chinese babies on the Pacific Coast seemed extraneous in view of the pressing needs across the Atlantic. Then Robert E. Speer lifted his voice in New York one night, challenging the great audience before him not to neglect their more intimate, normal responsibilities in the mass terms of the war catastrophe. Donaldina Cameron went out of that meeting strengthened in her belief in the success of her mission; and her friends, who had gone with her, sensed the reflex as she discussed his words with them.

Yet in spite of this spiritual encouragement there was little in a material way to reward the hopeful traveler who soon was of necessity forced to return to California. She came home to a Board meeting, serious in its tense discussion of her project.

One by one the members had admitted that this new venture of their superintendent was a mirage, attractive to contemplate, but impossible of attainment. Each in her own way had tried to raise funds with small success; and now Miss Cameron's return with only two thousand dollars seemed to be the closing argument. Then Mrs. Robinson, a quiet, older woman, who had sat silent through the discussion, spoke:

"There are ways we know not of. If this thing is meant to be, let us cease our striving, and wait on our knees."

And up in the New England woods, where the Tooker family had gone to their week-end cottage, Mary Tooker was walking along the pine-scented trails, thinking upon the smiling courage of their California guest, who had doughtily refused their invitation to share this respite because she must return home to report at the approaching Board meeting. The Tooker sisters, of course, had given liberally, but was it enough? And even as she thought the words, she knew it was not what they wished it to be. The picture of the homeless Chinese babies, with their potential good conserved, haunted her. Quietly, she retraced her steps and hurrying to the village sent a telegram to her New York banker and a letter to Donaldina Cameron. This letter arrived in time to turn the yearly report from a plea to a paean.

There was an old-fashioned house in East Oakland which had long appealed to Lo Mo as a suitable place in which to locate her younger family, and its purchase was soon arranged. In the autumn of 1915 it was in readiness to receive the twenty-seven younger children, orphans or half-orphans, and the eight 'teen-age assistants assigned to "Tooker Home," so called in memory of the father of the two friends whose substantial gift had made it possible.

Here Lo Mo could come to visit and watch the children at their play in the big yard shaded by its shiny-leaved magnolia. True, it was better that she should be free to give heart and soul to the distressing problems of rescue and rehabilitation; but how she missed the little ones, her babies. At the sight of her approach, the old wooden fence would be lined with climbers, each vying with the other for the first wave of her friendly hand. And then, before she could go in to confer with Nora Bankes, she must stop to see Ah Luen's display of mud pies, or the flowers Kum Mui had picked for her. She would have her moment of play and greeting and then, with the promise of more on her return, would climb the well-worn steps to discuss the incidental cares with one of these women who were her staunch supporters in the mothering of the babies. Perhaps she would have to arrange for a bed for some new child cast on her sympathy for protection, or perhaps she would be planning to what school an older girl must be transferred. Whatever the problem was, she was sure of co-operation. Nora Bankes had been her assistant at Nine-Twenty for several years, and had gained invaluable experience in the Chinatowns of southern California before that. It had meant real sacrifice for Lo Mo to spare her for this task, but she knew that under such guidance the new venture would succeed. It was only two years, however, until she had to bid farewell to this true co-worker, for the strain of the innumerable daily tasks into which Miss Bankes had poured herself proved too great. With only a part-time Chinese teacher and the group of schoolgirl helpers, who in turn needed much mothering themselves, she finally was forced to retire in complete exhaustion. After that for many years Lo Mo was met at the door of Tooker Home by Emma Mills, a strong-spirited though frail young woman who had stepped from much the same background of lack of experience that had "prepared" Donaldina Cameron for her work.

As this wholesome separate Home for the small children became better established there were calls from many sides to take orphaned and stranded Oriental children into its sheltering doors. The family grew so large that another house across the street was rented as an extra dormitory.

Soon more and more tiny tots were brought to Tooker Home. Like the shoe of Mother Goose rhyme, it had so many children its sponsors did not know what to do. There was no available house to rent, and a cottage was purchased where all the smaller members were cared for by Ann Wharton, a Red Cross nurse—"The Little Colonel" from Tennessee—just returned from four years' service in China. Her first assistant was a tall granddaughter of the Home, who had been sent to Lo Mo by a mother who wanted her child to have a few years of the same refining influence which had blessed her own life. Then had come N'Goh, who had learned to love babies with the six dolls brought her by Lo Mo to ease her own loneliness in her own first frightened days at Nine-Twenty. Lo Mo's busy hands had often interrupted serious tasks in order to teach this little play-mother to sew for her rag and bisque babies, and now N'Goh was overjoyed to serve in a place of real responsibility among flesh-and-blood infants.

In the days when Tooker Home was giving N'Goh and other Chinese girls such training in future motherhood, Lo Mo was finding the burdens almost too much to carry. After Nora Bankes went to Tooker, Tien added the duties of assistant to those of matron and interpreter. They had a part-time American teacher and a Chinese instructor who divided her time between San Francisco and Oakland. Six years of schoolgirl freedom in her wonderful Eastern experience had hardly ripened Tien to meet the pressing cares that bore down on Lo Mo day and night. She tried to spare her leader all she could. But nerves, those fragile stabilizers of human poise, were strained to the breaking point.

Funds were low. Two Homes were running where one had been supported before. Maintenance charges, salary overhead, those ghosts which stalk every meeting of welfare Boards, hung over the ones who planned the budget. Funds were administered from the East. Those who were so far away could not realize what was happening to these two who answered loyally all the calls which poured in upon them. There was one, though, who saw it at first hand. For more than fifteen years John H. Laughlin had brought his knowledge of Chinese ways and peoples to the upbuilding of this transplanted bit of old China in America. In his superintendency of Oriental work of the Coast, he was in and out of the Home on the hill on daily errands of ministry. He saw Donaldina Cameron's hair grow whiter; he watched Tien's efforts at self-control when struggling girls refused their proffered food and impatient officials called her from her own meals to interpret. Someone must be found to help.

In his routine travels from place to place, he was continually watching for another willing aide for Miss Cameron. Weary in the summer heat, he rested one Sunday evening in the vespers of the vine-covered Highland Park Church in Los Angeles. A young woman rose to sing. There was something in the eager spirit reflected in her face that brought a vision to his mind. He pictured her under the leadership of his friend on the San Francisco hillside.

A few inquiries told him that Ethel Higgins, with her sister and mother, lived in the house owned by the superintendent of his Chinese work in Los Angeles. A Mount Holyoke graduate, she had taught several years in Northfield Seminary before coming West; and he coveted her help on the teaching staff of the San Francisco Home.

He did not, however, broach his plan to her, but came back to Nine-Twenty enthusiastic over his discovery. Miss Cameron should go herself to Los Angeles and try to win the interest of this admirably fitted young woman. There was an immediate sympathy between these two—the slight dark-eyed Ethel Higgins with her vibrant singing voice, and the tall soft-spoken Lo Mo. The desire to come north was strong; but doctors warned against taking her mother from the relaxing southern climate. The dream seemed futile.

Inspired by this new vision of helpfulness, however, Ethel Higgins volunteered her time and talents in the Los Angeles work among Chinese. This was in 1915. Visitors from everywhere were pouring into San Francisco to wander in the City of Ivory built on the shore of the

Golden Gate to commemorate the opening of the Panama Canal. Ethel Higgins came north with friends to join the throngs who journeyed to the Panama Pacific Exposition. She came in July when dripping summer fogs cooled travelers from the sweltering East; but they dampened her hopes for bringing the mother to this northern city.

She did not, however, spend all her time studying the exhibits of the International Palaces or watching the fountains sparkling in the gorgeous courts and gardens. There was another attraction in San Francisco that drew her irresistibly to the hillside above Chinatown.

When the doorkeeper answered Miss Higgins' ring at Nine-Twenty, Lo Mo had just come down the back stairs attracted by the aroma of cookies baking in the auxiliary kitchen off the staff dining room. She stepped into the hall, a plate of spicy sweets in one hand and a fascinating little Chinese girl clinging to the other, as the doorkeeper announced the visitor. Years afterward Ethel Higgins stood by the deathbed of this same Chinese girl—one of the last of the very young domestic slaves rescued by Miss Cameron in Los Angeles—and then declared that it had been the sight of this homey picture, so different from the formality of most institutions, that had subconsciously crystallized her decision to come back some day as a member of Lo Mo's staff.

That opportunity came a year later. Her mother's health had improved; and when Miss Cameron made a second trip to urge her again to come north, the way seemed open. This time she came as assistant superintendent.

Ethel Higgins not only filled an important place on the Nine-Twenty staff; she came at a time when Lo Mo's heart was torn with grief. From out of the San Benito Valley had come a call to the bedside of her brother, critically ill. He who had scarcely known a day's illness in his life, who in boyhood had been adjudged to have a perfect physique, was taken from his family in the prime of life through a three-day sickness which struck like lightning.

Donaldina had come back to Nine-Twenty buoyed only by the glimpse of immortality she had seen in his farewell and the pressure of her sister Annie's hand as they stood together, silent, beneath an evergreen oak at the hour when the sun was dropping. "Love never dies," Annie had said, and Dolly could come back to pour more of herself into the effort to make these words true for many who had never sensed their meaning.

Ethel Higgins and her New England mother thus came into the harassed life of Donaldina Cameron when she most needed the support of mature judgment and sympathy. In the close relationship of the next two years, when Mrs. Higgins' apartment close by welcomed Lo Mo for brief respites from the turmoil of Nine-Twenty, this bond grew closer. Then as a fatal illness struck the older woman and life ebbed away, there could be sensed a feeling of profound comfort in leaving her daughter associated with the friend whom both so greatly admired. Upon her death in 1918 her two daughters made a substantial gift in her name to enlarge the Industrial Department of the Home, a phase of work which especially appealed to this descendant of the practical Pilgrims.

From the earliest days of the existence of the Home, the Industrial Department had had a vital part in the rehabilitation of the rescued girls. At its looms they were taught not only to weave the homespun bags and scarfs for which the yearly bazaars became famous but also to teach fingers used to dull drudgery and evil habits the craftsmanship that builds character.

During these busy years Tooker Home had continued to grow. The time had now come when expansion in the East Eleventh Street neighborhood could go no farther. Donaldina Cameron went forthwith to another of her staunch and tried friends, that generous-minded man of the seas, Captain Robert Dollar.

"We know your interest and want your advice," she said, and he immediately arranged to devote a forenoon to a survey of the Oakland Home. From basement to attic, he climbed all over its many stairs; he listened to the children sing; he examined every corner of playground and garden; still he made no comments.

"Must hurry back to a meeting in San Francisco," he told his young friend; but he asked her to walk to the train with him.

"What do you think of Tooker Home and its present problems?" asked the superintendent of Nine-Twenty.

"That's no place to take care of all these children," he replied in his decisive way. "Tell your Board to go out and find any piece of property they think adaptable and I'll buy it for you," adding with a twinkle in his deep-set blue eyes, "you'll have to put up a suitable building, too."

The president of Occidental Board, Mrs. H. B. Pinney, happened to be at an Oakland meeting a few days later with an old friend, Mrs. Carrie Judd Montgomery. She spoke of the promise Captain Dollar had made to Miss Cameron, and the two started roaming over the eucalyptus-clad hills near Mills College in the outskirts of that city. Mrs. Pinney stopped for a view of the Bay from a wooded knoll.

"This would be an ideal location. Do you know whether or not it is for sale?"

"Yes," replied Mrs. Montgomery. "It happens to belong to us at present; but forty years ago when this was all the Mills estate, I walked over this piece of land with Mrs. Mills herself and she stopped at this very place, saying this was a spot she would like to dedicate to service. And it has stood idle ever since!"

Mrs. Pinney hastened back to Nine-Twenty. Would Lo Mo share her enthusiasm? Indeed, yes, and more, for Mrs. Mills had ever been a warm friend to her and of her work; and many a time in the early days girls from Nine-Twenty had been allowed to camp out on this site when Lo Mo had asked the privilege of taking them on vacation trips out of the city fogs. In fact, the carpet on the floor of Culbertson Hall had been purchased with part of the small legacy left by Mrs. Mills to Nine-Twenty. It almost seemed that the spectral hand of this friend of the past had guided them to the site of the next future step.

Donaldina hurried to Captain Dollar with her news. Would he come and give his expert advice? Not only did he agree to that but he brought a group of astute business friends to appraise his findings. These men were all enthusiastic, and Captain Dollar turned to the Board women.

"Are you satisfied?" he asked.

Noting the approval in their faces, he did not wait for reply but turned to the owner, Mr. Montgomery:

"What is your price?"

"What do you think it's worth?" replied the other.

"Name your price—then I'll say whether it is worth it," insisted the Captain.

Mr. Montgomery's answer apparently satisfied him, for his next question came without hesitation:

"When can you give the deed?"

"What are your terms?" was the answering inquiry.

"Cash. Get the deed and everything ready. I'll mail you a check as soon as they are in order," and with these words the deal closed, giving to the Board over two acres of choice property on which to carry out their cherished project. And never did a Dollar birthday pass after that without a visit of gratitude from the children and grandchildren of Lo Mo, bringing their songs and flowers to say "Thank you" to this grand old man who later established a school of his own for Chinese children and young men in Poo-Tung across from Shanghai.

Students at Mills College were soon finding courses in international relations literally at their doorstep. For in addition to the proceeds from the sale of Tooker Home, friends soon provided the extra means to erect a Chinese-style building designed by Julia Morgan. In this attractive Ming Quong Home just opposite the Beulah Gate of the college, scores of girls grew from childhood under its vermillion roofs. The square court guarded by blue porcelain Foo-dogs became the scene of carefree play hours for children brought into its sunshine by Lo Mo's ceaseless questing among the dark alleys and narrow pavements of freedom stifling Chinatowns.

Lo Mo's visits to this second family across the Bay now took on a double meaning. She never stepped off the Key Route train at the bright orange-colored waiting room which stood between the college and Ming Quong (Radiant Light) without a tightening of her throat as she watched the group of happy girls running to meet her down the shrub-lined roadway. And her gratitude to those who had provided this perfect setting was enhanced by the satisfaction she had in watching Emma Mills's joy in the use of its modern facilities. Then, too, she was already beginning to sense the continuity of her work in the lives of some of the assistants to Miss Mills, girls whose early days had been spent at her knee, and who were now passing on to a new generation the atmosphere of trust and culture which they had absorbed at Nine-Twenty. There was Ida Lee, she of the merry eyes and musical voice, who having grown to womanhood in San Francisco had acted as assistant teacher for the young children at Nine-Twenty. After a few years of advanced kindergarten training in the state of New York she had returned to help at Tooker. Then had come another interval of study at Los Angeles Bible Institute, and she was back to bring her love of life to this larger family at Ming Quong Home.

Perhaps no one helper eased the daily burdens of Emma Mills's life in the same way as did another quiet "daughter" from Nine-Twenty. Hung Mui Chew, the child who carried the basket of eggs on that earthquake exodus, had been brought to the home by a Chinese neighbor as a three-year-old, left behind by her fleeing foster mother in the maelstrom of a vicious tong war. No word came back from China whither the woman had gone; but this child, like so many others, was safe in the new foster home. In the grammar grades when Tooker was provided, Hung Mui was one of those who had journeyed across the Bay, ever loyal and helpful to these wonderful friends of hers. By the time she had finished her course in Oakland High School it was decided that she should go on to Santa Barbara State Teachers College, there to prepare herself in a home economics course to return to the staff at the new Ming Quong Home. This studying, as well as her course at Los Angeles Bible Institute, was made possible largely through her own efforts at self-support, always with the goal of repaying her befrienders through service to others.

The constructive rehabilitation work carried on by Lo Mo and all her helpers on both sides of the Bay had its influence in the establishment of still another Chinese hospice. In 1919 a young Baptist medical missionary, Dr. Charles R. Shepherd, came to San Francisco to work among the Chinese. He soon recognized a duplication of effort in the conventional work of the many boards and agencies endeavoring to transform Chinatown; but the unique value of the activities at Nine-Twenty appealed to his progressive mind. Here was a woman with a definite conviction of a specific need, the vision needed to meet it, and courage sufficient to overcome all obstacles. On the other hand, Miss Cameron recognized in the growing interest of this young man a possible solution for a problem which had long perplexed her.

There was no place for the little sons of the broken homes and the delinquent family circles whose daughters were carefully sheltered in the new Ming Quong Home. In the old Tooker Home, and occasionally at Nine-Twenty, a small boy would become temporarily a part of the family; but Lo Mo's work was primarily to rescue real and potential slave girls. In Dr. Shepherd she sensed one who could take the stranded boys from the overcrowded alleys of Chinatown and build them into useful men. In the extremity of her present problem here was one who could relieve Nine-Twenty of the seven small boys to whom it had fallen heir because no one else claimed them.

Thus it was that Chung Mei Home, the only refuge for Chinese boys in America, was Dr. Shepherd's answer to Miss Cameron's plea. It was first established in a fog-stained, old-fashioned house on the edge of the marshlands of North Oakland, with one of the earliest "daughters" of Nine-Twenty—Mrs. Chin Toy—as matron. Called in her youth "the Madonna" by old Dr. Condit, Mrs. Chin Toy became the only "mother" some of these stranded youth had ever known.

Dr. Shepherd imbued these boys with his own sense of responsibility for their betterment. Their wood cart, lettered "Help the Chung Mei Boys to Help Themselves," became a familiar sight in the East Bay as they supplied residents with wood and kindling chopped by their young hands. That undertaking, together with the proceeds from clever minstrel shows, written and produced by their indomitable "Captain," eventually netted ten thousand dollars, with which they purchased five and a half acres of wooded hilltop in Contra Costa County. Lo Mo shared Captain Shepherd's pride in the accomplishments of his singing troupe—her "stepsons across the Bay."

CHAPTER XII

. . . . BY FAITH ALONE

THE LIFE of another "stepson" left on the threshold of Nine-Twenty helped to bring about a transformation in the career of one of the most amazing of all Lo Mo's "daughters." The story of his foster mother goes back into the night life of old Chinatown, where "light glows redly through fish-skin lanterns . . . . inviting into restaurants with rustling bead curtains, softly glowing lanterns, and heavily carved teakwood tables."

In the inner circle of the powerful tongs the name of Oie Kum was the toast of the most festive banquets. She was the favored one, owned body and soul by the leader of a great tong. When Oie Kum entered the banquet hall, her black hair combed and dressed by the hands of her little mooie-jai and piled high with glittering ornaments, all others were ignored. Through the years of her popularity she added to her scarlet earnings by extensive trade as a peddler of opium. Gradually she became known throughout Chinatown as "Ah-peen" Oie, from the native word for their favorite drug. With this augmented income she at length succeeded in buying her own freedom from her grasping owner, and also in becoming part owner of a younger slave girl whom she kept at her lucrative business in a house just down the hill from the Home. Several times the place was raided, and there developed between the owner of the house on the alley and the custodian of the red brick Home on the hill one of those bitter contests of intellect that only persons of strong will arrayed on opposite sides of a struggle can understand. The name of Ah-peen Oie, spoken shudderingly by the rescued slave girls who knew her power, was the one name in Chinatown that almost struck terror in the calm heart of Lo Mo.

There was instant action, then, when a typewritten note came to Nine-Twenty, urging help "without delay" to relieve one "in great distress" at the dreaded address off Commercial Street. But when the rescue party entered the house, it was not the shrinking mooie-jai whom they had expected to spirit away who waited for them. Taciturn and alone, there sat Ah-peen Oie herself. A thorough search revealed no other girl. Scarcely believing it possible, the intrepreter turned to ask Oie Kum if she had sent for them. Sullenly and yet pleadingly, she admitted authorship of the note. She wanted to gain the shelter of the Home she had fought so long.

Her Scotch wariness aroused, Lo Mo refused to be duped. Let this slaveowner and opium vendor into the family she had so carefully guarded? Never! No telling what were the cunning plans evolving in the head of this notorious woman. Miss Cameron turned away in disdain.

But Ah-peen Oie was desperate. Had she not heard Hip Chang, her former owner, strike a bargain with Wong Dick to sell her for three thousand dollars, in spite of the money she herself had paid for freedom? She had been blamed for the loss of the slave girl rescued by this tall "Fahn Quai"; and Hip Chang held her responsible for the money loss. Then, too, Sing Choy was threatening to turn the highbinders on her to collect the two thousand dollars she still owed on the last ten-thousand-dollar opium consignment. There was no way out. She must give in to one enemy or another, and, after all, she had heard that life in the brick prison was not what she had trained her slaves to believe.

Ah-peen Oie clung to the hem of Lo Mo's skirts, pleading earnestly through the interpreter, Yoke Lon, that she "wanted to change her life." Wisdom said "No," but that intuition which was always her unerring guide urged, "Try."

Lo Mo thought of her friend, the matron of the city prison. She conferred with her by telephone, then turned to the anxious woman: "If you really mean what you say, will you be willing to be held at the city prison until we have time to decide?"

This was a stern test of sincerity; but "I'll go anywhere if you say I'm safe," answered Ah-peen Oie. Willingly she changed her finery for prison garb and waited expectantly for word from the one person who now held her respect.

Back at Nine-Twenty there was consternation. The wise women on the Board who had backed every effort of their daring superintendent debated seriously over "the visionary experiment." There could be no good in a woman whose life was so deeply intrenched in evil. Their rooms were full of girls for whom all had fought. The danger of allowing this scheming slaveowner in their midst was too great to risk.

But Donaldina Cameron turned for help and guidance to the Book known and loved from childhood. From its pages there stood out Jesus by the well of Samaria. Spent and worn, He had asked help from a woman His friends despised. She had gone to spread the gospel among a race that was shunned. Quietly Miss Cameron thought back over the days of her sheltered girlhood. Who was she to pass judgment on this one who had fallen through whose fault no one knew?

She was alone in her decision to give Oie Kum a chance. But she did not take her into the protected family circle. There was a room on Joice Street with a separate entrance. For years this had been the schoolroom, but since the Board of Education had provided the new public school for Oriental children that phase of the work had passed and the room stood unoccupied. It was cleaned and put in order. Then its new inhabitant was brought here to live under lock and key. She was not allowed to take part in any of the Home's routine activities. Her three meals a day were carried to her by Tien Wu and her Chinese girl helpers.

Illness, which had been making its insidious way into the body of this forlorn woman, reached a climax which took her to the Lane Hospital for a serious operation. In spite of the skill of one of the city's best surgeons supervising the work of that charity ward, it looked for a time as if this life with all its hopelessness was nearly over. There seemed little response to the kindness of nurses and the visits of Lo Mo and her staff; but the vital force that had made Oie Kum a leader in her old life was still pushing her forward into the new though as yet unknown one.

She was brought back to her barren room to convalesce, still held as a "prisoner of hope."

Then came one of those strange coincidences which are sometimes woven into the fabric of life, giving the humble a feeling of being a part of some unseen plan. A few years before, Tien Wu had been in China and there had heard of a remarkable Chinese Christian woman, Miss Amy Law of Canton. The father of this woman had been one of the early merchants of San Francisco's Chinatown. One day a few pages from the Gospels had strayed into his hands. Strange thinking, this. He must stop its spread among his idol-worshipping clan. Yet he could not escape its searching words. He would challenge the native pastor of the old Chinese Church on Stockton Street to a debate. If the pastor could defeat him in argument, he would embrace the new doctrines; but he felt secure in his ancient Confucianism. With all the learning of the cultured scholar, he was sure he could out-argue the earnest young pastor; but there had been more power behind that individual than either of them comprehended. Once convinced, the older man had thrown all his influence, means, and personality to the furtherance of this new way of life. He must carry his news back to the family he had left in China. His keen young daughter sensed the appeal of this strange new story told by her father. Pioneer among liberated Chinese women, she abandoned all else to the cause in which she was to become known as "the most spiritually minded woman in South China," where her name had first come to Tien Wu's attention.

And now Amy Law, worn by years of devoted service, had come to America for a brief visit and rest. Tien Wu brought word of this visitor to Miss Cameron, and the proffered hospitality of the Home was readily accepted by this one so opportunely in their midst. The story of Ah-peen Oie was passed on and a key to the Joice Street door was made for Miss Law. Each day for the two weeks she stayed in San Francisco, she spent serious hours with the voluntary prisoner in the old schoolroom. No interpreter was needed. No one but those two know what went into these conversations; but no one who has since looked into the face of her who was once the "toast of the underworld" can doubt the reality of the message explained by her newfound friend.

Amy Law sailed back to South China; but Lo Mo knew that her faith had been justified. Gradually freedom was granted to the woman in the back room. She took her place with the other workers by the looms in the Industrial Department. Then came an opportunity for her to prove her willingness to serve. The supervisor of the Chinese kitchen left suddenly. There was no one to take her place; Tien Wu suggested, "Try Oie Kum."

No task was too humble for this strong spirit, who had suddenly come to see life values in their true proportion. Daily she stood over rice pots and heaping pans of well-scrubbed greens. With hands accustomed to dainty ways, she herself served those who had been her slaves. Less than a year after she had come to be a prisoner in the dark back room she was given the key to the service entrance of the Home where she presided with the dignity of the mistress of a mansion.

Then one morning Lo Mo was awakened by a commotion in the lower hall. Leaning over the bannister she saw the fair-haired English housekeeper bending over the short dark Chinese assistant and both of them concentrating on a bundle in Oie Kum's arms.

At sight of Lo Mo, Oie Kum ran quickly up the stairs: "Baby, Lo Mo, baby—see." And with a glad light glowing in her dark eyes she looked appealing at her friend. Lo Mo knew the story behind the longing heart. Many times since her new life had begun, she had pleaded, "Do you think I could adopt a baby?" and had turned, sorrowful, at the answer. "We must wait and see." She had told Lo Mo of the baby she herself had once borne. As a child of fourteen she had been married in China and she had been brought to this country, apparently, as far as her own respectable family knew, the wife of a prosperous merchant. Sick and bewildered, about to become a mother when she landed, she had seen this tall "Fahn Quai" at the dock but had shrunk from her, terrified, when the kind hand clasped hers in passing. She too had been warned by her husband to beware of this "agent of a foreign slave market." But it had not been long until she learned of the real slave market. Her baby had died at birth and she herself had been sold into the life from which Lo Mo had at last rescued her.

In the bitterness of her early loss she had turned against all that was good; but now that she knew the ways of love she longed for a chance to mother some babe who knew no other. This very night the unsatisfied prayer of her heart had woven itself into her dreams: An old Chinese man had stood in her door, asking her to take the baby he held out toward her. Sorrowfully she had replied that she "could not afford to support it"; then she had awakened weeping. As she had lain there awake in the early morning hours, mentally stirred by the ancient superstition that dreams of babies bring bad luck, a feeble cry had come to her ears.

"At first I thought it was a kitten, Lo Mo, but it kept on, and I thought I better look. See what I found," and she held out the baby boy.

"And there was a man sent from God whose name was John," answered Lo Mo, as she looked into the radiant face before her. And from that day no other arms held baby John save Oie Kum's and the partner who soon after that came to claim her as his wife.

For in the days of her illness there had appeared at the Home a young rancher from one of the valley towns. Years before he had met the enchanting Oie Kum and had tried to extricate her from the tangled life she was leading. But she was proud and indifferent. Then had come the great change. When she lay ill in the hospital he had learned of her whereabouts and had come to her new-found friends to offer help. As the years went on, Lo Mo came to understand and respect this quiet young man. At last, when John was three years old, she was willing to give in marriage this "daughter" too, as she had so many who had gone forth to make happy homes throughout the land.

There had been problems of deep perplexity before that happy day, for there were others to fear among those in the dark background of

Oie Kum's life. But she placed one condition on her promise to marry. She owed large sums of money in Chinatown. She had learned to cook, and cook well, too, and her experience included not only her service at Nine-Twenty but a year following at Chung Mei. Dr. Shepherd had been in that astonished rescue party who had answered her note of long ago, and when he needed assistance in his work she had gone with willing hands.

Now that a home of her own was offered, she stipulated that she be allowed to cook for the men on the big ranch run by her future husband and his father. If she could do this and earn enough to pay her legitimate debts she would be safe. Gambling and opium debts were sifted from those which would be legal and her debtors were called to give an accounting in black and white.

In the heat of the valley she labored from dawn till late at night, but her contented spirit eased fatigue and with light heart she sent installments back to her friends at Nine-Twenty to pay her creditors. At last there was but one hundred dollars left to pay. This she brought herself. The old merchant to whom she owed it was called to Nine-Twenty. When the purpose of the visit was explained to him, he answered:

"Oh, that debt was wiped off the books at Chinese New Year's seven years ago. She is living a good life now. I don't want her money."

But Oie Kum was insistent. She owed the money. It must be paid.

"You will have to tell him so yourself, then," said Tien Wu; "I cannot persuade him."

It was hard for Oie Kum to face him. She had seen none of her old associates since she had left Chinatown. But she came down and held out the hundred dollars.

"I am a Christian now. I owe the money. You must take it."

He rose with a low bow, unprecedented for a merchant of his class before a woman such as she had been, and accepted the currency with all the courtesy that those who know these gentlemen behind counters of Chinatown love and respect.

"If that is what your religion teaches, I want to know more of it."

CHAPTER XIII

TWENTY-FIVE YEARS A "MOTHER"

WHILE few lives have been as dramatically changed as was that of this woman who became universally loved and respected by Chinese and American friends alike, yet every life that touched Lo Mo's carried away something of that inner strength which bore her "on eagle's wings" through the years of perplexing tasks.

She was nearing the completion of twenty-five years in Chinatown when an invitation came to her to bring a group of her younger children to San Diego to speak before a large meeting. In Los Angeles she was joined by Ida Lee, then a student there. When they reached San Diego, they boarded a streetcar with their excited charges.

At the corner of Fifth and G streets, Lo Mo turned suddenly to her companion:

"Ida dear, will you take the children on to the Hall? I have a feeling that I must get off here. There are a few minutes to spare, and I'll have time to see Mrs. Thom."

But no sooner had she stepped from the car than a strange man, sunning himself in the doorway of a garage, untipped his chair and rose to greet her.

"Why, Miss Cameron!" he exclaimed, "how did you happen to come to San Diego? I almost telegraphed you last night."

She looked up, astonished, to greet a neighbor of the early years. With the glare of the afternoon sun in her eyes and her mind intent on her hurried errand, she had not at first recognized this old acquaintance; but in a moment she was all attention as he poured out the tale he had saved for her ears. He wanted her to know the tragic story of a Chinese girl recently arrested in San Diego. This girl had been helped from her career of slavery by a man who loved her enough to risk his life in an attempt to free her. But money was scarce, the former owner was close on his heels, and he had robbed a corner store to get the means of transportation to China. In the fatal shooting fray which followed, the girl had been wounded and taken to a hospital, where she was being held as a possible accomplice in the robbery and murder. Miss Cameron's informant did not think the girl in any way guilty; and he craved for her the protection of the Home at Nine-Twenty.

The children and the speaking engagement were left to Mrs. Kelley, who had also gone south for the meeting, while Lo Mo took Ida as interpreter and hastened from the hospital to the police court and back to the hospital. The girl was frantic. Two nurses had been required to guard her from taking her life. When Lo Mo arrived with the sympathetic Ida Lee, there were hours of pleading and explanation. Only a Chinese woman who knew from daily contact with other despairing souls into what depths of fear and mental chaos this sobbing girl had been plunged could possibly begin to pacify her. Finally late in the evening confidence began to be established. She promised to make no further attempts on her life and to trust herself to the sanctum of the Home from which these protectors had come—these strangely persuasive women who guaranteed her safety from the owner she feared worse than death.

In the meantime Lo Mo had been able to arrange with the authorities to release Suey Leen on bail, provided she should be taken to San Francisco in her personal custody. In addition to her gunshot wound, this girl was a seemingly hopeless opium case, and it was necessary to carry her on a stretcher into the seclusion of the Pullman drawing room, where Ida acted as patient guardian all night. When the train reached Los Angeles the next morning they were met by a trusted American friend to whom they had telegraphed to bring his automobile. Again the stretcher was brought into use and Suey Leen, exhausted from fear and physical weakness, was carried to the closed car and driven to a private hospital in a quiet part of the city. That evening this process was repeated and at last the party boarded the *Owl* for the final lap of the strange journey.

A taxi brought the returning wanderers with their unexpected charge into Joice Street the next morning as guests and visitors were excitedly coming and going, making plans for the twenty-fifth anniversary party to be held that night. Ida Lee jumped out first with the quartet of singing girls who had started with Lo Mo on the adventurous journey. As Tien Wu opened the door to admit them she was overjoyed to see Ida, whom she had urged in vain to come "home" for the great occasion; but this was no time for celebration. Hurriedly Ida sent the children into the bustling hall and pulled Tien down the steps to the waiting taxi where Miss Cameron still sat supporting the half-fainting stranger. Together they almost carried the girl through the crowd of curious daughters who had gathered to welcome Lo Mo. No sooner was their burden set down inside the big doors than Suey Leen was seized with a terrible hemorrhage.

Kind hands among the older girls quickly helped the newcomer, worn with fatigue and emotion, to the top-floor bedroom which was always in readiness for emergencies. Tien Wu was afraid the girl would not live through the day, exhausted as she was from loss of blood and endless fears. And the kind interpreter had to interrupt her supervision of the many surprises for Lo Mo in order to ease the struggles of the unexpected guest.

That night when visitors from far and wide were assembling for the Anniversary reception, shrieks and groans from this third-floor sufferer echoed through the house. Tien hastened from the astonished guests in Culbertson Hall to try once more to calm her.

"There are many people downstairs," she told her; "you really must be quiet. This is a very big time—a party for Lo Mo—she's been 'mother' to us for twenty-five years. All her friends are helping to make her happy. Please just try."

Suddenly the sobbing ceased convulsively; Suey Leen seemed to sense the sympathetic atmosphere of this strange new home where everyone moved under the scepter of love in the hands of the woman who had brought her here.

"Take this," she said to Tien Wu. "Tell your Lo Mo this opal ring is my gift on her anniversary, my pledge to stay and learn from her."

That ring on Lo Mo's finger became to her a constant reminder of one of the most poignant examples of a rebuilt life she ever knew; yet there were painful weeks before Suey Leen began to be normal. At her own request the co-operation of San Francisco's internationally known health officer, Dr. Hassler, was sought, and the girl was taken for treatment to the Isolation Hospital, where at last she was cured of the insidious opium habit. Then, rehabilitated in body and spirit, she was ready to return to San Diego as witness in the trial of her erstwhile lover for robbery and murder. Lo Mo and the interpreter from the Home were with her, and in spite of their advice to the contrary as well as that of the district attorney and the sheriff, Suey Leen begged for the privilege of a personal interview with the prisoner. So earnest was her plea, however, that she had important things to say to him that the authorities reluctantly granted the request, with the stipulation that the interpreter and the prison guard should remain beside her. As the result of this hour of sober discussion, the prisoner yielded to the persuasion of his former consort in evil to change his plea from the "Not guilty" advised by his attorney to the "Guilty" that was the truth. He was sentenced to life imprisonment in San Quentin.

Suey Leen returned to Nine-Twenty, where she was committed by court order to Lo Mo's guardianship. As soon as she was physically able, she went to work as a maid in one of the city's large homes; and Sunday after Sunday, when her household tasks were done, she would cross the Bay, her Bible under her arm, to read words of encouragement to the prisoner behind the bars. But always her great desire was to return to China. At last the opportunity came and Suey Leen crossed the broad Pacific to study in Miss Amy Law's School, there to prepare to teach her own people the way of life she had learned from the teacher who wore her opal.

The pathos and distress of this newest member of her household did not, however, spoil that April evening in 1920 for which Lo Mo's widely scattered family had planned so long. Tien's letters had gone out all over the United States and even to South China inviting daughters of other days to share in a surprise gift for their "mother." Before Miss Cameron had left for San Diego generous gifts had poured in by every mail, and Tien, puzzled over the responsibility of the proper expenditure of such an amount of money, had finally decided to consult Lo Mo as to her own wishes.

Thinking always of others, Lo Mo had been overwhelmed at this thought of herself. She knew the girls would not want it spent for the Home at Nine-Twenty; but perhaps they would be willing to provide a scholarship in her name in the school for the blind at Canton, where one of her earlier "daughters" had served on the staff. In these distressing postwar days she felt that even more than ever personal desires and pleasures must be set aside to relieve the suffering of the world. She thought back to Dr. Speer's speech at the beginning of the war when she had been trying so hard to raise money for her Chinese babies. He had said not to forget the normal demands of daily living; but he had not justified the gratification of personal desires. She begged of Tien to send the money on to China; but that wise young woman had other ideas, and more than that she felt keenly her responsibility to those who had contributed to this gift "just for Lo Mo."

Then the absence of Miss Cameron in southern California had given her the opportunity for which she had hoped. She had scarcely waved good-bye to Lo Mo when the painters and floor men for whom she and her fellow-conspirator, Ethel Higgins, had arranged arrived and went to work. The room where Donaldina Cameron lived must be made worthy of her. Hardwood floors replaced the rough painted boards made shabby by the coming and going of many small feet whose owners had here sought solace. New wallpaper, white-painted woodwork, fresh curtains on the windows, from which she now could look up at the magnificent hotels and apartment houses that replaced the Nob Hill mansions there before the fire—in these and other touches Tien Wu poured out the expression of the girls' devotion to Lo Mo. Then on her bed was laid the piece of brocade silk from which they had hoped she would have a dress made for the party they were planning. This was the real disappointment of the southern California delay. It would have been such a pleasure to have Lo Mo appear at the reception planned entirely by her girls in a dress their gifts had bought. She who had spent of her own meager allowance to satisfy their childish longings for bright colors and trifling adornments should be arrayed in the best the artisans of their race could provide.

But Donaldina Cameron's tears of joy had been shed alone in that remade room when Tien had opened its doors and slipped quietly away to escape the words of reproof she really could have expected. She knew what this tribute would mean to Lo Mo; but she knew as well that her friend would have expected her to heed the earnest request made before she left for San Diego.

When Lo Mo did appear for the family dinner party held before the reception, she was radiant in the lovely gown of lace, with silver slippers, lent by her friend Eleanor Babcock to ease the disappointment of the girls over the failure to have the brocade made in time. She had somehow brushed aside the fatigue from the tiresome journey, the worry over her distraught new burden, the emotion of the room surprise. The years had touched her lightly. True, there were lines in the face that had been so smooth. The lips that in repose drew together in a firm straight line were relaxed tonight in gracious smiles. But in her eyes, those mystic eyes inherited from her deep-souled father, "time paused . . . . and touched her not." Soft with remembrance, gay with quick humor, prophetic in their look toward the future, they sparkled with the iridescent light that baffles one who would describe them. Hazel, they are called, but often in their gray-brown depths is seen that glint of green that endears them to the jade-loving Oriental.

But the friends who gathered round that intimate dinner table were not thought of in terms of race. Evelyn Browne (now Mrs. Bancroft), daughter of the friend whose guiding hand had brought Donaldina Cameron into the inmost lives of these girls from old China, had composed a song that Mae Wong, sweet singer of the Home, now sang to the familiar tune of "Silver Threads Among the Gold."

There was no time to linger in this intimate group. Guests were arriving, eager to offer congratulations. Board women waited for Lo Mo to head the receiving line. Gifts were ready to be presented. Among these were a silver basket full of roses from the Occidental Board; a silver dish from the children of Mrs. Wing's kindergarten; a gold watch bought with the remainder of the world-wide response to Tien's letters and inscribed "from the girls—April 15, 1895, to April 15, 1920." Then one of the children handed her a large, silvered box tied with a broad, red satin ribbon. It looked like a mammoth box of candy. The girls pressed around Lo Mo as she lifted the cover to disclose an album bound in rich black-gold brocade. Inside the flyleaf in silver letters were the Chinese characters which, translated, described her as "Light of Womanhood and Mother of the Flock." Its heavy pages disclosed pictures of all who had been associated with her in the years of her work at Nine-Twenty, with blank pages ready for many more to come.

Not in portraits alone were her quarter-century of memories made vivid for Donaldina Cameron in this season of congratulation. All the stirring events of the forty-seven years of Occidental Board's history lived again in a pageant prepared for a national Jubilee celebration in which the red brick Home was the center of activities for the San Francisco Bay district. This was presided over by Mrs. Rawlins Cadwallader, daughter of John McArthur, another distinguished Scotchman of California pioneering days. Mrs. Cadwallader had succeeded Mrs. Pinney as president of the Board, and had guided its destinies until the support and administration of the Home passed to a national organization, into which Occidental Board was incorporated after nearly fifty years of loyal and useful service.

The program of that meeting back in 1920 illustrated in retrospect as in vivid present-day reality the episodes of this great adventure in race friendship. In the pageant of "The Pictured Years" parts were taken by many who had participated in the actual scenes it recalled.

Detachments of police were assigned from the Chinatown Squad to help in the dramatized raids in cellars and over roofs. Inspector Robinson played again his part of messenger between his Chinese friends in need and this haven of refuge on the hill. He brought the "half a handkerchief" which had been mailed to him as a token; and he and Detectives Barron and Richards climbed the fake stairways and unbolted doors that would not yield. An *Arabian Nights* scene was based on the faith of Hoormah, the Nestorian matron during Miss Culbertson's régime, she whose serene assurance of help when the rice bins were empty, at the time of the bitterest opposition to anything Chinese, had been rewarded by an anonymous goldpiece. The exodus from crumbling brick walls to welcoming barn doors during the disaster of 1906 was followed by a prune-picking episode explaining the then latest effort of these girls toward self-support; while the climax of the story was a tableau showing a home where the Oriental wife and mother, a former ward of the Board, was proudly viewing her daughter in cap and gown, diploma in hand, ready for service in the modern world.

CHAPTER XIV

WAR WORK AND SUMMER CAMPS

As the curtain fell on "The Pictured Years," audience and actors mingled in congratulatory groups around Miss Cameron. In the midst of the crowd, sprightly Suey Ching—she who years before had been lost, and found again at the Sacramento parade—slipped up just as Lo Mo was answering the questions of an Eastern visitor about the prune-picking experience.

"Yes, that was quite an undertaking. Suey Ching here could tell you many funny things that happened in those hot days in the orchards, and some not so funny, too," she added as Suey Ching, still clad in the blue denim overalls of the pageant, sighed reminiscently over the weary picture this brought to mind.

"You see, our girls couldn't enlist in the regular army, but these were their uniforms," indicating Suey Ching's overalls; and Donaldina Cameron, with the high spirit of her chieftain ancestors, proceeded to explain to her visitor how they had answered Herbert Hoover's clarion call to join the Conservation Army in the tense period of World War days. When the plea went forth to every rancher and every housewife to save the fruit rotting on the ground for lack of men to pick it, Lo Mo's patriotic spirit, that same flame that had flared in childhood play in the barnyard Fourth of July, had been quick to respond.

"We always try to give our girls a sense of independence and this fruit-picking furnished an opportunity for many things," she continued. "In it they could be taught patriotism and at the same time be self-supporting, while they could reap many benefits from the summer sunshine of the Santa Clara Valley without any expense to the Board."

But the guest who had seen only the pantomime repetition could not really sense that the opportunity for all this had come only because Lo Mo herself had been indefatigable in carrying out the details of her project.

Among her many acquaintances had been the head of the fruit-growers' association in San Jose. She went to him with her proposition. She could provide twenty girls to cut the apricots which were just then ready to be spread on the trays for sun drying. In a few days a long-distance call informed her that a Mrs. Williams, whose orchard was in the foothills east of San Jose, would be glad to employ her crew.

All of the family who were old enough and fit to be trusted outside the sheltering brick walls of Nine-Twenty were packed off on this new adventure. They had no camp equipment, and many of them had never been off the pavements of Chinatown before. Mrs. Williams provided a few rusty bed springs, but for the most part the party slept on straw bags on the bare ground. Lo Mo had stayed over to help settle camp, and had shared the general confusion when an unexpected late spring rain found them utterly unprepared that first unforgettable night. When daylight again brought sunshine, she had had to leave her charges with Ethel Higgins and return to pressing duties at Nine-Twenty.

Life among the itinerant laborers, white, Mexican, and nondescript, was as heroic in its way as that among the highbinders and tongs of Chinatown. The picture of this New England-bred Mount Holyoke graduate with her Chinese assistants and charges sharing the common necessities of life with the rough-and-ready wandering fruit-picker tribe was another of those unpainted portraits of war time reflecting behind-the-scenes loyalty of the women of America.

Scarcely had the last of the golden crop on Mrs. Williams' ranch been harvested when Lo Mo came down to negotiate a prunepicking job for her laborers. This was offered across the valley on the road toward the hills of Santa Cruz, just outside the quaint town of Los Gatos with its high white steeples and rose-laden arbors.

By this time the Bailey family had moved down from "The Canyon of the Little Greenhorn" to a brown-and-white Los Gatos cottage with a garden full of orange blossoms and syringa. Whether it was the fiction of being near them—for she was far too busy to see much of them—or the bending pepper trees on the Silker prune ranch that settled Donaldina Cameron's mind to bring her family here, or whether it was just plain business judgment and attraction to the sympathetic young ranch owners, matters little.

Camp housekeeping was upset a second time almost as soon as Mr. Silker had deposited his load of workers after a late night truck ride across the valley. This time there was a three-day downpour which threatened the prune crop itself. There were long sheds on the ranch where the girls slept on rows of narrow cots. In this Noah's Ark they were crowded till the sun shone again on Mount Hamilton and the meadowlarks supplemented the burr of the four o'clock alarm calling them to go to work when the storm was over.

From this early hour till the heat drove them in for a noontime siesta they worked with feverish haste, picking their way through the 'dobe mud over ground steaming with fermenting fruit. Then as soon as the soft afternoon valley breeze made it possible to breathe and work again, they were back at their job until the purple shadows of evening sent them wearily to their cots once more.

The storm cleared on a Sunday, and Lo Mo herself, donning overalls, led the way to the orchard. If the fruit was to be saved, it had to be gathered then and there. But the summer heat was intense, and Sunday was meant for rest. Rebel as they might inwardly, however, Lo Mo's daughters could not lag when she set them such an example.

This first summer was decidedly an experiment. Those in charge knew not what to provide. Supplies ran short, and Ethel Higgins with Tien Wu had to make many a bus trip to join the Saturday-afternoon throngs in the bustling Farmers' Union in San Jose. One hot day the two of them stood on the sidewalk, laden with bundles—a large sack of fresh corn, ten loaves of bread, six cartons of eggs, and other bulky necessities. The Los Gatos bus passed them by.

"You stay and guard the provisions. I'm going to stand in the street and make the next one stop," Miss Higgins called to Tien Wu.

This scheme worked, and as she resolutely demanded that the driver wait for her load she saw her Chinese friend gather all the bundles under her arms and run into the street. They literally fell into the laps of the amused passengers, who kindly assisted them to get settled. Then came the problem of disembarking; but this was more easily accomplished, as eager helpers from the camp ran through the orchard to welcome their returning leaders.

Camp life had its pleasurable side, however, for girls and leaders alike enjoyed the freedom from the tense atmosphere of the city. Tien with her accordion and Yoke Lon with funny songs whiled away the rest hours, while campfires in the orchard for a brief respite before bedtime furnished outlets for pent-up spirits. The girls composed their ditties, the same sort of rollicking rhymeless verses that any group of carefree vacationists would improvise, as they toasted marshmallows, and in spite of weary limbs and sunburned shoulders were paid in fellowship as well as in coin. One evening in particular Lo Mo was part of the campfire group. She had listened with intent amusement to the round of jovial song when she turned to Ethel Higgins with the request for a favorite ballad—"The Better Land." The old English ballad, crooned by Donaldina's beautiful mother under the Southern Cross, was in Ethel Higgins' earliest memories of songs her mother had sung her under New England elms in the Indian summer haze.

By the next summer, after the rainstorms on the Silker Ranch, the Nine-Twenty outfit was better equipped. This time they picked three hundred and fifty tons of prunes in the two camps established on the hundred-and-fifty-acre ranch near Los Gatos where two groups, one from Nine-Twenty and another from Ming Quong, were employed. Yoke Lon shared the supervision with Tien Wu, and learned much that helped her in a later season when she was in charge of a group of berrypickers on a ranch near the oceanside town of Santa Cruz. While these girls did not make any fortune, they did pay all their own expenses and had some savings to take back to Nine-Twenty when they returned, tanned and vigorous, for their winter's schooling.

The berrypicking experience stretched to three months—four or five weeks longer than usual—because there actually was not room at Nine-Twenty for the campers to return until other accommodations could be provided for some of the twenty newly rescued girls. Yoke Lon's responsibilities were shared part of the time by Miss Tooker's niece, who drove over the winding redwood-lined highway from her Los Gatos home to assist in the supervision of this berrypicking. Day by day Inez Bardeen donned her blue overalls and accompanied the girls to the berry patches, red with the luscious fruits. Yoke Lon's task then was to do the camp cooking, both Chinese and American, for in addition to the girls they had two boarders, Lo Mo's nephew and a friend, who were earning college expense money by joining the fruit-picking army.

As a respite from the back-breaking labor of bending over these berry patches, the girls and their friends from the Nine-Twenty camp found the doors of a cozy seaside cottage always open for their refreshment. Here Lillian Waghorn, former housekeeper at Nine-Twenty, the one who had shared Oie Kum's joy in the finding of little John, had retired to spend her days with her white-haired English father. This granddaughter of Cooling Castle, transplanted from the downs of Kent to the supervision of the daily tasks of a Western Chinese Home in her desire for Christian service, had always been close to Donaldina Cameron. Now she was glad of this opportunity to see the "daughters" of her friend, and to welcome to her home with its treasured keepsakes the girls she had helped to train.

Both berrypicking and the prune season interfered with the school routine of these girls from San Francisco, for the fall term in this Western city starts in August. Therefore, when the immediate pressure of war necessity ceased, these more strenuous occupations were abandoned for the earlier work among the apricots. With their reputation for efficiency established, there was no difficulty in finding annual employment; and a well-equipped sanitary camp near Sunnyvale, halfway between Palo Alto and San Jose, was ready for them every July when the firm golden fruit was ripe for cutting.

CHAPTER XV

RESCUES IN FAR PLACES

IN THE DAYS of readjustment following World War I, Donaldina Cameron was in the East discussing various phases of her changing work on the far Pacific Coast. She sat in the rooms of her Board high above the bustling din of Fifth Avenue explaining to them her desire to go to Washington to lay some of her problems dealing with immigration and slave traffic before the Department of Labor.

"Better than that," spoke up her friend, Dr. Halsey: "I'll give you a letter to President Wilson. You remember he was my classmate at Princeton. He would be able to give you the most constructive advice."

Thus armed with an introduction to the President of the United States she started with high hopes for Washington. But as usual in her interrupted life, she did not foresee whither her path led. She was no sooner in her room at the Grace Dodge preparing to place her letter before the President than a note was slipped under her door asking her to come at once to the Chinese quarter.

News of Lo Mo's whereabouts and plans passed quickly from one Chinatown to another wherever she traveled. From Vancouver to Tucson, from Honolulu to Boston, there were homes full of welcome—homes that might not have been except for Lo Mo. This nation-wide co-operation not only meant pleasure for her, but it insured allies in her ceaseless war against the highbinder. There were safe hiding places in every distant city. While secret messengers warned of Fahn Quai's approach, there were always daughters and granddaughters ready to inform her of new cases needing her aid.

No wonder she forgot her larger objective when she read this urgent epistle from one of her Washington daughters. Without a second thought, she rang for a taxi, and was soon on her way in a very different direction from that which she had contemplated. When the taxi brought her to the door of the waiting girl she found a story not of

Chinese highbinders but of a vicious American woman who had preyed on the Chinese community until she had enticed this girl's husband away to the underworld of New York. Then Miss Cameron did appeal to the federal authorities; but not to the Department of Labor. This time it was the Department of Justice which furnished the allies she needed. Back she traced her steps to New York, where the elusive pair were located through some dependable Chinese friends. When she returned to comfort her Washington daughter and help her to arrange the immediate future, the time for the appointment with the President had passed, and other plans kept her from presenting her letter.

Lo Mo reurned to California still in possession of Dr. Halsey's treasured note; but more important, bringing with her the disillusioned "daughter," who chose to return to Nine-Twenty rather than to accept the proffered protection of her old father-in-law who wanted her to go with him back to China. In the years of devoted service this girl later gave at Tooker Home, Lo Mo felt she was more than repaid for the abandonment of her well-laid plans in Washington.

While her journeys were frequently interrupted by such calls for help, she was often cheered by restful visits in homes like that of Suey Leen. One New Year's Day it was possible to stop over in Detroit for a holiday luncheon with the family of this loved "daughter," who had been the sweet singer at General Assembly when Henry van Dyke was so entranced with the "flower garden of Oriental children." Suey Leen was a rarely talented child, left an orphan at ten by the death of her father, then the most gifted designer of poetic and artistic signs in Chinatown. Board members attracted by her birdlike soprano had persuaded one of San Francisco's finest vocal teachers, Mrs. Mariner Campbell, to train her voice. Now Lo Mo sat in the pleasant Detroit dining room and told the family about the little Chinese children on the Pacific Coast.

Suey Leen's nine-year-old daughter listened eagerly to the *keng gai* (reminiscences) shared by her mother and Lo Mo. She laughed over the funny picture Lo Mo described of her mother running down the steep Sacramento Street hill buttoning the many fastenings of her long black sahm while the one-armed switchman, true friend of the Nine-Twenty family, held his cable car at the foot of the hill and Lo Mo called back, *"Fi dee,* Suey Leen, *fi dee."* Then her eyes grew rounder as Lo Mo told of the many needs of the orphaned children in San Francisco. Before Lo Mo started to pay some other calls, Suey Leen asked this little daugher to play on the piano the perfectly memorized pieces she had prepared for this visit. Then, as soon as the door closed after her delighted listener, Mae Seen turned to her mother.

"Please may I have my bank, mother? I want to help Ah Pau's (Grandma's) babies."

The rattle of the toy bank indicated that its coins were few; but Mae Seen slipped out while her mother was busy preparing the New Year's dinner for which Lo Mo was returning. A group of Chinese employees from the Ford factories who always made a pet of the pretty little girl were in the upstairs flat. To them she took her story and the shiny bank. When Lo Mo came back for dinner she was greeted by Mae Seen with dancing eyes.

"See what I have for my little sisters in California," she announced as she emptied twenty dollars from her bank into the lap of the surprised Lo Mo.

She was a true daughter of her sweet-voiced mother. In the records of old Nine-Twenty was a letter written by Suey Leen, aged eleven, when she was a member of the Occidental Red Cross League, a patriotic activity inspired by Evelyn Browne's zeal during the Spanish-American War. How well she taught her Oriental pupils is reflected in an announcement of this society, of which Yuen Qui was president. The secretary, Kum Ying, wrote: "We try to help the soldiers all we can by sewing for them. And we always remember them in our prayers, because we think that they are right, and we know that God will help the right. We are very glad that the American soldiers are not fighting for land or money, but to make men free." Then Suey Leen, who had never spoken a word of English until she had come into the Home the year before, wanted to write a letter of sympathy to the soldiers. Here is her letter just as she wrote it, faithfully copied from the old reports.

DEAR SOLDIERS,

I write these letters for you. I am very Sorry you go to war. I hope God help you. I live These Country. I give These text for you: "Be thou faithful unto death And I will give thee a crown of life." I was born in These Country. I am native daughter. God bless you, good-bye.

SUEY LEEN

Lo Mo was growing accustomed to being called "grandma"; but to the inquisitive public the effect was as strange as "mama" had been on the Ferry Boat strangers years before. One afternoon she was on her way to visit a neat but unpretentious home above a Chinese laundry, on one of the narrow chestnut-shaded side streets of old Philadelphia. Here two clean, chubby-faced Oriental children hung on the whitewashed wicket fence anxiously watching each approaching street car. When the conductor let her off at the corner, they shouted, "Here comes grandma!" and unlatching the gate ran gleefully to meet her. She saw the other passengers on the passing car crane their necks to see the finish of this unusual greeting, but she went gaily on to join the father and mother at the feast spread on the table upstairs from the steaming laundry, where work had been halted for her reception.

Lo Mo had brought the mother of this family East with her on her own first transcontinental trip. She only wished that good old Dr. Hemphill could share her pleasure in watching the consummation of the real-life love drama he had arranged. She could hear him now in the parlor of Nine-Twenty explaining to Quai Gum the meaning of the engagement ring he was presenting in behalf of his friend Wong John, who had written to him as former pastor to find him a bride. With all the lilting poetry of his Celtic nature he had explained its stones—diamond white for purity, the blue sapphires for constancy and faithfulness.

As they sat around the festive dinner table Lo Mo laughingly recalled her own first meeting with Wong John. When she had arrived in Philadelphia with Quai Gum, Wong's American teacher met them at the train and escorted them to her home, where he sat waiting for his timid bride. It was not Quai Gum, however, who received the first embrace; for as they made their way down the long dark hallway—one of those pitch-black relics of stifling "back-parlor" days—Quai Gum was suddenly overcome with shyness and slipped behind Lo Mo's skirt just as her fiancé came forward to plant the kiss intended for Quai Gum on the brow of her Scotch escort!

Some years later Lo Mo and Tien were welcomed into the New England home of a beautiful girl, once known as "the belle of Chinatown." Choie N'goh had been the highly prized possession of one of the powerful tongs. Her close friend, Leung Ying, was a recently rescued member of the Nine-Twenty family, and she had volunteered to lead a party that sought to bring Choie N'goh into the new life that she was experiencing. Thoroughly disguised, she had taken the would-be rescue party, including Lo Mo, Tien Wu, Inspector Robinson, and Detective Barron of the Chinatown Squad, to the hotel where she thought her friend was staying; but no sign of Choie N'goh could be found. Up and down the streets of Chinatown they had sought her in vain, and had finally gathered around the coal grate in the Nine-Twenty sitting room, pictures of despair.

It was then ten-thirty, but John Robinson had an idea, perhaps only to give zest to a disappointing evening.

"She might be at the theater. I have some tickets. Do you all want to go?"

They slipped into the Oriental audience, looking eagerly for their quarry. There were many slave girls with their owners in the expensive front boxes, but no sign of the charming one they sought. Five minutes went by. Then Leung Ying squeezed Tien's arm in excitement.

"There she goes now. See that tall one in the blue sahm," she whispered as a girl with queenly bearing slipped into a seat two or three rows in front of them. She was accompanied by two men, handsomely dressed and prosperous in appearance.

"Let's not attract attention," Lo Mo warned. "Let her enjoy the play a while. We'll all watch them."

But there had been other watchful eyes. Such a party as Lo Mo's could not come into a theater without due notice. Tien's quick eyes caught a look of warning passed down from the front box to the man next to Choie N'goh, then a whispering between them. There was an exit near where they sat. Lo Mo answered Tien's inquiry with "Better act now."

Detective Barron had stayed at the rear to guard the entrance, and Tien hurried back to where he stood. Sensing danger, the man accompanying Choie N'goh endeavored to slip her out through the side exit; but before they could reach it, the detective blocked their way and took Choie N'goh into custody while the eyes of the audience turned from the painted actors on the stage to this drama of real life in their midst. From the excited throng in the theater the rescue party made their way to police headquarters for proper registration.

Then they all walked gladly up the steep hill to the Home, the willowy Choie N'goh chattering excitedly in Cantonese with Tien and Leung Ying, who led the way, while the American helpers formed the rear guard. As they watched the group ahead of them, Detective Barron remarked:

"If your Mission accomplished nothing else, the whole effort would be worth while for what we've done tonight."

But he could not look down the years to see how true the sequel to this night would make his words. Once the Juvenile Court had settled the question of her guardianship, Choie N'goh entered wholeheartedly into the life of the Home, learning quickly the many lessons that went into the shaping of her womanhood. In time she went out to work in a San Francisco family and was free to go and come among friends of her own race. Then a young Chinese gentleman came forward with an offer of marriage; but signs were posted around Chinatown: "Whoever marries Choie N'goh must pay $7,000." Her friend had no such fortune, and he knew his life was in danger if he should press his suit without it. He left for another city, and Choie N'goh's heart was broken.

Then some years later the Chinese pastor was visiting friends in the East and among other pictures of his San Francisco associates showed a portrait of the beautiful Choie N'goh. One of the group fell in love with her picture. Correspondence followed. Then came a summer visit to San Francisco. Things were done in a more modern way than when Dr. Hemphill had practiced matchmaking.

Even so it seemed wiser for a Board member to chaperone them on their first drive through Golden Gate Park. With true California pride, the hostess turned to call the visitor's attention to the beds of gorgeous asters before the park conservatory.

"Miss Nichols," he had replied, "do you think I have eyes for anything else when Choie is with me!"

At that attractively spread New England dinner table Lo Mo was well aware of the truth of that statement; she knew, too, that Detective Barron had spoken well.

The trip which took Lo Mo and Tien to this home together was one for which they had long made plans. It came in the winter of 1928 when distressing problems had broken up most of Donaldina Cameron's long-needed year's furlough, and took them into twenty-seven homes in fourteen cities.

After a brief business stop in New York, the two went to spend a week in New England as the guests of Mrs. H. B. Heylman, formerly Mary Tooker, and her sister Gertrude. In all her various trips before, Lo Mo had never stopped in this historic part of our country, original home of Charlie Bailey's family and that of Ethel Higgins. With her deep regard for places touched with romance and history, she felt the same thrill of enthusiasm which had swept over her at her first breath of the heather-scented air of the Highlands. The autumn foliage was still brilliant when they motored up through the hills along the winding rivers of New Hampshire to the Heylman summer home on Lake Sunapee. Tien Wu, who had spent her Eastern summers during the years of her schooling at Camp Diamond, Maine, was radiant with memories.

But their week of relaxation spent among the rocks, trees, and lakes, with the far view of Mount Kearsage to lift them up, was all too short a preparation for the plunge into vital problems waiting them in New York. They had scarcely taken off their warm traveling coats in the Heylman home when the maid handed Lo Mo an air-mail special-delivery letter forwarded from San Francisco. This letter was from the girl whom she and Chief O'Brien had rescued without a warrant so long ago on Stockton Street. In it Lai Gum, who was now married and living in the East, gave an address and telephone number of another slave girl living in Chicago who was in desperate need of assistance. Lai Gum wrote that her husband, on a recent visit to China, had learned from the father of this girl, Quai Fah, that she had been taken from Fresno and sold by the highbinders for seven thousand dollars to tongmen in Chicago. The father had appealed to his younger friend to help in her release, and of course as soon as he returned to discuss it with his wife Lai Gum had turned to Lo Mo.

Miss Cameron and Tien were frantic over the delay their vacation had prolonged. Immediately they took down the receiver and called the Chicago telephone number given in the letter. "They do not answer," came back Central's disconcerting report. Three nights in succession they tried at the hour specified in Lai Gum's note, with the same baffling results. A tong war was in progress in Chicago and they both feared what might have happened.

Their next planned stop was Philadelphia, and they went on, much disquieted. As soon as they were in their hotel rooms they debated over the next move. "Tien, go telephone once more," said Lo Mo with that same intuitive instinct which had brought results so often; and in a moment Tien hung up the phone in excitement.

"Lo Mo! She's there! I've spoken to her. We must go at once!"

They had missed the night train, but there was one early in the morning, and the two were its eager passengers. They sent a telegram ahead to a Board secretary in Chicago.

"Please have dependable man with closed car meet us," it had read, naming place and hour.

At the Chicago station, Tien tried to telephone Quai Fah again to assure her that they were on their way. "This is strange," she said to Lo Mo as she stepped out of the booth; "they say the telephone is disconnected."

Nevertheless, the two continued on the quest they had started. At the Moody Institute where they had asked their escort to meet them, a tall man stood ready for orders.

"My car is outside. Where can I take you?" he asked in pleasant tones.

He looked somewhat surprised at the address Miss Cameron handed him as he ushered her into the seat beside him.

"I suppose Mrs. Dean explained to you the nature of our errand," she began.

"No, I haven't the remotest idea," he replied, and listened in amazement as the story unfolded.

They parked the car about a block away from the place to which Lai Gum had directed them, leaving Tien Wu in the back seat. They found themselves in a quite disreputable tenement district, and her escort gave Miss Cameron his arm as they threaded their way among the ragged children and gossiping, slatternly women on the cluttered street. The number they sought was on one of the most forlorn of the unpainted buildings, and as they climbed its long flight of dingy stairs they wondered how human beings could live in such a place. High up on the floor which Quai Fah had specified in the few minutes' talk she had had with Tien from Philadelphia, they turned down a long passage. A bright Yale lock on one of the far doors attracted their attention.

"This must be the room," explained Miss Cameron; "they always keep these girls under strong locks."

She and her gallant friend were debating over their next move when they heard footsteps on the stairs. Miss Cameron leaned over the banister and saw a man, evidently Chinese, coming up.

"Let's walk down this long dark hall. There's usually a turn at the end," she whispered. "We can watch from there and he probably will not notice us."

The hall proved a cul-de-sac from which there was no escape. The Chinese paused at the door, key in hand, staring with hard-faced threat at Miss Cameron and her tall young escort.

She spoke up, quickly, "Any American people live up here?"

"What you want?" he grumbled back.

"I'd like to see American lady," she insisted. "Not any here at all?"

"No!" he scowled menacingly.

"Any families live here?" she went on calmly with the air of an interested welfare worker.

"No!" again; this time more emphatically.

"You live here?" continued his fair questioner.

"Yes, I live here," he admitted.

"You have wife—American?"—for this sometimes happens in this low stratum of society.

"No, I have Chinese wife."

With that Miss Cameron assumed the guileless curiosity of a "slummer." "I'd like to see your Chinese wife," and, turning to her companion, "wouldn't you? Did you ever see a real Chinese woman? Do let us come in a moment," to the astonished man with the key.

The Chinese glared hard at the intruders. Then, as though impelled by an unseen hand, he slowly turned the key and opened the door. There were voices within, and the moment the knob was turned, her escort pushed his way in, holding the door wide for Donaldina to enter.

Miss Cameron's quick eyes spied a door to the left of the entry.

This opened and a Chinese man, partly clad, looked out. She brushed past him into the inner room, where a girl stood beside the couch. "Thank God!" breathed Donaldina Cameron. The man snatched his clothes and disappeared into another room. She turned to her escort, who had remained close to her side, "Fly for Tien; she to be waiting near. Speed!"

He stopped only to ask, "What will you do?"

"I'll bolt this door!" she replied, as her escort dashed from the room.

At the first sight of the visitors, the girl had sprung toward them.

"Are you Quai Fah?" asked Miss Cameron.

"Hi. Ney ma ma?" she replied eagerly, meaning "Yes. Are you mamma?" Then looking anxiously—"Tien Fuh?"

"She's coming. Hurry, dress," commanded the older woman. Quai Fah was all ready for flight and she picked up her bundle of clothes secreted under the couch. Strange to say, no one touched the door until, at the end of three minutes, which had seemed like a year, Tien's voice and that of their new friend accompanied a tap. Miss Cameron unbolted the door, to answer Mr. Radcliffe's surprised question:

"Where are the men?"

Those individuals were nowhere to be seen. Evidently they had fled by fire escape or secret exit, believing their intruders disguised authorities who were out after tongmen. At that particular time local and Federal officials were bearing down on members of the fighting tongs and these men were taking no chances of arrest.

Quai Fah was the gainer by their fears and walked in trembling gratitude down the long stairs, clinging tightly to Tien Wu's arm.

"You don't know who I am?" she asked as they settled in the comfortable big car. Then as they drove hurriedly along under the roaring elevated trains Quai Fah explained that she was the girl for whom Tien and Miss Cameron had made a futile raid in Fresno, four years before. Then she told of her pitiful existence as the property of the tongmen from whom at last they had rescued her, of her daring attempt to mail the letter telling of her plight to her father in faraway China, of the long months of anxious waiting for help to come from some source, of her joy in hearing Tien's voice over the long-distance wire, and of her fear that her owners would move her again before they really could find her.

But Quai Fah's ended problems were the beginnings of new ones for her rescuer. Here was Lo Mo, halfway across the continent from the protecting doors of Nine-Twenty, with a girl whose life was in danger at every turn of a street, and with pressing plans in her itinerary which she could not change by a premature return to California.

As usual, unexpected aid was near. She returned to Moody Institute to find an invitation to lunch at Marshall Field's with Mrs. Milton Stewart of Pasadena. This constant friend of years, whose husband expended a fortune on work among Chinese in their own land, had poured her interest into Lo Mo's family in San Francisco, to which she had been attracted through their Union Oil associates, the Fenns. She was returning from a Canadian trip and was overjoyed to find Miss Cameron in Chicago on her way to California. She did not, however, have much opportunity to ask all the questions she had planned concerning the Ming Quong babies and their merry-eyed instructor whose place on the staff had been provided for by Mrs. Stewart's own generosity.

Donaldina Cameron, flushed and exhilarated after her morning adventure, was glad of a sympathetic listener. Her tale finished, she said:

"Now that is chapter one; but what of the next? She should be in the safety of the Home, but neither Tien nor I can take her there now."

Then Mrs. Stewart volunteered. "I'm leaving tonight on *The Chief*. Do you think I dare assume the responsibility?" It was indeed a responsibility to take this newly rescued girl without even an interpreter; but her brave friend's pluck in the morning adventure inspired Mrs. Stewart to attempt this strange task. She generously provided the money to buy transportation, an amount that was later refunded by the Chinese friends who had planned the rescue. An upper berth was secured above Mrs. Stewart's own, and Lo Mo returned to complete the plans for the evening getaway. There was need for the utmost secrecy to avoid possibility of a writ which would hinder all plans. Once more the knight-errant of the morning was called upon to help. Quai Fah was disguised in American clothes and the party parked in Mr. Radcliffe's car on a dark street near the station. Then just as the train was about to pull out, the tall young man hastened through the gate with the disguised Quai Fah leaning on his arm. He turned her over to Mrs. Stewart with a sigh of relief and drove Miss Cameron and Tien back to their rooms to make preparations for their interrupted journey.

On the *Chief* the oddly assorted traveling companions aroused a vast amount of interest among the fellow-passengers of this luxurious train. Finally one of them could restrain his curiosity no longer.

"I beg your pardon," he asked of Mrs. Stewart, "but are you a private detective?"

She was glad to be relieved of this role, as well as to place her charge in more experienced hands when Ethel Higgins, who had come in response to a carefully phrased telegram, stood ready to receive Quai Fah in the Pasadena station.

The northern journey was made in safety and Quai Fah spent one contented month in the wholesome family circle at Nine-Twenty. Then Lai Gum and her husband arrived in San Francisco from their Eastern home on their way back to the land of their ancestors. They took her with them back to China, where she lived under the loving protection of those whose happy life would never have been possible had it not been for that day when Sergeant O'Brien took Miss Cameron's word in place of a warrant for "that childlike one in the rocking chair."

CHAPTER XVI

WAR ON THE TONGS

Quai Fah's own desire for escape from her Fresno slavery four years before had been thwarted at that time; but it had meant release for another, to whom this freedom had been a boon undreamed. Lo Mo's party, aided by Dr. Shepherd, had combed the Fresno Chinatown till two o'clock one morning in a futile search for the girl for whom they had come, only to discover Bo Lin, a Chinese "paper bride," whose story revealed that she had been bought from her mother in China for five hundred dollars to be taken to San Francisco as an entertainer. To permit her entrance into this country a pseudomarriage had been performed according to Chinese custom. Bo Lin had come with eager hopes, planning to send back money to support her widowed mother; but once landed, like so many other deceived young girls, she had found herself in helpless slavery, the property of a vicious owner, who took her from place to place, finally establishing her in Fresno. Most of her earnings went to her owner, and the rest to the "husband." For a period, when her "husband" once left her, she did manage to send a small sum to her mother in China; but upon his discovery of this "treachery" when he returned, he had threatened to kill her. The slaveowner, however, had recognized Bo Lin's value and paid the "husband" a thousand dollars, in return for which he relinquished all further claims.

When finally she was so unexpectedly released by the police officers of Fresno who aided Miss Cameron's party on that cold winter night in 1924, she was turned over to the Juvenile Court of San Francisco, which committed her to Lo Mo's custody.

Among Bo Lin's possessions at the time was found a half-finished letter to her mother. This was brought to court and translated as part of the proof of her ill-treatment in Fresno. Judge Murasky, who awarded Bo Lin to Miss Cameron, declared that never in all his years of experience had he read a document so expressive of the finer sensibilities of a child or so revealing of the worth of salvaging a human soul. In the letter, after describing the mental and physical suffering which she had endured in this land across the seas, Bo Lin quoted a proverb from the old Chinese writers in which sons were called the "pillars of the house" but, to prove her filial devotion to a mother without sons, said she had come to America with the longing to prove that a daughter could be a pillar, too. She still had hopes that a way would open for her to do this; and then she said she hoped that after this had been accomplished there would still be some years left when she could enter a Buddhist monastery and there expiate the unwitting sins of the present.

As soon as Bo Lin began to sense the friendly atmosphere of the Home which sheltered her, she told her new friends of a forlorn girl, ill and despairing, whom she had known in her Fresno days. She would go with the rescue party if they would attempt to give her friend the freedom she herself was enjoying. Fresno Juvenile Court authorities readily secured the warrant for Tang She, and the raid was planned for an hour when, according to information gleaned from Chinese friends, there was to be a festive midnight banquet.

On these occasions the painted slave girls slipped silently about among the inlaid teakwood chairs, serving their lordly owners with dainty hands from lacquered trays of cigarettes and clinking glasses of *ng-ga-pa* (a favorite Chinese liquor). Quite often authorities chose these times for a raid, for the slave girls were then adorned with all the finery they possessed, the only form of wealth they could call their own. Sensing this official habit, tongmen always guarded particularly against raids when a banquet was in preparation.

So it was on the night when Bo Lin led her new-found friends to the Bing Kong headquarters. She pointed out slips of red paper posted on the bulletin board in the long hallway, and explained that these red slips, bearing the names of slave girls and their owners, were posted as warnings to other tongmen to keep hands off their pretty possessions. But when Bo Lin showed the raiders the slips bearing the girls' names on that April night, the owners' names had been removed. Bits of torn paper left sticking to the boards showed only too plainly the hasty effort to destroy damaging evidence at the first hint of an impending raid.

The officers made their way past the guards and seized Tang She and one other exceptionally attractive girl, whom Bo Lin positively identified as a slave, from the festive banquet hall; but the rest of the painted servitors were quickly spirited away.

The two new charges were taken by Lo Mo to the Y.W.C.A., where she and her party, consisting of Bo Lin, Ethel Higgins, and Tien Wu, were staying. Early the next morning Miss Cameron went to the Juvenile

Court for a warrant for Gum Oie, the unexpected one they had brought with Tang She, and prepared to bring them both before the judge for legal custody.

In the meantime Tien Wu and Bo Lin were doing their utmost to explain the purpose of their seizure to the dazed and frightened Tang She and Gum Oie, and to dispel the fears implanted in their minds by their owners. Bo Lin understood their terror, for her owner had been especially vehement in her tales about the dreadful Fahn Quai; one of the worst of these warnings had been that Miss Cameron was in the habit of draining blood from the arteries of newly "captured" girls and drinking it to keep up her own vitality.

While their countrywomen were thus trying to win the confidence of the girls whose custody Lo Mo sought, she herself was busy laying the backlogs for the hearing in court, and a former district attorney of Fresno County and his client, Yick Foon, head of the Bing Kong Tong, were exercising their keen intellects toward finding a way to remove the two girls from the influence of their rescuers before these women had had time to win their confidence.

Their coup was sprung at noon while Lo Mo's party sat at luncheon in the spacious dining room of the Y.W.C.A. As the newly rescued girls were chatting more easily with Tien and Bo Lin, suddenly all eyes were turned toward the entrance. There the young American Secretary was talking earnestly with the attorney, Yick Foon, and two other men. Instantly recognizing the group at the door, Miss Cameron motioned her party to follow and attempted to lead them out through the side door of the dining room. But the men were upon them at once, seizing the two girls and dragging them toward the main exit. Bo Lin struggled frantically to get out of the group, while Tien Wu and Lo Mo clung to the girls the men were dragging. Ethel Higgins managed to slip through the crowd and get to her parked car, in which she sped to the home of Judge Austin, loyal friend of the work, who lived near by. At the door the Y.W.C.A. secretaries and assistants sprang to the defense and were roughly tossed aside, one with her blouse nearly torn off. Tien Wu was the last to let go her desperate hold on Tang She. Alongside the seven-passenger car in which the former district attorney and his Chinese allies had come she was ruthlessly thrust away, and the slave girls were unceremoniously bundled in. Their captors followed and whirled them quickly beyond the reach of those who would free them.

Investigation showed that the American attorney and his client had taken advantage of the technicalities that often hindered Lo Mo's efforts to rescue slave girls. The Juvenile Court, of course, has no jurisdiction over married persons, or over girls whose age could be proved greater than twenty-one. Therefore, importers of slave girls were careful to protect themselves by threatening their prey until the girls falsely assumed such a status. Entirely unknown to Lo Mo, and even to Bo Lin, were the facts that Tang She had been legally married in order to be admitted to this country, that is, "legally" if the age she gave were correct; and Gum Oie had been admitted as a "native daughter" over twenty-one. This deception was accomplished through a favorite trick of importers. They would present a picture taken in infancy in the United States and swear that the girl they sought to bring in was now of age, thus removing the possibility of Juvenile Court interference even if she was later found living an immoral life.

The only way Lo Mo ever rescued such girls was by winning their confidence to such an extent that they would voluntarily ask for guardianship and reveal their true age. But this took real courage. As Bo Lin and others confessed, their owners filled their minds with dire threats both as to what would happen to them at Nine-Twenty and as to what they would do to them in case the attempted escape failed.

Although Tien had not yet found out all the complications of the cases of Tang She and Gum Oie, she was progressing rapidly to a point where they were beginning to have confidence. This was then the crux of the battle for time between Lo Mo and her legal opponents.

The latter had been too quick for her this time, and the Superior Court judge to whom the former district attorney had gone for co-operation had not taken the trouble to verify the facts back of the evidence presented by him. Tang She's alleged marriage and Gum Oie's landing papers both placed them outside the reach of the Juvenile Court, and the judge had signed a temporary release empowering the attorney for the tong to take the girls away from their rescuers and return them to the alleged husband and father.

Within a few days after the capture of the girls at the Y.W.C.A., Miss Cameron and her legal advisers demanded a hearing in the case of Tang She. The beautiful Gum Oie she never saw again, as she had had no warrant for her. Poor Tang She, intimidated and crushed with the weight of her hopeless life, followed the way of so many unenlightened Chinese slave girls and told in court the story her owners had taught her. The law was powerless to release her without her own willingness to be helped. Immediately after the trial was over, she was removed from Fresno, where public sympathy had been deeply stirred. When last heard from, Tang She was dragging out the wretched life of a slave in a northern city. Miss Cameron later heard that Gum Oie had been murdered in the San Francisco underworld.

The *Fresno Republican* reflected outraged public sentiment in a column-length editorial, closing with these words:

To little Tang She, who sat in darkness, there came a great light. It was the light of American justice, shining with the benevolent aspect of Occidental Christianity. It glowed for a minute. Then the writ of habeas corpus, coming down to us from our Anglo-Saxon ancestors, came in, and kicked little Tang She back into slavery.

This editorial was written following a mass meeting at which Miss Cameron and her assistant, accompanied by ten of their rescued slave girls brought from San Francisco, were asked to speak. Two other friends of the work, Duncan Matheson, head of the San Francisco Detective Bureau, and Attorney Robert Borland, added accounts of their experiences. Parts of Captain Matheson's speech sum up the whole situation clearly:

If it had not been for the evil influence of Americans, I do not believe that we should have had such a problem as the tong problem with us. But we have it.

The tongs were organized to protect the narcotic, gambling, and slave-girl traffics in this country. Tong wars are caused when members of one tong rob the tables of another tong member's gambling house, steal another tong member's slave girl, or become an impeding factor in the narcotic trade of the other tong.

The tongs have become a great harvest for American lawyers who can provide protection for their various vicious transactions.

The highbinder tongs have become so well organized that they hire regular gunmen to kill at so much per head. Silly, sentimental women often interfere with the execution of these criminals and make it all the easier for the vicious system to continue. Respectable Chinese often give the authorities tips on how to combat the menace of these tongs, but they fear to appear in court. They will die prematurely.

The American school has been the greatest factor in reducing the Chinese problem to its simplest terms. Instead of ninety-five per cent of the Chinese being opium smokers as they were twenty-five years ago, less than five per cent use narcotics now.

Our problem is one of enlisting and crystallizing public sentiment to such an extent that we can get legislation which will put the tongs out of business and thereby do away with the organizations formed principally to protect these interests.

The elements of law and order in the Chinese are stronger today than ever, and if it were not for the baneful influence of the tongs, the Chinese people would be a definite asset to California.

Back in San Francisco, a new ally was lending the force of his powerful personality to this fight for a clean Chinatown. When Sergeant

Jack Manion came to head the Chinatown Squad in 1921 the Chinese and their friends at Nine-Twenty found a consistently sympathetic and strong supporter. He came to this work an enthusiastic follower of his boyhood friend, later Chief O'Brien. Within four years after he took over the Squad there were no more tong wars in San Francisco, slavery and gambling were wiped off the records, and his boast that "ours will be the cleanest Chinatown in the United States" was fully justified. But he, too, referred much of the credit to his Scotch friend on the hill.

It was she who came to him after about three years' acquaintance with the wish: "I should like to catch the owners of a house at 654 Jackson Street." This was a difficult place to raid, as it was kept by an old-time Chinese woman who insisted that Miss Cameron was the godmother of her daughter, and John Robinson the godfather.

With such pretensions of respectability it was hard to secure evidence of the suspected evils. The doors of the house were heavy and hard to force. By the time police could get in, the inmates had fled.

But Sergeant Manion was determined to know what went on behind those doors. Miss Cameron was invariably correct in her suspicions. There must be a reason for her desire to raid this house. He circled around the Jackson Street neighborhood at various hours. There was a skylight, always open in the daytime but closed at night. If it was not locked, it afforded a chance to enter.

"If you will get sufficient information from some of your girls to justify a warrant, we'll see what we can find," the Sergeant had reported.

This was soon forthcoming, a vagrancy warrant issued for a girl known to be in Mrs. Chin Bow's custody. As there were several girls possibly involved whose entrance papers were questionable, Inspector Robinson was asked to go with them on this raid.

At five o'clock on a stormy St. Patrick's morning Sergeant Manion and two other officers called at the Home. Miss Cameron, Tien Wu, and Miss Higgins were all ready, while Robinson met them at the appointed corner, where they were all to keep out of sight until a given signal from the police should call them into action. The Sergeant and his men climbed carefully to the roof, carrying with them a long, stout rope. The skylight *was* unlocked! The rope was securely fastened to a chimney near by. Then with the loose end in his clenched hands, the Sergeant let himself in as the other two payed it out inch by inch. The first officer followed safely; but the second man caught on the rope in the dark and came down with a thud. Mrs. Chin Bow screamed with the most violent of Chinese curses. Whistles blew. Miss Cameron and her waiting allies swarmed in the front door, quickly opened by the first officer. They were too many for the startled Mrs. Bow. Before she could knock her warnings on the doors that lined the narrow hall, police opened them, disclosing the girls they sought and their patrons.

"Why are you here?" demanded Mrs. Chin Bow's daughter of Inspector Robinson, in a frenzied moment off guard. "I thought we were always to be warned of a raid. Why didn't you let us know?"

"Why should I? We give no advance tips on raids. How did you think you could get away with this?" indicating the opened doors and the group of slave girls huddled together close to Tien Wu.

"But we paid Yick Yee. Where is the diamond ring we gave him for you?"

Honest John Robinson looked aghast; but he knew at once that these women had been duped by another vicious highbinder custom. A sporty youth whom they had kept supplied with bribe money and flashing jewels had promised them absolute safety in their trade. And the girl continued: "He said to us, 'With John Robinson as your godfather, you will never be suspected, but you had better send him this ring as a safeguard. I'll just tell him it is a memento of your regard for him.' "

That had been at Chinese New Year; but John Robinson had never seen the ring nor did he know the dashing Yick Yee, who disappeared from Chinatown soon after this raid.

Mrs. Chin Bow and her daughter were both arrested, and the girls were booked for Angel Island as inmates of a house of ill fame. Most of the girls were ordered deported, but Yum Gue, the youngest, just sixteen, was made a ward of the Juvenile Court and turned over to Miss Cameron. Then came months of litigation. Yum Gue was represented by an American lawyer who insisted that she give her age as twenty-one. She swore under oath that she had never said that she was sixteen, but when faced with a charge of perjury changed her mind and admitted that she was in her 'teens. Finally, after several hearings, the case was won by Miss Cameron, and Yum Gue began her life on the hill.

Thus ended the career of one of the last of the professional slave-owners' houses in Chinatown; but many had been the exciting adventures shared by the Irish Sergeant and his Scotch co-worker in the rescue of the twenty-five or thirty girls brought in during his early days on the Squad.

Sometimes the rescue would be quite unexpected. There was the case of "Satan."

"Never did figure we could do anything with 'Satan'," mused the Sergeant as he thumbed over old records and came across the picture of a wild-eyed creature staring out of a page of his big case book. "She came in as the 'daughter' of old Lew Chong, who was arrested under the

Opium Act in 1923. We found her in 1925. I happened to call at a residence under suspicion down on Washington Street. I noticed this girl there and called Miss Cameron's attention. We got a warrant and went after her. It was daytime when we found her, still in bed. She claimed to be sick, and how she did fight against going to the Home. There was quite a case in court. She changed testimony many times, said the man we found her with was her 'father.' Finally Miss Cameron persuaded her to tell the truth and she seemed ready to accept the changed life offered. But the owner wouldn't give up. The case came into court again the next year. Miss Cameron won out, though—and what's more, she made a fine girl out of her, too.

"Then we found another girl, who is still in the Home, down on Portola Alley off Washington Street. This alley is notorious because of the numerous raids. Finally, I believe, the name was changed to Cameron Alley by the Chinese because of this. The girl we found down there was living with an old narcotic peddler and user, and she had a lot to unlearn when she was delivered to Miss Cameron.

"The owners used to tell these girls that the food at the Home was poisoned, that they would become slaves to *old* Miss Cameron, and all sorts of wild tales. Miss Cameron had not only to rescue them but to win them by her kindness to eat the very food that was set before them.

"Then there was Barbara. We found her at No. 12 Ross Alley. I noticed her there when I was making my rounds; but she was one of those who had been warned against Miss Cameron. She insisted she was not a slave girl and refused to leave the place. Then she disappeared. Some time later Miss Cameron found her in Santa Barbara—that's how she got her new name. She was owned by a Hop Sing man and there was a fight to get her. I had to go down as a witness. She was the same girl I'd seen at Ross Alley, all right. We won the case, against her wishes, but I know she's lived to thank Miss Cameron, too. Went to her wedding up at the Home one night. She made a pretty little bride.

"There were lots of others, like Ah Wong, who we rescued in the Hip Sing Tong Building; and another girl, I've forgotten her name. We found her sleeping in a cubbyhole in a cigar factory on Jackson Street, between Sansome and Montgomery, a little out of the regular Chinatown."

One story the Sergeant told with a twinkle: "There was a baby born at the Home who has a good Irish name. He is called Horace Patrick after Captain Horace McGowan and John Patrick O'Connor, two officers who went to rescue the mother just before he was born. The Judge let her stay with Miss Cameron at this time. First she denied she was a slave girl, and was very unfriendly. Gradually she began to realize what these people meant to her, and it wasn't long till she was out assisting with the rescue work herself."

One of the hardest things these keepers of the peace in Chinatown had to face was the secret strength of the highbinder tongs. When Lee Young, prosecuted on a white-slave charge, was securely behind the bars of San Quentin, they felt a real battle had been won. He was a member of the Suey Tong, as was his father, too. But in spite of the fact that the father was the priest of a Josh House on Spofford Alley, the old Chinaman was part owner of a young slave girl possessed by Lee Young. One of the best criminal lawyers in San Francisco was retained by the tong to protect the rights of these two members in the fight before the Grand Jury; but he lost to the representatives of Nine-Twenty and the old priest returned to China, where ownership of slave girls was then condoned.

The story of Tom Ling who sought to rescue his own cousin from the slavery which Lo Mo is fighting is a vivid illustration of the far-reaching power of the highbinders. He was a Chinese citizen of the United States with a successful business of his own in New York City. While in Chicago attending a banquet of the On Leung Tong he was introduced to a group of slave girls held there for immoral purposes. One of these girls, Gum Leen, seemed to sense something familiar in this clean-appearing young stranger. "Are you really a 'Tom'?" she whispered, referring to the family name that binds each clan together. Being assured by signs that only those of close family connections can understand, she confessed that she, too, was a "Tom." Later he learned that she was his mother's sister's child. But members of the tong had noticed this underhand conversation. A warning was issued to Ling to avoid further intimacy. He was determined to free his little cousin, however, and opened negotiations for her release. Returning to New York, he placed a mortgage on his business and came back to Chicago to pay $6,650 to the president of the tong. With his receipt and bill of sale he took Gum Leen to New York, where she was safely ensconced as a member of his own family.

It was not long, however, before bitter threats pursued him from the blackmailing tong in Chicago. Gum Leen must be returned to her former owners. Her cousin again went to Chicago and was offered the alternative of paying one hundred and twenty-five dollars a week till two thousand dollars more should be paid or "returning the said Gum Leen to the said immoral life and paying her earnings to the On Leung Tong."

She was left as a hostage in an apartment in Chicago, while Tom

Ling crossed prairie, desert, and mountains to the Pacific Coast to the haven in San Francisco where Gum Leen had found refuge four years before when she had been rescued from her notorious owner, Oie Kum, only to be snatched away from her protectors by a deceitful use of the law.

Miss Cameron welcomed Tom Ling with eager attention. Where was this girl they had sought far and wide? Of course she must be brought at once to San Francisco. As she sat in Attorney Borland's office listening to Ling's tale of bitter struggles, she thought back over the years of their search for Gum Leen.

She saw the picture of this girl so piteously in need of rescue and the "husband," Lim Se Quong, determinedly swearing that he had married her in China when she was sixteen. The court and the Consul became convinced by his intriguing story of promised protection. Then Lim Se Quong and Gum Leen had disappeared. Lo Mo remembered her anxiety on a trip to Chicago when she had learned that Gum Leen was there in bondage, then her appeal to the Juvenile Court and police for aid in rescuing the girl, and the power of the tong in effecting the escape of the two they sought. A year later, she recalled, Gum Leen had again been located; but when the Chicago police had battered through to her prison, they had found only her clothing. Again the tong influence had been at work, and the police raid had been "tipped off."

Now here sat the girl's own cousin, and final rescue seemed in sight. It was agreed that it would be unwise for Lo Mo to go after Gum Leen. Her movements were too closely watched in the Chinese underworld. But Miss Higgins was not so well known at that time. She hastened to Chicago, to the designated apartment where Gum Leen sat ready. They rushed to the street and a waiting taxi, thence by the first train back to San Francisco.

But her own safety was not all that Gum Leen sought. When she had first been spirited away from San Francisco, her baby boy had been snatched from her. In the long years of suffering, her anguish had been multiplied by longing for the sight of this child. Sergeant Manion was called in to help, and his diligence was rewarded when he found the boy in the custody of an old Chinese woman on Pacific Street. Then followed the joyful courtroom scene when Judge Graham handed to Miss Donaldina Cameron the custody of this boy and his long-sought mother.

A few years later Attorney Borland's office saw the climax of another story which further emphasized the declining power of the slave ring under the ceaseless attacks of Miss Cameron and her Chinese allies. Lo Mo's part in the beginning of this adventure came in response to an unexpected call from a former Chinese acquaintance.

"But we thought you had returned to the Orient for good," was the surprised greeting to this visitor at Nine-Twenty.

"We think so, too," replied Mrs. Chan, "but we come back once more. Daughter my friend's cousin come with us. That's why I come see you." And she explained how the friend had persuaded her to chaperone this girl from Canton to join her "father" in San Francisco; and how she had recently been married to a seemingly respectable merchant from Reno.

"I think you people at the Home better watch King Lon," she continued. "Her 'father' not come. We go up to Reno after she get married. I don't like how things go there. He say he have lots money. No sign. Drive old Ford belong his friend. His 'big restaurant' just chop suey house. We leave King Lon envelope addressed to you, and twenty-dollar bill in her suitcase."

"And where can we reach you if we want more advice?" questioned Tien Wu.

"Oh, taxi outside. We sail China in half-hour!"

And so the resourceful Tien was left to do her own sleuthing. She immediately called for Sergeant Manion and he started his detectives on the job. In a very few days he returned to say that he had found that the husband was the gambling king of Reno and the restaurant a disreputable dive, adding, "You had better start your rescue party right away."

It was impossible for Miss Cameron to leave at the time, but Ethel Higgins and Tien Wu prepared for an immediate start. The services of Dr. Shepherd, who had so often assisted in complicated rescues, were sought and obtained. Disguised with a beard, a cap with a bent visor, and a shabby old lumber-jacket, he was often able to scout around for information where the staff from Nine-Twenty would be recognized. In fact, his disguise once became almost too successful when he narrowly escaped arrest as a vagrant; but this time there was no chance to grow a beard and he came in his own role.

The three met "as if by accident" on the station platform when they alighted from the train at Reno the next morning. Immediately Miss Wu was put in a taxi and told to wait for orders, for she would be the most easily recognized of the trio. Miss Higgins turned to the station agent.

"Is there a Presbyterian Church in town?"

"Dunno; better ask the Western Union man."

That individual, somewhat better informed, pointed the way to a Community Church, at the parsonage of which these early morning callers took the pastor by surprise. He was virtually an acquaintance, however, for he had known of the work of the Home through his wife, a San Jose girl, who had heard both Miss Cameron and Miss Higgins tell of their exciting raids. He was immediately sympathetic when his aid was asked in locating the address given them by Mrs. Chan.

Walking to the study window, he pointed out a yellow apartment house about a block away, saying, "I believe I did hear that the place had been recently bought by a Chinese."

It was decided that Mr. Case, their new aide, and Dr. Shepherd should go on a scouting tour in search of information. They rang the manager's bell, which was answered by a white man.

"Have you any vacancies?" asked Dr. Shepherd.

"Just one—a nice sunny apartment," answered the manager, as he escorted his prospects to the elevator.

"This seems to fill my needs," concluded Dr. Shepherd after careful inquiries as to price, janitor service, and other details; "but I have just one question. What about the other tenants? My wife is very sensitive about her neighbors; and I'm sure she wouldn't live in a house where there might be any Orientals."

"Well—er—, as a matter of fact, the house has just been purchased by a Chinaman, but he doesn't live here. Just now he has his niece visiting, but she is staying with us in our apartment and it will be only a matter of a few days. I am sure your wife would not see anything of them."

"I'll have to talk it over with her, anyway. I'll be back in about a half-hour. Will you be here?" asked Dr. Shepherd.

"No, but my wife will be. I'll just take you in and introduce you," and the manager turned the key in the door of his own apartment, where sat not only the Chinese girl, a picture of despair, but her old husband as well.

Dr. Shepherd and his new co-worker could not go back fast enough with their news to the women waiting in Mr. Case's study.

"Let's park down the street a way, if Mr. Case will lend us his car a few minutes," suggested Miss Higgins; "we'll send Miss Wu around the corner to watch the back door."

Tien Wu hurried off, and the others were about to climb in Mr. Case's coupé when he exclaimed, "We'll have to hurry. Looks like the Chinese and his wife are getting into that sedan in front of the apartment!"

They followed the car as far as a service station, where it stopped for gas. The Chinese stepped out of his car to talk with the station operator. Ethel Higgins warned Mr. Case to hasten after Tien Wu while she walked over to the sedan, opened the door, and spoke in Chinese to its forlorn occupant.

"Where are you from?" asked this girl, but before Miss Higgins could explain in her sketchy Cantonese, Tien Wu came up.

King Lon was overjoyed to see one of her own race, and readily acceded to the invitation to "step out of the car a minute to talk." Miss Wu was careful not to touch her in any way, for Attorney Borland had warned them not to use force, as the Nevada kidnaping laws are stringent.

Before her new acquaintance could fully explain the reason for their coming, King Lon's husband joined their group.

"Who is this?" he demanded of his wife. "And what are you talking about?"

"Oh, we are of the same race. We like to talk."

"So am I," he interrupted; "I like to listen to your talk." But Dr. Shepherd, who spoke Chinese fluently, joined the group and engaged the man in rapid conversation.

"Are you content?" almost whispered Miss Wu, edging away from the group.

"No, no," replied King Lon, "I am afraid for my life. I don't know what he is going to do with me. He keeps me shut up all the time."

"Well, we're here for no other purpose than to help you. There is our car; get in it if you want to escape."

"What about my clothes?"

"Never mind your things. Your life is more important," and Tien Wu was edging impatiently toward the open door of the coupé with its engine still chugging.

King Lon stepped voluntarily into the car, where Miss Higgins was already waiting. Tien jumped in after her as Dr. Shepherd slammed the door, shouting, "Step on it, Case, step on it!"

They sped out of town, hoping Dr. Shepherd would detain the infuriated husband till they could reach the state line. It was late November and the mountain roads were slippery with snow and ice, but the speedometer showed a steady "60" as they covered the fourteen miles to the border.

"Now they can't touch us without extradition," sighed Miss Higgins. "How far is it to the nearest train stop?"

"It is thirty-five miles from Reno to Truckee, and we've covered the worst of it already," replied Mr. Case.

"Can you really take us that far?"

"Well, I can't leave you here, and anyway, we've come this far, I want to see you safely in Truckee."

Miss Higgins consulted the time table she always carried. The next train for San Francisco left Truckee at ten-thirty that night. It was still only eleven in the morning. The roads from Truckee on were hopelessly blocked by snow.

"I'll take you to the Hotel," volunteered Mr. Case.

"By all means no!" Ethel Higgins spoke with the authority of experience. "That is the first place they would look. Find me another minister."

There was only one in Truckee, and he turned out to be a stranger, just moving into the parsonage next to the prim white Methodist Church. Taken unawares by the unusual request of his callers, he looked up in alarm: "The minister's house would be their first thought after the hotel—"

"Then, why not the church?" Miss Higgins interrupted.

This seemed possible, and he led them into the ladies' parlor, where an airtight stove was soon stoked up to warm their shivering bodies. Miss Higgins pinned a couch cover over the window, as there were no blinds to be drawn, and then turned to Mr. Case.

"I have just one more request to make of our kind friend. Could you take me to the railroad station to buy our tickets for tonight, and to the store for some food for the day? Then we shall be seen no more till train time, and we shall be eternally grateful to you."

A section and an upper berth were reserved on the night train and the agent warned not to reveal their numbers to any curious questioners. Then Mr. Case left his party securely hidden in the church for the day, while he turned his car back to Reno, where neglected family and duties awaited him.

Once alone with her two rescuers, King Lon began to tell her story. She had been brought to America with promises of education; but immediately upon her arrival in San Francisco, strange-looking men and women were brought to call upon her. The appraising way in which they looked her over and questioned her had made her suspicious. Then she had heard them talking over a price of six or seven thousand dollars for her. She knew what that meant, and refused to be sold. Then there had been quarreling and discussion.

"Well, it's no use," he had heard one of them say; "I can't risk it if she is unwilling herself. Since that 'Fahn Quai' up on Sacramento Street has stirred up all the authorities to watch for slave girls, there is too much chance for her to escape."

The women who had paid her passage over were desperate. They must make some money out of the venture. Then the Reno gambler had come looking for a second wife—his other one was in China. He offered to pay $2,750 for her. While she did not like this either, marriage even of this sort seemed less evil than out-and-out slavery. She was really only sixteen, but she had been browbeaten into claiming nineteen for the sake of the marriage, which Miss Wu now told her had been illegal.

It was about three o'clock in the afternoon when King Lon's story was interrupted by a knock at the door. A woman's voice called for Miss Higgins. She went out cautiously to discover that she was wanted on the telephone at a neighbor's house. It was Dr. Shepherd, calling from Reno.

"You'll have to come back," came his surprising message.

"Not for anything," replied Miss Higgins; "I'm out of Nevada, and I'm going to stay out. How did you know where to call me?"

Then he explained that the service-station men had read the license number on Mr. Case's car and had immediately reported to the district attorney that the Chinese had come peaceably into their station when two women and two men had dashed out of a parked auto and dragged the girl, screaming and fighting, from the side of her bridegroom of six days. As a result the Case house was full of police and the chief of police had ordered all their telephone messages to be relayed through police headquarters. Mr. Case had called his wife to let her know where he had so mysteriously disappeared, only to find himself facing a warrant for arrest on a charge of kidnaping.

"You see you'll have to come and save our friend from arrest," concluded Dr. Shepherd. "There is a local train from Truckee to Reno that will get you here in time to catch the through train on which you have reservations back. Leave Miss Wu to get on the train with King Lon. She'll manage all right."

Miss Higgins put down the receiver; then called San Francisco. She must consult Robert Borland. "We have our girl," she told him first. "Where are you?" "Truckee." "Keep moving," he cautioned emphatically. "How!—there is no train till ten-thirty and the roads are impassable!" "Then, walk!"; but when he heard Dr. Shepherd's story, he replied, "You'll have to go back!"

When Miss Higgins returned to the church several of the neighborhood women were gathered around Tien Wu and her charge; and Miss Higgins challenged sympathy to action. Were they willing to guard these two Chinese till train time and then start them safely for San Francisco?

Assured of their willing co-operation, she almost ran to the station through slush and mud. The train was standing in the yard ready to go. She called to the brakeman to hold it while she bought her ticket.

"You are Miss Higgins?" asked the agent.

"Yes," somewhat cautiously. "Why?"

"A message just came from Reno. You do not have to go!"

No sooner had Miss Higgins settled back in the church "prison" for a refreshing cup of tea than another neighbor appeared. "You are wanted on the phone," she said.

It was Dr. Shepherd again. He explained that Borland had called the Reno district attorney and cleared matters on the kidnaping charge; but he went on to say that the Chinese had left Reno in a high-powered machine. "Turn out the lights. Lock yourselves in, and lose the key. I'll come as quickly as I can find someone to bring me. Be ready for me at the back door."

For two endless hours the three sat in darkness in the silent church, not daring even to speak to each other. King Lon proved her stamina, for she never once flinched. Then the whir of a heavy car was heard speeding up the street. They scarcely dared to breathe. It went by on one street, and turned the corner. Back it came, circling the church. But it did not stop.

Another hour, and the sound of wheels crunching the snow under the very window where they were huddled made them jump. Miss Higgins peeked out through the merest crack. It was Dr. Shepherd!

They ran to the back door and shoved out their suitcases. Before Miss Higgins could warn Dr. Shepherd of the skiddy stairs, King Lon literally jumped into his arms and down they both went, sliding, unhurt but shaken, to the snow below. Dr. Shepherd took off his heavy lumberjacket and threw it over the shivering girl, heretofore protected from the weather by only a narrow woolen scarf.

"Now, Bill—all the speed you've got," he called to the six-footer at the wheel, and he explained to Miss Higgins that Bill Claussen had come in response to his request that Mr. Case find him a boy "with guts and a good automobile."

The car headed for Reno. "Why?" demanded Miss Higgins.

"There's a flag station just this side of the state line where Bill says we can stop the train," answered Dr. Shepherd.

There was another cold hour and a half before the strange party climbed into the welcome warmth of the Pullman. With a hasty explanation to the conductor, Miss Higgins secured the only available drawing-room on the train, and tipped the porter with a request to "be ignorant." He had just replied, "I'm sho glad you got her in time," when the grinding brakes announced their stop in Truckee. Inside the drawing room with the curtains securely drawn and the door safely locked, the three women listened in silence to the buzz of excitement in the station.

Dr. Shepherd, on the other hand, had donned his disguise and was mingling with the crowd during the fifteen-minute stop. Nearly the whole town was gathered round the train, stirred by the dramatic hunt of the Chinese with their Reno police officers who had ransacked hotel and town for the past few hours. On everyone's tongue were the words, "Kidnaped Chinese bride."

True to his promise, the porter had locked the door to their Pullman. The sheriff walked through the train till he came to this barrier. He swung off and found the conductor.

"I have to search this train. We're looking for a Chinese bride kidnaped in Reno this morning."

"Kidnaped Chinese bride! What kind of passengers do you think I carry on my train?" protested the official, but the sheriff demanded to see "Section 1 and Upper 3, Car 42."

"Certainly, but they are unoccupied." Having satisfied himself of this, the sheriff remained to watch till the last "All aboard!" was called.

"Guess they got cold feet," he remarked, as he swung himself off the step, and the disappointed crowd dispersed.

When the jubilant quartet slipped off the train themselves at the Berkeley station next morning, they went immediately to Dr. Shepherd's home in the machine from Nine-Twenty for which they had wired ahead. They drove out the four-mile Berkeley pier to hear the newsboys calling "Extra—big kidnaping in Reno"; but it did not take Attorney Borland long to assemble reporters and revamp their story, with King Lon in his office to tell them the real truth. For fear that officers might be waiting at the Home, Ethel Higgins and Tien Wu had thought best to drive direct to the lawyer's office. Then Borland explained that after receiving Miss Higgins' message from Truckee he had called his college friend, Les Summerfield, Reno district attorney, on the phone. "Go ahead and prosecute if you wish—but I suppose you don't know that the girl is only sixteen!"

"Keep her there," came the quick response over the miles of wire, "but why didn't you send your friends to me in the first place?"

"These women have to act first and ask questions afterward. I did give them your name, but things happened too fast for them."

The district attorney had been convinced, but not so the husband. He demanded his money back from the conspirators. Mrs. Chan had gone off to China; but the others, "friends" who had intrigued her into bringing King Lon over, were called upon to refund the remaining amount.

For weeks King Lon had to be guarded at every step, for until the husband saw some possibility of monetary return he was desperate. He sent messages and envoys, but she refused ever to see him again. Finally she sat one day in the attorney's office facing her "husband's" agent. She pulled a five-hundred-dollar ring from her finger and threw it across the room. "Take this back to him and tell him to leave me alone forever—but please send me my things."

The answer was final. Two days later her suitcase arrived, apparently untouched, for inside was Mrs. Chan's letter and the crumpled twenty-dollar bill!

CHAPTER XVII

RESULTS IN OTHER LIVES

MORE THAN two thousand girls have called Nine-Twenty "home." Among them are many who had no connection with tongs or slavery. As Lo Mo became in fact "the Mother," her help and advice were sought by Chinese families who wanted their young people to share the family life created within those red brick walls. Orphaned or half-orphaned girls were often brought to her as wards. Sometimes illness or business demands in the Old Country broke up local homes and Lo Mo was persuaded to keep the schoolgirl daughters. These normal young people were a boon to her, as she made them the nucleus about which to weave the family atmosphere which was her surest instrument in helping the less fortunate ones.

As she sat among the gratified parents who thronged the Stanford Memorial Church on a June morning in 1928, she watched one of these girls of hers at the head of the procession of black-gowned graduates, the first Chinese woman to receive her degree from that university. Donaldina Cameron looked proudly at the well-poised young woman who stepped up to accept her diploma from President Ray Lyman Wilbur, at that time president also of the Institute of Pacific Relations, and thus especially concerned with the successful outcome of lives such as Yoke Yeen's. She thought back to the day when a timid little girl from the backwoods of faraway Siskiyou County had knocked at the door of Nine-Twenty and begged to be kept in the United States so that she could have an education and then go back to help her countrymen in China. In response to Lo Mo's surprised question as to how this child, Yoke Yeen (Jade Swallow), had sought her out, she had heard a tale of struggle that had roused her determination to make possible what was now climaxing before her eyes in this inspiring commencement scene. Only in those days she had never dared to dream of her little friend so far advanced as this.

The story of Yoke Yeen's childhood, as she had poured it out in that first interview and in the years of companionship that followed, told of her babyhood in San Francisco Chinatown, where she had lived with father, mother, an older sister, and two brothers until she was five. During these years the sister had been married to a man older than her father and had gone to live in a Siskiyou logging camp. Then for some reason the mother returned to China, and little Yoke Yeen was sent to her sister's home. Two babies were born in the lonely mountain cabin, and much of their care fell on the young aunt, scarcely out of babyhood herself. Schooling, even then her dearest desire, was had only at the price of a beating from her old brother-in-law whenever he discovered, before her sister could protect her, that she had run away to the country school. Ten years of this precarious existence had passed, but still drudgery and disappointment could not quell the ambition surging in the heart of this quiet little Chinese girl.

She was fifteen when her father decided that he, too, would return to China and take with him the two sons and this daughter now grown to marriageable age. But Yoke Yeen rebelled inwardly. She did not propose to spend her life slaving as her sister had done. She had an inner urge to do big things; and she knew she needed education. Now her opportunity had come. She would go with her father to San Francisco. But beyond that she had her own plans, which she confided to no one except the sister who had pointed the way to Nine-Twenty.

Her sister's knowledge of this haven had come to her at secondhand, but from one whom she knew she could trust. In those far-off years when the sister, too, had been a carefree child in San Francisco she had been the special protégé of another daring woman who gave her life to the upbuilding of Chinese girls in America. Deaconess Drant, a woman of unusual height and deep, stirring voice, had been a familiar figure on the streets of old Chinatown. Although their busy lives contained no time for more than casual visits, there had been a silent bond of admiration between the stately deaconess and the gentle guardian of the red brick Home. Often, as their daily paths would cross, the deaconess would ask in Old Country style, "And how is The Cameron this morning?" and the pictures she presented to her little Chinese protégé had always filled the child's heart with a longing to know Donaldina Cameron.

And so it was that Yoke Yeen had presented herself at the door of her sister's dreams. Could Miss Cameron keep her until she had enough education to be ready to return to China and be useful there? Wisely, Lo Mo turned to Judge Murasky. He listened sympathetically.

"By all means get your father's consent to remain if you can; but if he refuses, you are old enough to choose, and I'll issue letters of guardianship," he had promised.

A two-hour session with her father and Miss Cameron left him stubborn and resolute. He *would* take this child back to China. She knew that would end all hopes of education. The girls she saw coming and going in this Home looked so contented and attractive. This friendly woman before her was willing to keep her there. Her father *must* let her stay!

Appeals and persuasion proving of no avail, she had returned to claim Judge Murasky's promise. Ever cautious and wise, he determined to try his powers with the father. A citation was sent ordering him to appear before the Judge. Then with kindly incisive questions this friend of many children drew from the father his own confession of lack of parental guidance; got him to tell how he had sent her off, an unwelcome visitor, to the family of her old brother-in-law; and finally showed him that he had forfeited his parental right to plan her future.

With her father's mark at last on the precious paper giving her to the custody of Miss Cameron, Yoke Yeen had watched the boat bear her father and brothers out of the Golden Gate, leaving her behind to study with all seriousness. With avid interest she had applied herself to the precious lessons taught in the grammar grades, which were as far as the schooling in the Home went. Then one Sunday afternoon she and five other girls had gone to Lo Mo begging permission to go to public high schools. Until this time the carefully guarded girls had not been allowed outside the Home for education, except the rare few who were adopted and educated by such private philanthropists as Tien Wu's guardian.

Lo Mo had taken her group of sanguine girls to the home of Mrs. Pinney, then president of Occidental Board. They sat in her living room looking out of hilltop windows across the Bay, with its white-sailed yachts and glistening ferry boats. Mrs. Pinney, wise counselor of young girls, with her vigorous mind and her strong grasp of things which make for the strengthening of the inner life, looked from one to the other of her visitors. She knew that their wistful spirits were following the boats on the Bay with mental eyes awake to the adventures they represented.

"What do you intend to do, if you do go on through high school?" she had questioned each in turn.

One chose music, another nursing, a third business. The other two just wanted more school life. When it was Yoke Yeen's turn to reply, she poured forth the ambition which has ever impelled her toward her goal. She wanted education so that she could go to China and help its burdened women.

Mrs. Pinney suggested that they try to send her to Lux, an endowed public school which includes industrial training with its scholastic courses. The admission requirements of Lux were restrictive. Only once before had a Chinese girl been admitted, the daughter of a pioneer merchant, a girl who became one of the leading dentists of Chinatown. The Board turned to Mrs. John F. Merrill, who had organized the Chinese branch of the Y.W.C.A. in San Francisco, and through her influence Yoke Yeen was given a chance.

But even this schooling required fees for materials, and the budget of the Home did not provide for "extras." "I'll earn my fees if I can go to school," begged Yoke Yeen, and then the way opened. Not far from Nine-Twenty lived a group of business women who needed someone to prepare dinners at their apartment. Yoke Yeen's training in the Home, reinforced by the domestic science she would have at Lux, prepared her for this task, while her grace and willing spirit made her a welcome addition to the busy household.

She graduated with honors, scholastic and social, for she was twice president of her class. Then she had come to Lo Mo with a further plea. Could she go on to college? She had made her way thus far, and she could do so much more with a college training. There was such a need for educated women in China. She had set her heart on a medical course—the longest and most expensive! What could Lo Mo do? Again she turned to the resourceful Mrs. Pinney. Friends of hers down the Peninsula agreed to take the ambitious girl into their home while she made her way through San Mateo Junior College. Her goal by this time was Stanford University, and Mrs. Pinney, who now lived in Palo Alto, knew that a good record in a junior college would ease the way for her application to be one of the five hundred women then allowed in the university according to the terms of the founding grant.

Two years of quiet, effective work passed by, and at last Yoke Yeen had come, radiant, to Lo Mo with a green slip from the Stanford registrar. She had been admitted to the university.

Together they boarded a train for Palo Alto and sat with Mrs. Pinney on her wisteria-draped veranda. They feasted their eyes on the bright flowering shrubs of the spacious grounds, one of the pioneer places of this garden-loving town, as they focused their combined minds on the problem of finances.

"How I wish I could send you myself!" spoke the ever-generous Mrs. Pinney, "but just now that is impossible. However, Mrs. Wright is in town. We'll go to see her."

The visit to Mrs. Wright proved the beginning of a new relationship for the aspiring girl, who had already attracted the interest of this former Board president. Taller than most of the girls, and always ready with an appropriate verse or reading, Yoke Yeen had been one who had always helped to make the monthly Board meetings attractive. Now Mrs. Wright listened with understanding attention—she had granddaughters of her own in college and realized all that this meant to her eager young friend. When Mrs. Pinney finished her plea, Mrs. Wright turned quietly to Lo Mo and the waiting girl.

"Jade," she said, for that is the name by which Yoke Yeen was known to her American friends, "I want to see you through Stanford. A medical course is so difficult that you cannot divide your attention between your studies and outside work. All I ask is that you bring me good reports each quarter."

When Yoke Yeen's name appeared on the list of new girls to live in Roble Hall, the girls' dormitory, the dean of women had received a letter from one of the leading upperclass sponsors—a group of women who assist with the welcoming of strangers each year. This girl, who after graduation became secretary to a United States senator from her home state, wrote:

"May I ask the privilege of rooming with this Chinese student? I am sure it would be a broadening experience for me and perhaps I could be of some assistance in return."

In the two years before her degree was won, Jade's really serious struggles with the difficult subjects that make up the premedical course were eased by congenial friendships made among faculty and students alike. This slender Oriental girl, her own innate good taste encouraged by the years of association with Lo Mo, always dressed in clothes of simple attractiveness which marked her among her schoolmates. The privilege of a cup of tea served with true Chinese courtesy attracted many a campus leader to enjoy a relaxing moment in Jade's room at Roble Hall, with its Chinese-blue draperies and daintily embroidered table covers.

She had little time for conventional college activities, but her loyal interest in the student Christian association drew her into intimate contact with those of similar spiritual interests, and her gracious manner assisted her in finding the various odd jobs offered by the student employment office. In spite of Mrs. Wright's warning, Jade was determined to be of as little burden as possible to her generous friend. There were vacation periods, and odd moments between times, when she could earn some "extras" by collecting laundry and cleaner bills, selling selected Oriental goods, and caring for children, whom she aways loved. It was this latter occupation which won her the privileges of Dr. David Starr Jordan's treasure-filled home, for often his two grandchildren had been intrusted to her care.

Now, as Lo Mo joined her other friends in the congratulatory group mingling with the graduates on the broad pavements of the inner quadrangle there were anxious inquiries as to "what next?" Those who had watched Jade's successful struggle knew that her goal was not yet reached. The coveted medical degree was still ahead, and that must be hers before the longed-for time should come when, as she expressed it to the dean of women, she could "return to China to make good all the faith others have put into my education. And then," she added, "I do hope my mother and father will understand why I stayed in America. You see, I don't blame them for the way they treated me as a child. They only did what they thought was right; and I wouldn't feel right about them if they hadn't been true to their own convictions."

Her entrance into medical school was postponed for one year more while Jade followed the wishes of her Occidental Board advisers and devoted her time to a course in a Philadelphia Bible college. At last in the fall of 1929 she was enrolled in the Women's Medical College, writing regularly to Lo Mo and Mrs. Wright of the privileges and opportunities that were hers. There her capacity for winning friends continued to enlarge her experience, one of whom, the dean of Hackett Medical College, encouraged Jade's ambition to serve her countrywomen in China.

As the years of her quest grew longer, Lo Mo and her associates found their only reward in such records as that of Yoke Yeen. One day another of these "daughters" who went out from the Home to a life of service herself as an efficient church board secretary, sighed:

"How I wish we Chinese girls of the Coast could build a monument to Lo Mo."

"No," answered a friend, "that is not necessary. You girls are her living monuments."

These "living monuments" were found in many lines of work, among them a serious student nurse taking her place among her American classmates in the hospital of the Affiliated Colleges, the University of California Training School on the high hillside which overlooks all of San Francisco and the Golden Gate. Lo Mo took a group of friends to the "capping ceremony."

"I want you to meet my foster mother," said Choy Har proudly, as she brought up her new associates, from superintendent to classmates, to introduce them to Miss Cameron. In reply Lo Mo invited them to visit Choy Har's "other home" with the hospitality she encouraged in all her "daughters" at Nine-Twenty or Ming Quong.

"Homecoming Day" at Ming Quong always brought these girls and their friends to share that infectious spirit.

"Ida Lee has saved the most frivolous part of her program till the last," Lo Mo explained to the guests who were spending a spring afternoon in the spacious living room. Three black-eyed Chinese lassies tripped past her, dressed in full Scottish regalia as Ida Lee seated herself at the piano. At a nod, her young charges started singing "Comin' Thro' the Rye," acting out its well-known phrases in clever pantomime. Then with a flourish they ended with a perfectly executed highland fling.

"And where did they learn to do this?" asked an astonished visitor.

"Oh," gaily explained Lo Mo, "Ida found it in one of her physical drill books and thought it might please their Scotch mother."

And so internationalism became part of the daily play of these school children who learned year by year what the friendship of another race could do to brighten their lives.

Older girls were there that June day, back from school and work to act as hostesses to the friends whose bounty had given them this home and shelter. These girls with deft hands and smiling faces passed among the guests serving punch and sesame-seed cakes with all the grace that comes to daughters of cultured homes; for was this not indeed their home, and did they not honor their Lo Mo with all the homage any girls could feel?

In the courtyard outside, the kindergartners of the present Ming Quong family played "Farmer in the Dell" and other games of childhood, as gay and merry in the afternoon sunshine as any group of little children at a birthday party.

To please some late guests Ida Lee called them from their play to repeat the songs of the earlier part of the program. Like soft petals of spring blossoms they seemed to waft into the room in their pale pink trouser suits. Solemn faces lighted with true hospitality as they sang their welcome song. What genuine love of music Ida had passed on to them in their happy hours around the piano!

Several times they sang; then noiselessly filed out to the waiting supper tables in the big dining room. In groups of six or eight they ate together at round tables set by small helpers, fresh white aprons tied on over "dress-up" suits. Voices full of childish eagerness rose in their song of grace ere chopsticks clicked over steaming bowls of rice.

Upstairs Lo Mo took some lingering guests to watch the golden sunset over the Gate across the Bay, for the illness of Miss Mills and several changes of staff had brought her to spend a few months among the little ones she so loved—a welcome respite from the pressing cares at Nine-Twenty which even at sixty she continued to carry with the same minute attention to details seen in her whole life.

"Perhaps you would like to see how we live," she invited as she led the way through immaculate halls. "Our youngest sleep in here," pointing to four tiny white iron beds, "and the larger bed belongs to their big sister, Ah Siew, a granddaughter of the Home. Left motherless at seven, she knows how much these other babies need the mothering she has come back to give. She is assistant to Hung Mui Chew, our nursery director, and how dear and patient she is with these tots! Never while I have lived on this hall have I heard an angry or impatient word; yet her charges, like all normal children, are often trying and full of mischief."

The room for the little children was equipped with painstaking understanding of the needs of its occupants. Dolls nodded their rag or china heads on the pillows, and dressers just high enough for very small girls to reach the top stood by each bed, "made by a Japanese carpenter in Berkeley especially for this room," Lo Mo explained.

As the door into the room belonging to the older girls opened, the western sunlight streamed across the picture of a thoughtful face on the neatly arranged dressing table. The sight of this face with its halo of sunshine led Lo Mo to indulge a moment of reminiscence:

"That is the picture of the mother of two of our youngest. She died last winter, leaving her babies and all she had in the world to our care. Ah Fong, the four-year-old, was the little one with Miss Yue just at the foot of the stairs."

The story of Ah Fong's mother made that day at Ming Quong indelible. Yute Tai was one of those sad, cruelly mistreated "mooie-jais" whose rescue had occurred in the days of confusion following in the wake of the San Francisco earthquake. Armed with a court order and application for letters of guardianship, Miss Cameron, Tien Wu, the sheriff, and another officer had gone for this little domestic slave, report of whose condition had reached them by secret messenger. There was no chance to warn Yute Tai. Accustomed as she had been to beatings and all manner of ill treatment, her terror knew no bounds when she was suddenly snatched out of the only shelter she had ever known and forced into a taxi with four utter strangers, among them the dreaded "Fahn Quai."

In all their years of rescues, Lo Mo and Tien remembered no such ride as this. Usually the calming words of friendliness spoken in Tien's musical Cantonese would gradually subdue the sobs. But this time no sound of comfort could be heard above the hysterical screams. Out Market Street they sped—court was being held in temporary quarters at the corner now occupied by Hotel Whitcomb. A curious crowd closed in on the sidewalk as the shrieking girl was dragged out of the cab and into the courtroom.

Fortunately the discerning Henry Monroe had arranged with Judge Cerf for a hearing after hours. But there was no stopping the hysteria.

With real understanding the Judge issued a temporary order and set the case over.

A curtain may well be dropped over the tale of that first night. Suffice it to say that finally the idea of firm authority and little deeds of hitherto unknown kindness pierced the benumbed brain of the wretched little thirteen-year-old slave. In a few days Yute Tai was able to tell her story to the judge, and Miss Cameron was made her legal guardian.

Then came months and years of struggle toward womanhood. "I can never learn" changed to "I will," and out of this scrawny, half-living child developed the most immaculate of dainty young girls, with a spirit of sweetness and helpfulness hard to equal.

At twenty, Yute Tai married a worthy young merchant. Together they established an attractive little home near his store in the Mission District. After three years Ah Leen was born. Then, four years later, came Ah Fong. But sickness and business depression overtook the devoted father, and soon Yute Tai found herself a widow. The store and its furnishings were sold at auction, the funeral and other expenses were met, and she with her two babes moved into two small rooms in Chinatown. With the electric sewing machine she had saved from the store, Yute Tai worked to support her little ones. A devoted mother, she kept both home and babies clean and attractive, and many were the visits "home" to Nine-Twenty.

Then came a day when the carefully guarded little Ah Leen must venture, alone and frightened, through the Stockton Street traffic. Mother lay desperately ill. The friends from the Home were sought and came. Before Yute Tai would allow herself to be taken to the hospital these friends must take her precious daughters "home."

Flu-pneumonia was too severe for the worn mother, and she called for the lawyer to come to her bedside. Willing her all to the care of the friends who had remade her life, Yute Tai closed her eyes in death.

"Is there anything you want—are you afraid to go?"

"No. I have no fear. I am trusting all to Jesus. Pray Him to forgive my sins."

And with the peace "which passeth all understanding," this girl, who had learned of life eternal, passed on, blessing the lives of those who stood around her.

Truly her spirit was in the happiness of that Home-Coming Day at Ming Quong Home as little Ah Leen and baby Ah Fong waved their childish good-bye, standing on the steps in the evening shadows—a picture never to be forgotten, little pale pink figures hiding shyly in the folds of Lo Mo's blue dress.

No matter what the important occasion Lo Mo had to preside. The times she loved best were the wedding days. When Quai Fong chose an August evening for her marriage to a young merchant from southern California, Lo Mo promised a "big wedding."

Multicolored dahlias transformed Culbertson Hall. Only the touch of loving hands could make a room look as that one did. The men of the bridal party stood before a screen of pure white blooms, faultless in their evening clothes. Even four-year-old Ah Quong in his navy-blue sailor suit never for a moment forgot his solemn-faced dignity as he stood holding the wedding ring on its white satin pillow.

Yoke Lon, she whom Lo Mo had held up for the farewell kiss that morning long ago when Miss Culbertson had left the Home, struck the familiar chords from Lohengrin. Her musical education had begun in childhood when Professor Otto Fleischner had trained her to become accompanist for Suey Leen, as well as to sing the alto that had lent its mellow quality to the Home quartet. In her rich native dress of green brocade she fitted appropriately into this gardenlike scene. Black-haired bridesmaids marched slowly down the aisle, preceded by tiny Ah Fong, granddaughter from Ming Quong Home. The petals she strewed before her seemed almost a part of her pink-clad self.

Then all eyes looked upon the bride. Those who knew asked themselves the question—was this white-robed maid with lacey veil really the same person who had struggled against the kindness of the beloved Lo Mo on whose arm she leaned tonight? No—she had the same name, and the same features, only softened by love; but a new soul had been born within this erstwhile mooie-jai.

The service proceeded in Chinese. Then, "Who gives this woman?" and Lo Mo stepped up to place the hand of her "daughter" tenderly in that of the eager bridegroom. A simple gesture; real mothers do it every once in a while. Older sisters sometimes take the father's place; but there was a specially poignant blessing in this gesture from one who had been father, mother, sister, all—the first one to show this girl the path to happiness.

Other friends were there who had helped along the way—the generous "godmother" whose means had insured education and now the appointments of this beautiful wedding; Attorney Borland in full evening dress to do honor to the bride who owed her freedom to his legal advice and skill; and teachers whose patient instruction in handicraft and books had pointed the way out of the dark past. Sergeant Manion was there—he of the Chinatown Squad whose hand had brought freedom to so many. Strong Knight of Columbus though he was, he recognized the utter sincerity of the work in this Presbyterian Mission Home. These people, young and old, were his true friends.

Choy, black-haired little six-year-old, only son of the Home at present, clung constantly to the Sergeant's knee. That was as high as he could reach on this giant friend of his, but he knew from the pat of the big hand resting on his head that his protector was near. He exulted in the rare treat of masculine presence in the room.

"We have to be very careful how we order Choy around here. He is always boasting that he will call you to arrest us, if we do anything he doesn't like," laughed Miss Cameron, as she greeted them in the reception which followed the ceremony.

"That's right, Choy, we men have to hang together. Choy says he is going away to school soon."

"Yes, he is going south with me this week, to the Voorhies School at San Dimas. This was founded by a young man who is using his inheritance to care for homeless boys. It will be so much better for him to have normal relationships with other boys. There is another Chinese boy there, too, to keep him company. I am so grateful to the one who told me of this place. Chung Mei is too crowded, you know, and anyway he is younger than most of Dr. Shepherd's boys."

Choy's mother, Gum Leen, once Oie Kum's slave, had gone back to China, but she knew this little "native son" of hers would have a chance for a life she could not have given him because he was protected by such friends.

Good-nights were said and the couple ran out of the door in a shower of rice and rose petals. Mentally, Lo Mo followed them to the land of bending pepper trees where so many years ago she, too, had been young and full of dreams. A few days later she followed the bridal couple in reality, when she journeyed south to place Choy in his promised school.

Her visit to the honeymoon home with its cheerful, rose-draped bedroom and well-furnished living room left a picture that sang in her heart as she traveled north again to meet the pressing problems that waited at Ming Quong and Nine-Twenty.

A week or two later friends of the Chinese family were puzzled to receive these invitations from Oakland:

We very much desire the pleasure of your company for afternoon tea, in honor of a dear friend, next Thursday, from three to five o'clock.

Cordially yours,

MING QUONG FAMILY
DONALDINA CAMERON
TIEN FUH WU
ETHEL V. HIGGINS

There was mystery in this note. Ida Lee's name was missing from the hostess list. Yes, it was true. There she stood, in white satin native dress embroidered with pink blossoms. A corsage of lilies of the valley told the story that sparkled in her merry eyes. At last she was going to the one who had waited for her for ten long years. Her heart torn between her adopted babies and the man she had promised to marry, the Chinese director of Ming Quong had finally reached the day of decision.

She stood beside Lo Mo receiving the congratulations of the room full of friends, Chinese and American alike, tender appreciation in her regard for this leader to whom she owed much that makes life abundant. There was poignancy, however, in the parting. Lo Mo had been so deeply sympathetic in the heart struggles that had preceded this happy day. And now she was so gaily thoughtful in the little things that make such days red-lettered for daughters.

"Yes, we are leaving tomorrow night for Pasadena. Ida and I by train and a few others in the family car," answered Lo Mo to the friends who gathered round. "Mrs. Milton Stewart has invited Ida to have the wedding in her lovely home. Then Ida and her husband are going right on East. He is an officer in his own church and has many friends who are waiting to welcome her."

A young Chinese student was one of the next to offer good wishes. "And who is he?" inquired a recent friend. "Oh, he is one of our finest grandsons," answered Lo Mo. "His home is in Arizona, but he is studying medicine at an Eastern college. His mother knew Ida when she was a small girl, and he was passing through Oakland just in time for today's party. We are very thankful when the children of our girls turn out as he has."

Always rejoicing in the happiness of others, Lo Mo made that trip to Pasadena with Ida memorable for this one who had been so close in the years past. Ethel Higgins, intrepid driver on many rescues and camping trips, followed with the family car loaded to the gunwales this time with suitcases of wedding finery, gifts, and guests. In place of special honor rode the choice wedding cake baked with devoted interest by Lo Mo's sister, Annie. The car also brought Emma Mills, and the Chinese teacher from Ming Quong, Mrs. Lee, that devoted co-worker by the same name though not of the same family as Ida, whose little daughter Suey N'goh was joyous in anticipation of being flower girl.

One and all they joined in the pride of welcoming this new son-in-law into the ever-widening circle of Lo Mo's family. A graduate of an Eastern university, he held a responsible position in the design department of a transcontinental railroad, and he was a man whose personality won friends for his race as well as for himself.

Guests gathered round to congratulate this couple whose tastes and ideals furnished such a congenial background. The huge wedding cake was being cut. Suddenly Lo Mo was overwhelmed by the sense of separation from the "daughter" on whom she had come to lean in their common interests at Ming Quong. She stepped through the French doors upon the veranda, white in the moonlight. No one should see her do other than smile tonight. But a strong arm rested about her shoulders She looked into the eyes of her stalwart nephew, her own kin in the ways of the flesh as well as the spirit. No words for a few quiet moments. Then, "a gorgeous moon tonight," and both their spirits were bathed in the flooding moonlight of the old San Benito Ranch home, the present entirely forgotten. But Donaldina Cameron had few moments for introspection. No sooner had she returned from this journey of romantic interest than there was the fall bazaar to manage, in addition to the regular calls incident to her rescue and rehabilitation work. The girls in charge of the Industrial Department were discouraged over lack of funds; but Lo Mo never failed to rally her creative play spirit. They would call the three-day festival "A Street in Canton"; intriguing pictures in the daily press and gay Oriental posters would beguile seekers of the exotic to Nine-Twenty.

Many willing hands helped in the preparation, but it was Donaldina Cameron herself who directed every detail and who wrote the letters which brought responses from her scattered family. Great truckloads of queer-shaped Chinese melons and vegetables with names and tastes unknown to American housewives came down from Oie Kum's ranch to fill brightly painted market baskets in the transformed Culbertson Hall. Wares from antique shops, whose owners were gratefully willing to aid Lo Mo, were displayed in gala booths. Mrs. Fenn came up from Lindsay to supervise the publication of a Chinese cookbook adorned with colorful figures and dangling tassels. Then during the festival an ancient lantern-painter decorated fishskin lanterns to order, the handicraft from the basement looms found delighted purchasers, and kindergartners taught by "Auntie Wing," T'sang Tsun of the old days, sang on the afternoon programs. Mae Wong and Janie Chew at length balanced the books of the Industrial Department with lighter hearts.

Tired, but gratified by the appreciation of her girls, Lo Mo now turned to the planning of the Christmas season. This was when she and Tien most missed Ida and Ethel Higgins, who had replaced Miss Mills as Director of Ming Quong. Both were full of music—a special necessity in the Home this year. She felt that the many new girls in the household must learn the meaning of the season through the universal language of music. Her opening wedge to these hearts, whose memories were so full of darkness, would be in the proper interpretation of the Christmas story.

The streets of San Francisco were gay with the stars and wreaths of a municipal "White Christmas." On the one time that, with careful chaperonage, the newly rescued girls from Nine-Twenty were allowed to join the nightly throng that circled around the star-tipped sequoia in Union Square, she knew their senses were touched by a dim realization of the meaning of the season that knits all hearts.

The traditional Christmas atmosphere of Nine-Twenty must be preserved; but Lo Mo felt her reserve of strength and time unequal to the task. Then others came to help. A pageant was translated into Cantonese by the Chinese pastor and Lau Sz Nai, a member of the staff who had spent thirteen years in China. A friend with years of experience came to direct rehearsals. The Industrial Department sparkled with tinsel and white robes. An artist friend painted the scenery, while clever Chinese hands wired the star and draped the cheesecloth sky above the Syrian plains. Christmas Eve came. Three American college girls, home for the holidays, appeared to lead the choruses and sing the solos behind screens.

All was excitement at Nine-Twenty. Guests were coming from every corner of Chinatown, as well as a few chosen American friends. Hands that had so recently toyed with the bamboo mah jong counters of the underworld were busy arranging the straw for the lowly manger. Eyes that had so long looked down on evil were lifted up to behold the Star of Bethlehem. Voices that had spoken submissively to harsh masters rose in musical Cantonese to sing "Joy to the World" in adoration as the pictured story of the birth of the true Master was enacted. The Wise Men in their robes of gorgeous hue brought frankincense and gold with that courteous generosity innate in Orientals. Shepherds on the plains rose with mystic wonder in voices expressing hearts which really were learning the story for the first time.

A Christmas tree heavy with gifts stood at the side of the stage. Before the pageant round-faced children, the ones who look so placid and unresponsive to the casual outsider, had played excitedly around its base. Now and then a brave finger would poke a wooden animal and its owner would run giggling to hide behind the others.

The curtain was drawn. Lo Mo stepped quietly from the seat where she had watched each detail of this Oriental presentation of the story which had ruled her life. Golden beams from the amber-lighted star shone across her soft white hair. Her voice was tender as she thanked the audience for their silent attention.

"The gifts on this tree are the girls' own expression of their love for the Giver of all good gifts. Out of their own savings they have bought these toys and tokens to brighten the lives of the little brothers and sisters of Chinatown. We hope you will all stay while the older girls distribute the presents."

Choie Ying, a child who just two months before had come with Lo Mo from the Detention Home, looked up with beaming eyes as her two younger sisters each received a package from Lo Mo's own hands. The disheveled hair and blue-denim garb of the days so lately passed were forgotten as she stood there, quietly happy in her dress of soft holiday color, her shining black hair neatly combed, her eyes full of unspoken admiration for the gracious woman on the edge of the platform.

Choie Ying approached her more nearly. Still her hands would not touch the soft, clinging silk of the scarf which hung from Lo Mo's shoulders. Almost reverently she turned to her newest friend, the very girl who had shrunk so terrified from the dreaded Fahn Quai in the midnight flight from Stockton such a short time before. She spoke in Cantonese; translated, she said, "Isn't Lo Mo beautiful tonight?"

"She is—'Quan-Yin' come to life," replied that other, groping in her pagan lore for an expression of the strange thought stirring within her.

CHAPTER XVIII

MORE DAUGHTERS FOR LO MO

Lo Mo's likeness to the Chinese Goddess of Mercy—she who had in tradition begged for a thousand arms that she might bear all the sorrows of womankind—was tested every day. Mae Wong expressed the comparison understandingly: "My people bring all their troubles to Lo Mo. She knows the real way out of difficulties. She can talk to God. In my country before they know Christianity they only make sacrifices to Quan Yin." Mae could speak with authority. She was parted from her own substantial village family in China through artful deception. After she had been brought to this country in childhood the wisdom of new friends led her to this haven where she had grown to young womanhood. Her own decision to give up more remunerative and carefree outside employment for the Home where her talents could be of real benefit proved how truly Lo Mo had wakened her spirit of service.

But in the group who made up audience and cast at the 1930 Christmas pageant were many who were just beginning to understand Lo Mo's tender mercies. Choie Ying herself had been reported to her by Sergeant Manion in the busy days following Ida Lee's wedding. He had already taken the little schoolgirl, whom he had discovered in a private house devoted to evil ways, to the Juvenile Court for protection. The court could furnish this protection only through an agency, and the Sergeant knew to whom they would turn. He therefore brought his story to Miss Cameron. She knew the family well. An older sister was living a life of abandonment in a Northern city, a brother was in a state institution for the feeble-minded. She realized that the ill-kept family home from which this 'teen-age girl went daily to her sordid tasks was no place to leave the child. Here again was a problem like those of old. "But you know," she had said to her old friend, "I dread to bring a girl with that background into our family. We had begun to think that phase of our work was passing, in San Francisco, at least—largely due to all you have done," she added, looking with a smile at the Inspector's star he had been showing her. This star made of unalloyed gold had been a gift from the Chinese Native Sons on the occasion of Manion's recent promotion from the rank of sergeant to inspector.

Their discussion of Choie Ying's case had given Lo Mo an opportunity to share with Inspector Manion some of the problems nearest her heart. She had told him about the seven homeless babies now housed in the third-floor rooms formerly kept for newly rescued girls, and of the long hours she had spent with Community Chest officials trying to work out some solution for the care of these waifs. She recognized that they did not belong in Nine-Twenty, a house which did not meet legal state requirements for baby care; but there was no other place where they could go. Of course, as she had said to the Inspector, the Babies' Aid would take them for their first three months; Ming Quong and Chung Mei would carry on after they were three years old; but what of the interim? The Foster Home plan which worked so successfully for most orphaned infants was too difficult to administer in crowded Chinatown: Lo Mo knew, too, how dangerous it might be for some of the Chinese girl-mothers she had sequestered to reveal their secrets to any official source where the facts had to be kept in writing.

"If only the Chest could find some place for my babies, and the new Y.W.C.A. Boarding Home could be finished to provide a home for our many business girls who are still living here, then Miss Wu and I could be free to look after more girls like this one, from all up and down the Pacific Coast," she had sighed as Inspector Manion stood waiting for her to turn the key in the familiar bolted door. "I am sure there are many like Choie Ying who need rescue as much as the old-time mooie-jai—and of course if we could travel about more, we would help to do in other places what we have done in San Francisco—only we wish we could always be sure of as real co-operation as you give us."

Yet, as at so many other times in her life, Donaldina Cameron could not choose her own path. This time it had led irrevocably to the old pressed-brick Detention Home. She had gone in response to the call that had followed Inspector Manion's visit. At the doorway the old caretaker recognized white-haired Lo Mo, and she stopped to chat over thrilling rescues of the days gone by, days when he had helped her and her newly appointed wards to dash out by back stairs to escape the lurking highbinders.

As she went upstairs in the elevator which had held so many distressed young people, she thought of the times when she had brought her own problems to Judge Murasky in his crowded Juvenile Court in this same building. The social worker who greeted her in the tiny upstairs office turned to her with relief born of experience; for she knew in whose resourceful hands she was placing the long, technically worded brief from the district attorney's office containing the deposition made by the grammar-school child brought in by Inspector Manion. Miss Cameron's practiced eye read between the lines of the legal words another story of a broken life. This thirteen-year-old eighth-grader had been taken by a chance acquaintance to call on a white woman married to a Chinese and living on the outskirts of Chinatown. A few days later the same woman called on Choie Ying's mother, asking if her daughter could come to work for her after school hours. Without further investigation the old mother had given her consent.

Choie Ying had presented herself at the given time. She was handed a broom and told to sweep the living room, but in a few minutes her mistress returned to give instructions about things of which Choie Ying had never heard. There was no escape. The doorbell rang and Choie Ying was forced without further words into her unspeakable calling. The part of her earnings she was allowed to keep and the dire threats of the emphatic mistress had locked the secret in the child's inmost heart. Back and forth she had come for several days until the ever-vigilant Manion had discovered her plight, arrested the employer, and brought the child to the Detention Home.

The social worker was watching Miss Cameron's face as she read the closely typed lines. She seemed to read the question rising to Lo Mo's lips as she glanced up from the bottom of the page.

"Yes, she is in need of medical care. She needs many things, but most of all, someone who can re-establish her respect for life." Then without waiting for Miss Cameron's answer, she went on.

"I'll call Choie Ying, and you can talk with her about her future."

The door had opened to admit the schoolgirl, her black hair uncombed, her eyes downcast, her garb the plain blue denim of the institution.

Miss Cameron stepped to the far corner of the room and drew her chair close to the despairing child. "Would you like to come and stay a while with Lo Mo?"

A nod of the disheveled black head answered "yes" to this. Together they sat talking in low-pitched tones of the great trouble which had so suddenly descended. With the wisdom acquired in long years of experience, and the vision of many another little girl like this now grown into useful womanhood, Miss Cameron looked beyond the pitiful figure in the chair before her.

"But I shrink from this, all the same," she confided to the social worker when the doors were closed. "We thought this phase of our work nearly over."

"Do you really think the slave traffic has ceased?"

"Not exactly. Inspector Manion and I were just discussing that question yesterday. We find that such girls are not often brought into San Francisco any more. Our police are too quick for them. But in other cities up and down the Coast, and even in the East, we are told that conditions are far from right. Our Board has often wished that Miss Wu and I could be free to float about more and help in other places; but we are tied down by the many details of work here."

And the next day more details had been heaped upon her, as the Juvenile Court Judge awarded Choie Ying to her custody, while the old mother and two smaller sisters sat by, weeping silently.

This seemed to be the beginning of a new chapter in the history of Nine-Twenty. Choie Ying was brought from the confines of the cheerless Detention Home to this ivy-clad brick Home where everyone moved about in cheerful obedience to the invisible scepter of love in the hands of the woman who had talked so kindly with her that morning when she had felt full of despair. Only a few days after Choie Ying had come to take her place in this household, the doors were unlocked to answer the ring of a taxi driver.

"Got two girls out here that can't speak English. They are asking for Tien Fuh and Lo Mo. Thought I'd better try this place," and he looked relieved when the doorkeeper, turning to a white-haired woman passing in the hall, said:

"Lo Mo, here is someone looking for you."

And so two more stranded girls found shelter. The taller one—a girl of real charm and resourcefulness—poured out her story to Tien Wu. She had been landed in Los Angeles as the "daughter" of an alleged merchant. Here she had made friends with a girl who had been in slavery for three years and whose owner had cruelly beaten her. In these days even slave girls have more freedom than in the years of barred doors and opium-smoking guards. They are allowed to go and come more or less as they please, but they are still filled with tales of fear about the red brick Home in San Francisco. These two, however, decided to risk all and try to find it. They had heard from some whose friends had found new life within its doors, and they doubted the stories told by their hateful owners.

Yin King had saved some money. In spite of their language handicap, they hid in a cheap hotel. Equipped only with the words, "China Street," still the Chinese name for Sacramento Street, "Tien Fuh," and

"Lo Mo," they had climbed into the taxi of the wise driver who had brought them to the doors which had just opened.

Yin King's great desire was to return to China; but her heart was burdened with the plight of other girls like herself. On the long trip out from China she had met a girl still detained at Angel Island. Offering to turn state's evidence, even though this would place her own life in jeopardy, she went before immigration officials with her story, and before long this girl, Suey Wong, too, was brought to the Home.

But Yin King was not alone with her tales of others needing rescue. The friend who had come with her from Los Angeles, Mui Qui, also had stories to tell. She had escaped from a slaveowner who had held her in the Chinatown of Stockton, that thriving city on the San Joaquin from which Henry Monroe helped Lo Mo release Bow Yoke over thirty years ago. According to Mui Qui, conditions in that Chinatown had not noticeably improved in the years that had followed.

While Lo Mo was still considering these items brought by Yin King and Mui Qui, a letter arrived from a Chinese friend, who inclosed a message from a girl named Fong Ping, living in Stockton, pleading to be rescued and brought to Nine-Twenty.

To corroborate Mui Qui's statement and the letter just received, Lo Mo called in one of the few other rescued girls then in the Home, whom she knew had at one time lived in Stockton. This girl, Leen Ho, had been a mooie-jai whom Tien Wu had met years ago in old Canton when she was there on a visit. At the time Tien had felt certain the child was destined for the slavery they all were fighting; but she had had no absolute proof and had left her with a heavy heart. It had been a relief, then, for Tien when the girl about whom she had worried so long appeared years later at the door of Nine-Twenty. Leen Ho had been brought first to San Francisco to live just two blocks away from the Home; but before she could escape to the friend she had remembered from her childhood, she had been taken away to the Stockton dive, from which at last she had made her escape about a year before this letter had come, bringing with her a foster child whom she herself longed to save from impending slavery.

Leen Ho and Mui Qui both offered now to go to Stockton to assist in the rescue not only of Fong Ping but of the many others they knew were in need. The raid was planned for the day after Thanksgiving. Tien Wu went ahead by train to arrange for Juvenile Court warrants. In Stockton she was met by Mr. Young, chief probation officer of that city, and taken directly to his office. With the wisdom born of long experience, Tien insisted that no one should know of her arrival. Even the warrants were not filed until the clock struck five, so that in no way could the secret leak out.

In the meantime an automobile was racing from San Francisco bringing the remainder of the rescue party, driven by a young Chinese friend, who eagerly gave his services to help to liberate more of his countrywomen. Miss Cameron, Mae Wong as interpreter, Leen Ho, Mui Qui, and a government official, to aid in the arrest of the owners, made up the party. Toward evening they parked outside the city limits near the municipal baths. They were tired and hungry, but they must not be seen before the appointed hour for the raid. Two raids were to be made simultaneously at two separate headquarters, and there must be no inkling of their intention. It was deemed safe, however, for Mae and the immigration officer to look for a wayside grocery. Soon they returned with rolls, ham, and red apples. A strange picnic party that was, under the eucalyptus trees in the fast-gathering fall dusk, all making common cause with the girl Tien Wu had seen so long ago in Canton.

They had scarcely finished eating when another car drove up through the twilight, bringing Tien Wu, Mr. Young, and his assistant, Mrs. Brown. The whole party waited an hour until it should be quite dark. Then, fortified by the arrival of two members of the Stockton police force, they divided—Miss Cameron, Mae Wong, Mui Qui, and one of the policemen in one car, while Tien Wu and Leen Ho led the rest of the party.

Simultaneously the two groups rushed into dark hallways on separate alleys in the unsuspecting Chinatown. Lo Mo's party dashed up the long stairs into a labyrinth with rooms on both sides of a twisty hall, an exit in the rear. They found ten or fifteen men and three older women consorting with them in a waiting room. One of these women, a hardened vixen about thirty years old, slipped by and started to escape down the stairs. Miss Cameron was after her immediately, pulling her back. She wrenched herself free and slammed the door of a room near by. The police forced the door. Too late! The woman, later found to be part owner, had escaped.

Mui Qui, so terrified she could scarcely stand, kept indicating with her thumb a tightly bolted door in front. This was battered open to reveal a hideous old woman weighing somewhat over two hundred pounds, Mui Qui's former owner, and mistress of this house.

At this moment heavy footsteps coming up the stairs startled them all. A huge Danish officer appeared, club in hand—"probably sent by the Chinese," flashed the quick mind of Lo Mo.

"Got what you want?" he called.

"Part, not all," was the cautious answer.

"Got all of our girls—Miss Wu sent me to help you," and with that he started kicking open all the remaining inner doors. Huddled close in a hidden lavatory were the girls Mui Qui had reported, their terror piteous when they saw the big officer and, at his side, the dreaded "Fahn Quai." They were quickly driven to police headquarters, while the old mistress was placed under arrest and taken in a separate car. A further search of the place for the part owner ended when they pried up the linoleum in the room where she had been last seen. Under a trapdoor a box was found and then a ladder to the room below, out of which opened a door to a back alley.

Tien Wu was like a mother quail as she huddled her charges under her arms at the sight of a queer group of Chinamen hanging around the courthouse door. Inside Captain Porter's office at police headquarters, the telephone was ringing every minute. "Yes, government officials?"—then, with his hand over the mouthpiece: "Doesn't this show the value of these slaves in hard cash? You better get out of here as quickly as possible. Lawyers and reporters are on your trail already. Inspector Washburn and his big car are at your service."

And so had started the whirring ride over the sixty flying miles, ending at two the next morning on the steep San Francisco hillside, another day already begun.

EPILOGUE

DONALDINA CAMERON almost lived a century. But that was not her wish. On her 96th birthday I took our youngest grandson to call.

"Just think, Cam," she told the wide-eyed boy, "in four more years I will be 100 years old," counting on her fingers as she spoke. Then she turned to me and whispered, "But I don't want to live that long. They make too much fuss over you."

She lacked two years of the hundred when she was hospitalized for a broken hip. As she lay there, gradually slipping away, Cam's father, our eldest son, brought her white roses, always her favorite flowers.

"I'm having a wonderful time," she said to him, "one foot in this world; the other in the next."

Soon after that, January 4, 1969, she took the full step. I saw her shortly before she left. Her last words to me still echo with the lilt that was so meaningful. She seemed to be in a coma, but as I leaned over to say, "Good-bye. I am going to Cam's birthday party," she roused, and a faint smile lighted her opening eyes. "Oh! Give him my love," she murmured.

The beloved "Mother of Chinatown" spent over forty years as the guiding light of the institution she had come to serve "for just one year" before the turn of the century. As retirement loomed she sought the fulfillment of a cherished hope. She had expected that Tien Wu, trained and sympathetic to every phase of the work, would be her successor. The Board agreed; but with characteristic modesty Tien declined. She persuaded Lo Mo that as "Auntie" she could keep in more intimate touch with her girls, and promised that she would remain as Assistant to whoever might follow Lo Mo as the new Director.

Then Evelyn Brown Bancroft, now the representative of the Presbyterian Board of National Missions on the Pacific Coast, discovered Lorna Logan, a recent graduate of the University of Washington. Miss Cameron made a trip to meet Lorna in Portland. She felt immediate rapport with this girl who was about the same age as she had been when Evelyn Bancroft's mother had brought her to San Francisco Chinatown from the Santa Anita Ranch. Lo Mo liked Lorna's quiet reserve and the twinkle in the deep brown eyes that seemed to reveal an understanding heart and a well-trained mind. She sensed that Lorna, a graduate in journalism, was equipped to interpret the needs of a new Chinatown with purpose and intelligence—a prophecy Lo Mo lived to see fulfilled for more than thirty years.

It was not long before Lorna was at Nine-Twenty, learning from the experienced Lo Mo as the young Dolly had from Margaret Culbertson. Duties differed, however. Calls for rescue were becoming less frequent. Cooperation with leaders of Chinatown plus the vigilance of American law enforcement officers had combined with Lo Mo's alert watchfulness in out-moding "yellow slavery," as had new laws in China. But the difficult adjustment of family life among the second and third generation Chinese-Americans confined in the crowded blocks of Chinatown drained their sympathies. More daughters from these homes were entrusted to Nine-Twenty via the Juvenile Court, or because their elders recognized that the spirit of this Home could soothe emotional disturbances. Lo Mo spent rewarding hours talking intimately with these young girls, in conference with parents and Board members, planning ahead with Lorna and Tien on how to meet changing conditions. As she began to bring her new assistant into these conferences she was delighted to see how readily Lorna, whose elder sister was a missionary in China, was winning the confidence of the Chinese community.

At the age of 70 Donaldina Cameron reluctantly became "emeritus" on the records of the Board of National Missions and returned to the sisters who had waited so patiently. But she never ceased to be chief counsellor to her successor, nor could any official act separate this mother from her flock. The little white cottage in Palo Alto to which the Camerons finally retired became a mecca for all who had ever shared her care and kindness. She listened with understanding to the problems of the Nine-Twenty staff and shared the joys and sorrows of every age group of her adopted "family."

She was freer now to accept speaking engagements, unconsciously interpreting to her listeners the laws of living revealed by the Master whose strength seemed to become hers in tasks that would have overwhelmed those who understood less. Sometimes those who heard Lo Mo describe the regenerated lives of the girls she had brought into the "family" questioned the "whole truth." One such young person approached her on a commute train to Palo Alto.

"You are Miss Donaldina Cameron?" she inquired. Assured by Lo Mo's smile she slid into the empty seat beside the older woman. "I so enjoyed your talk at college recently. But tell me honestly—those are not all *true* stories of real people, are they? I suppose you just weave them together as typical examples."

"By no means," Lo Mo interrupted briskly. "They are indeed true stories of real people. There is no word of fiction in anything I say! I only wish you could share some of these experiences."

That girl thanked her and went on her way to other duties, but Betty Eldredge from Pasadena rang the bell at Nine-Twenty one morning when Lo Mo was there.

"I have heard of your work," she told Miss Cameron, "and I want to give you my summer and my car."

Such unsought volunteer assistance seemed to come more often as Lo Mo told her story; but the problems of deportees and homeless Chinese waifs increased. Lo Mo's prayers were burdened with concern for the girls who must be deported because of illegal entrance. She knew that there were few places where they could be protected once they docked in China.

Sui Muie, the terrified girl who had shrunk from "Fahn Quai" on that long ride from Stockton, was even more afraid to be deported. During the months of investigation that followed the raid the rescued slave girl found an ideal in Mrs. Chan, an assistant at the Home.

"Oh, Lau Sz Nai," Sui Mui exclaimed one night to the white-haired Bible teacher, Mrs. Robinson, "I know that I am stupid; but there are many women in China as stupid as I. I could never be like Mrs. Chan, but I know I could learn to tell other women about Jesus! Do you think if I work hard I could take this book back and teach others?"

Sui Mui's wish was granted soon and unexpectedly. Dr. Mary Stone, a medical missionary, came from China as a guest. She was deeply impressed by the ambition of the young girl and offered to take Sui Mui back under her care. Later that same year Tien Wu arrived in Canton with a group of deportees. She was greeted at the dock by a radiant Sui Mui. She told "Auntie" how she had saved money earned by doing menial chores at the Home and in Dr. Stone's hospital. Now she was about to return to her native village to buy a small plot of land. She would farm like a man and at the same time teach other women the wonderful story she had learned in San Francisco.

Tien came home in time to help with a new problem. A teacher from the Methodist Girls' Home brought to their door one cold December morning a frightened young girl who had insisted that she *must* meet "Gum Mei Lun" (Chinese for Cameron). The girl had been misdirected by a child in the street. When they finally sat down in the privacy of "Auntie's" room, where the soft Chinese rug and Cantonese wall hangings shut out the loneliness of this strange country, Gwai sobbed out her story. Lo Mo happened to be at Nine-Twenty that day, and her heart sank as she realized that the illicit trade was much further from control than she and Inspector Manion had begun to believe. Gwai had been landed in Seattle the previous July, brought to San Francisco and sold. Night after night she had been taken to different hotels and forced to earn $25.00, $22.00 of which had been turned over to her owners.

This day her owner's wife had taken her to a beauty parlor, saying she would come for her as soon as her hair was dry. Gwai had managed to slip unobtrusively from under the drier and out a back door into an alley. She had been afraid to inquire of an adult about the way to the protecting home she had heard about, and the little girl she found playing in the street had sent her to the wrong place. Tien's assurance of shelter and a prompt report to the Immigration Service changed her life.

For over a year the case of "The Trampled Blossom," as reporters dubbed the dainty Oriental, dragged on in the courts. Finally the government gave her permission to stay at Nine-Twenty in return for her testimony about two other girls brought from China as her alleged "sisters." At three o'clock one morning Lorna unbolted the doors of the Home to welcome one of these girls, rescued that night by an Immigration Service raid in Salinas. Ah So proved to be a person of real stamina. As the result of the testimony of both girls the importer who had brought in all three was arrested, fined $5000 and sentenced to two years in the penitentiary. His three women accomplices were sent up for a year and a half, and all four ordered deported as soon as their terms were over.

This case seemed to close out the era of such "rescues," but the plight of homeless waifs like those Lo Mo had often sheltered in her own room became more pressing. In all of San Francisco's charitable institutions there was no provision for Chinese of the toddler age. Sanguine in her belief that once a critical need was presented to the right persons the right answer would be found, she and Lorna gathered a group of friends of both races around the fireside at Nine-Twenty one winter afternoon. Out of that meeting there developed an interracial, interdenominational organization pledged to provide a Christian home for dependent Chinese pre-school children. T. Y. Tang, a business leader with wide interests, became president of the board of directors.

After several rebuffs in their attempts to rent a suitable place, an old-fashioned home was found in Menlo Park on the sunny Peninsula. About twelve little ones were soon under the care of Miss Halcyon Kyle, a trained nurse, in what was then called "Gabriel Cottage." The summer passed smoothly, but in the fall an epidemic of trench mouth among the children overwhelmed the director.

At this point Yoke Yeen came home from Philadelphia—Bessie Yeen Jeong, M.D. on her diploma from Women's Medical College. She was ready for her internship, but her debt of gratitude to Lo Mo was too great to ignore.

She went at once to "Gabriel Cottage" and devoted herself to bringing health to her charges. She realized that this house was inadequate. Soon they were moved to a rambling old place with a large oak-shaded garden in Atherton, and Dr. Bessie's babies became the pets of Peninsula church people. A fund was accumulated for building a proper home. A Chinese architect, a friend of Lo Mo's, drew up a typical Chinese plan, moon gate and all, to be erected in the midst of an old pear orchard in Menlo Park. But the County Supervisors gave in to the protests of neighbors and the search of another site began.

In the meantime friends on the Babies' Aid Board in San Francisco became interested. Some of their own charges had been placed under Dr. Bessie's care when they became too old for the San Francisco institution. They offered property in the Richmond and new plans were drawn. By now Bessie had relinquished her responsibilities to other hands and completed her internship in Los Angeles General Hospital, where she was persuaded to remain on staff for one more year because of a serious epidemic of infantile paralysis. She and many others became victims, but she recovered fully and came home to Nine-Twenty to write her State Board examinations just as the new cottage was ready on Thirty-Seventh Avenue.

Although good positions were offered as soon as she passed the examinations, the call to help her babies was too strong. Bessie supervised the move from the Peninsula in 1937 and stayed a few more years to see the new home running well before opening her own offices, remaining as Medical Advisor. Her wish, seconded by the Board, to call this "Donaldina Cameron Cottage" was thwarted by Lo Mo's adamant refusal. It became "Mei Lun Yuen" ("Beautiful Garden of Family Relationship"), serving for many years as a sheltering home for little ones until the changing welfare policy of the city substituted foster homes for institutions like it and the Babies' Aid.

Although Donaldina Cameron consistently refused public recognition of her work, she did accept the invitation of her Chinese family to celebrate her 70th birthday on July 26, 1939, with a banquet in the upper room of one of Grant Avenue's traditional cafes. Professor Sao Chang Lee of the University of Hawaii (that summer on exchange at the University of California) stirred happy memories as he rose to preside, introducing himself as "Lo Mo's son-in-law." In explanation he recalled the days when he met his wife, then a member of the Mission staff, at Nine-Twenty. He spoke, too, of the time when as secretary of the Chinese Y.M.C.A. he had shared Lo Mo's concern for the neglected and homeless small boys of the neighborhood and of their combined cooperation with Dr. Shepherd in establishing Chung Mei Home in El Cerrito.

Captain Shepherd was also at the table and the three chatted with pride about the boys whose hard work had helped raise the funds that made this home possible. Dr. Shepherd pointed out to the professor his new assistant, Eddie Tong, their first college graduate, who was seated at another table. Then Lo Mo turned to Ethel Higgins and asked how her Ming Quong girls were doing in their new establishment in downtown Oakland. She was pleased to find that the site provided by Mills College near the Civic Center was proving so convenient for the older girls and that when they left the old building on the college campus they had brought the familiar blue Ming dogs to guard their new Home, as well as the latticed light fixtures which added to the Oriental atmosphere. Lo Mo was interested, too, in hearing of plans to take the younger children to an old estate in Los Gatos—included in the property exchange with the college.

Miss Higgins added her account of the girls who had grown up in the old Home, now making good in the outer world, and told the professor about Dr. Pauline Owyang, who like Bessie Jeong, had graduated from Stanford, then from its University Medical School and was now working in the San Francisco clinics of both U.C. and Stanford, as well as teaching pediatrics at Stanford.

Three years later, on June 7, 1942, Lo Mo finally very reluctantly agreed to a lasting form of recognition. She sat at dedication exercises for a remodeled Nine-Twenty and saw the unveiling of a tablet designating the old brick building as DONALDINA CAMERON HOUSE. The Board of National Missions had decided that with the substantial obliteration of the yellow slave trade they did not need such a large headquarters for their Chinatown work, and the interior had been changed to house Hip Wo School, where Chinese children were taught the language and culture of their ancestors. This school, operating under the auspices of Congregational, Methodist and Presbyterian churches, brought youngsters off the streets after public school hours to receive Christian-inspired training. Lo Mo rejoiced to see the doors unbolted and bars removed from the windows.

"Auntie Wing," tiny and bent, who had participated twice in cornerstone layings of the original and the re-built building, stood beside her. Evelyn Brown Bancroft read appropriate Bible verses. Inspector Manion spoke of the impact of the long years of rescue work in Chinatown. Lo Mo's namesake, Donaldina Lew, sang, and Lo Mo thought of the many times that lovely voice, trained by Auntie Wing among her kindergarteners, had delighted audiences in the past.

Lo Mo wrote a friend later that "this re-knitting of the old bonds between the past and present service at Nine-Twenty" should "strengthen the things that remain . . . things of the spirit that we long to have revived and made stronger."

She often visited the smaller house around the corner on Wetmore Street where Lorna, Tien and Mae were continuing their work of counselling; but now her sisters needed her more and more in the "little white cottage with a petunia-like walk, and blue morning glories climbing up its walls and over its windows," as Robert O'Brien described the Cameron home in Palo Alto in his "Riptides" column in the *San Francisco Chronicle.* He was writing to "remind San Franciscans of a debt of gratitude" the city owed "to one of the most fearless women San Francisco ever knew . . . one who did more than most to help the city's lost and friendless."

Mr. O'Brien summarized his conversation with Lo Mo, quoting her as being certain that "not enough credit has been given to those who made this work possible. I could have done nothing without the help of the Chinese and American men and women who stood foursquare in back of me." As well, she talked about the "happy reunions on high days and holidays when old Chinese friends come with gifts and sometimes with babies to show off. Surely there is no more grateful race. . . ."

During the war years Lo Mo was often surprised to see a uniformed figure at her front door. One day it was Oio Kum's adopted son in the blue of the Navy. She breathed a prayer of gratitude as she looked into the serious dark eyes of this young man who as a baby had been left on the doorstep of the Mission Home. They discussed his ambition to finish college once his days of service would be over and she realized anew what wise guidance he had had from his foster parents.

John survived. Not so Gum Leen's Choy. One day Tien brought Lo Mo a Purple Heart with an official telegram saying that Choy had been in the gallant company of the 9th Infantry who gave their lives in the Battle of the Bulge. Gum Leen herself had disappeared in the welter of war-stricken China. But her son, educated at the Voorhies School and later at Chung Mei, never forgot the foster mother and "Aunt Tien," whose name on his record made her the "next of kin." Dr. Shepherd wrote later of the $150 in war bonds Choy had willed to Chung Mei.

Choy's was not the only Gold Star on Chung Mei's service flag flying above a memorial rose garden on the El Cerrito hillside. Another of the eight red roses blooming in that garden stood for Chan. Like Choy, he had named Chung Mei as beneficiary of the $1000 life insurance policy he had taken out when he enlisted in the paratroopers. Dr. Shepherd told Lo Mo that Chan's friends at Pasadena Junior College had asked, "Why such a dangerous branch?", to which Chan had strongly replied, "America has given me everything—a home, and a country. I want the toughest job to defend her." This was from a boy who had been nicknamed "Bulldog" by his playmates because of his attitude toward the society he felt had so mistreated him! After Chan's death in Germany Dr. Shepherd told Lo Mo that he had been notified that Chan had taken out a second policy for $1600 which he had figured was the exact amount Chung Mei had spent on him.

The war ended and Lo Mo began to welcome home more of these

fine young "grandchildren." Among them was Dr. James Yee, whose mother had been one of her earliest staff members. He recounted for her some of his China experiences where he had happened to be at the beginning of the war. She smiled with pleasure when he said that the U.S. Government has assigned him to look after the property of the Embassy and told her of his later service with UNRRA. Now he was about to join the staff of the San Francisco City and County Hospital. She recalled for him the efficient help his mother had given her in the distraught days of the 1906 Fire and Earthquake, saying how proud she knew Mary would have been of her son's same response to emergencies.

In this period the death of Katharine Cameron left Donaldina alone with Annie, now in her mid-nineties. Although this tied her more closely to home, she did not lose touch with what was happening in San Francisco. Lorna was a frequent visitor after she returned from her sabbatical year in China, where she had mastered the Cantonese dialect. One day she related an incident that reminded Lo Mo of her own days of meeting ships. Lorna had gone to the airport to welcome a young Chinese doctor coming to America to do graduate work in an eastern medical center. As she waited for her guest to go through landing formalities Lorna had spied a forlorn young Chinese woman hugging a tiny infant as she looked beseechingly from one official after another. Excusing herself from the doctor, Lorna had spoken to the woman in Cantonese, learning that she was enroute to join her husband, a New York merchant, who had sent passage money and assured her that relatives would meet her in San Francisco, supply her with American money and secure a flight to the east.

The rest of the story sounded familiar . . . a phone call to Mae at Wetmore Street where they found native food, a clean bed and willing hands to relieve the mother of the tired infant. Just as Lo Mo would have done in days long past Lorna had searched and located the missing clansmen, settled the stranger in a comfortable hotel and notified the husband, whose letter of appreciation contained a substantial gift to the Mission.

Mae and Tien came to see Lo Mo regularly, too, bringing tales of their new responsibilities. Recent changes in immigration laws permitted Chinese to become naturalized, and immigrants from Cathay were coming into San Francisco at the rate of 800 a month. Among them were many war brides, timid girls from small villages who had known their husbands a matter of weeks and were completely confused by the bustling ways of this faroff land. Tien herself had been among the first to take advantage of the opportunity to become a citizen of the country she had served since childhood. Lo Mo laughed with them when they described Tien's day in the court where she had interpreted so many times. Her friends among the investigators had plied her with difficult questions, evidently just to hear her earnest answers. She had her papers now although for a tense moment her Mission friends had feared refusal when Tien had answered with a stubborn "no" when asked "Would you bear arms for your country?"

Mae, too, had led the way for many of Lo Mo's "daughters" when citizenship was promised to those who would acknowledge illegal but forced immigration in the past. She had now become a special court interpreter, assistant to Deaconess Maurer, the dignified Methodist "Angel of Mercy," who had once been Lo Mo's contemporary in meeting perplexed women from China.

As Lo Mo listened to her friends' stories she began to sense that the day was near when Nine-Twenty would be needed again as a Mission of the Church. Thus it was no surprise when Lorna brought word that the Board had requested Hip Wo to seek another location. Quite soon the Methodist Church offered its facilities to the school, and workmen were again engaged in another job of remodeling the old brick building.

By the time Nine-Twenty was ready for occupancy there were changes in the program and an enlarged staff. The Women's Work would continue under Lorna; but Cameron House would have enlarged usefulness. Now it would serve as a community center for the young people of Chinatown. In the Director of this work Lo Mo could welcome another kindred spirit. Dick Wichman, a recent graduate of the Presbyterian Seminary at San Anselmo, had read her life story and vowed to devote his own to the Chinese in America. He came as associate pastor of the Chinese Church, as well as Director of young people's work in Chinatown for the denomination.

Now there were American children sharing the living quarters of old Nine-Twenty. The Wichmans, with their two, occupied one of the newly remodeled apartments on the third floor; the Chinese pastor with his wife and four youngsters, the other. The second flood would be headquarters for Lorna, Tien and Mae, with rooms to house transient Chinese girls in need of temporary quarters.

On infrequent trips to the city Lo Mo watched the boys and girls of Chinatown respond to Dick Wichman's energetic leadership. They spent a year redecorating the first floor, brightening the dark hall with red lacquer and dubbing Culbertson Hall "Calsomine Hall" as they livened its somber interior to become a gay recreation center. A talented young Chinese artist designed and painted a mural to trace on its walls the history of the Home from Tong wars to modern games. In the basement they built an intimate chapel with a cross lighted from behind. Two black wrought-iron candelabra and a simple reading stand occupied the place of the wooden loom and whirring sewing machines of the old

Industrial Department. Here, in the years to come, young men were to receive their inspiration to train for the ministry—twenty-six of them—under Dick's buoyant guidance. His own colleague in the later years, Harry Chuck, was then an active member of some of the thirty-six clubs which provided outlet for active youth. There was space in the basement for these clubrooms—a Highland Room, its walls papered in plaid, a den with a log cabin effect, a large room lined with tumbling mats where possible fights could be finished off as wrestling matches and another with work benches and tools for craftwork.

Housewarming on the second floor took place on July 13, 1949. Lo Mo had told everyone that she could not make the trip; but when Caroline Bailey came for her and arranged for a friend to stay with Miss Annie, she gave her other "family" a happy surprise. She saw Lorna's desk installed in the room that had been her own bedroom for so many years—that room whose very walls spoke of the love of girls who had sent contributions from all over the world to decorate them on the 25th anniversary of her coming. The afternoon sun shone on the pale green of bamboo-trimmed wall paper. Bookshelves were filled with volumes that promised inspiration to those who were helping the women of new Chinatown. Off the adjoining hallway were two small offices where Tien and Mae could bring perplexed visitors for intimate talks. At the other end of the hall the large living and dining rooms were fragrant with flowers from grateful Chinese friends. Over the tea cups she visited again with little "Auntie Wing" and Bow Yoke, who had remained as caretaker when the rest of the staff had moved to Wetmore Street.

"Bow Yoke," she said, "you are the link between past and present. I have always felt comfortable about the old home because I knew you had not deserted it."

For nearly twenty years more Lo Mo participated in spirit in the expanding usefulness of the Home. She rejoiced in accounts of the gay yearly Carnivals; of the fun times in the playground built on the lot behind the building which she had purchased many years ago with a legacy from an old friend; and of the Day Camps in Golden Gate Park and Summer Camps sponsored for the young at various Conference Grounds away from the city.

While most of her contact was with those who came to see her, she did respond once to a request from Dick Wichman. He asked for a taped conversation. Instead, she had persuaded her niece to bring her to Nine-Twenty on the train and enchanted the Junior High Group by her personal story of early days. She was then past ninety!

It is not granted to many people to come full circle in their life work. Donaldina Cameron not only saw the fulfillment of her hopes and dreams in the accomplishments of her hundreds of Chinese "daughters" and "grandchildren" but also in the recognition that came to her colleagues. Although she could never bring herself to accept civic or national honors, it would have been a proud moment if she had sat at the banquet table hosted by the *San Francisco Examiner* in 1969 when a Phoebe Apperson Hearst medal was given to Lorna Logan as one of "San Francisco's Distinguished Women." (Her own post-humous medal had been voted in 1968!) It is an interesting coincidence that Mrs. Hearst herself served on Occidental Board in early days.

Perhaps, however, to her Scottish-Presbyterian heart Lorna's election as the first woman Moderator of San Francisco Presbytery in 1970 (and one of the first women to hold such an office anywhere in the USA) would have seemed the highest honor. She had lived, however, to know that this recognition of the work of Cameron House had come earlier when Dick Wichman presided over that body some years before.

Although her physical presence is denied to those who gather in 1974 to celebrate the Centennial of the work to which she gave her adult life Donaldina Cameron's spirit pervades the thoughts of all who survey this 100 years. Her name is cast in bronze at the entrance to the old building; but her faith and love live on in the hearts of those youth who are trying to make Chinatown a better place than it was when the Occidental Board of Foreign Missions was formed in 1874.

INSIDE COVER LEGENDS

YESTERYEARS, 1874–1934

Front cover (from top left, clockwise)

Donaldina Cameron with her "refugees" in Marin County after the 1906 earthquake and fire; rescued slave girl of the 1870's; Captain Robert Dollar's birthday with Ming Quong children; foster children at Mei Lun Yuen; a Chinese New Year's gift to Inspector Manion.

NEW FACES AND NEW PROJECTS

Back cover (from top left, clockwise)

Lorna Logan, successor to "Lo Mo"; Reverend Harry Chuck, Jr., Collegiate Pastor; Lambert ("Buddy") Choy, Director, Christian Service Department; F. S. Dick Wichman, Director, Cameron House, watches Mayor Joseph Alioto break ground for double-deck playground; youth reached for service through recreation; Tien Wu receives guests; Cameron House Welcomes You.

Photographs from the Cameron House Collection; montages by Larry Wilson.